THE VOLVO TOUR

Y E A R B O O K

Mark James

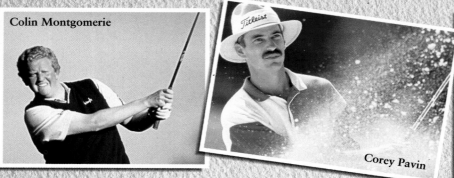
Colin Montgomerie

Corey Pavin

Paul Azinger

TITLEIST.
YET MORE PLAYERS.
STILL MORE WINS.
EVEN MORE MONEY.

Barry Lane

Sam Torrance

José Maria Olazabal

1993 VOLVO TOUR
Ball Count. Titleist: 3777, Next Ball: 1021
Tournament Wins. Titleist: 26, Next Ball: 8

1993 WORLDWIDE TOURS*
Ball Count. Titleist: 11642, Next Ball: 5495
Tournament Wins. Titleist: 83, Next Ball: 39

Joakim Haeggman

Costantino Rocca

Bernhard Langer

There's no other word for it - 1993 has been another spectacular year for Titleist.

No fewer than 18 of Europe's and America's best players used a Titleist ball in the Ryder Cup.

3 of the year's Majors were won with a Titleist ball.

And Titleist players earned no less than £45 million worldwide. That's more than all the others combined.

Further evidence, if any were needed, of Titleist's coveted position as the finest, most trusted and best performing golf ball in the world.

*Results based on US PGA, Volvo, Japan PGA, Canadian, Asian, PGA Australasian and Sunshine Tours as of November 8th 1993.

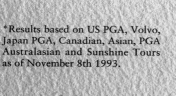

Titleist®
Nº1 ball in golf.

Titleist, St Ives, Cambs PE17 4LS.

GOLF Foundation

INTRODUCTION FROM THE PGA EUROPEAN TOUR

EDITOR
Chris Plumridge
PHOTOGRAPHIC EDITOR
Charles Briscoe-Knight
CO-ORDINATING EDITOR
Sue Rose
CONSULTANT EDITOR
John Hopkins

ART EDITOR
Beverley Douglas

PUBLISHER
Eddie Southcombe
ACCOUNT HANDLER
Dieter Lloyd

PRODUCTION MANAGER
Ken Holt
PRODUCTION CONTROLLER
Nicola Mirams
PRODUCTION DIRECTOR
John Petty

THE VOLVO TOUR YEARBOOK
1994 is published by HHL
Publishing, Greater London
House, Hampstead Road,
London NW1 7QQ, England,
on behalf of PGA European
Tour Enterprises Ltd.
Printed by BPCC Paulton Books
Ltd., Bristol.
Colour reproduction by Litra.
© Headway, Home & Law
Publishing. No part of this book
may be reproduced, stored in a
retrieval system or transmitted in
any form or by any means,
electronic, mechanical,
photocopying, recording or
otherwise, without prior
permission in writing from
Headway, Home & Law
Publishing.
ISBN 0 9519801 8 1

If any phrase encapsulated the 1993 Volvo Tour season then most surely it was 'Bonded by Mutual Respect'.

From the European and United States team rooms at the Ryder Cup by Johnnie Walker to the locker rooms of Campo de Golfe da Madeira and Valderrama, St Mellion and the Wentworth Club, on the Volvo Tour there exuded a tremendous sense of respect, and genuine esteem.

The members of the Volvo Tour set playing standards of the highest calibre, and their commitment to the game, in addition to their acknowledgement for the achievements of their peers, was warmly recognised by sponsors and spectators alike.

Yet in 1993 the sport transcended itself to unite all with a spirit of sportsmanship and harmony that truly supported the PGA European Tour's adopted philosophy for incentive and opportunity. Quite simply the performances of the players, both on and off the fairways, endorsed the reputation of respectability which golf enjoys.

You earn respect. It requires time and talent, character and integrity, pride and passion. All members have these virtues in varying degrees, but none more so in 1993 than Bernhard Langer and Nick Faldo.

Bernhard provided compelling evidence of his capacity to ply his craft in contrasting arenas. He won the US Masters at Augusta National. He won the Volvo PGA Championship at the Wentworth Club, and he won for a record-equalling fifth time the Volvo German Open at Hubbelrath.

More importantly he won with great dignity just as Nick did at the Johnnie Walker Classic in Singapore in February and the Carrolls Irish Open at Mount Juliet in County Kilkenny. Nick's performances enabled him to complete by the end of the Volvo Tour a record of 69 weeks in number one position in the Sony Ranking.

The names of Seve Ballesteros, Faldo, Langer, Sandy Lyle and Ian Woosnam are synonymous with all that is good about European golf, and there were many significant performances in 1993 to demonstrate why we can look to the future with increasing confidence.

Joakim Haeggman and Costantino Rocca became the first players from Sweden and Italy respectively to play in the Ryder Cup, and they were among nine new winners on the Volvo Tour. Indeed, Rocca was one of eight multiple champions during a year when, without question, the overall winner was the game of golf as reflected by the outstanding support the Tour continued to receive from all our friends and, specifically, Volvo.

KENNETH D. SCHOFIELD
EXECUTIVE DIRECTOR

CONTENTS

READY FOR THE NEXT GENERATION

BY MICHAEL McDONNELL

Royal Ryder: The Duke of York presents the Cup to Tom Watson.

Perhaps in times to come, 1993 will be remembered as a milestone in the development of European golf; the season when a truly multi-national spirit and character took hold of the Volvo Tour and the rolls of honour reflected the new exciting face of the professional game.

It was the year when Continental golf came of age and began to assert itself as never before. The best players were good enough for Ryder Cup duty and a Swede and an Italian joined their ranks for the first time. More than this, the Continental professionals assumed a more dominant role as players of impressive quality and class.

Even in Ryder Cup defeat, the Volvo Tour was to make an important discovery that its role and status in the world of golf are secure and no longer precariously dependent on momentary success. For years, it had been trapped by a combative ethic in which the merit of the Tour itself seemed to be assessed solely on how its best players performed against the rest of the world.

Such a view meant, for example, that past Ryder Cup matches took on great significance as biennial tests of self-worth as Europe's best professionals had a chance — for some their only chance — to discover how they measured up to their American counterparts who for so long had been acknowledged as the most dominant players in the world. In those terms, defeat was often greeted as a national disaster and invariably provoked acres of newprint which captured every mood from outrage to despair but rarely offered an ounce of sympathy or insight as another failure seemed to reveal more evidence of second-class citizenship.

Times have changed. When Europe was narrowly defeated at The Belfry in September, the consensus view was not condemnation or blame but simply regret that a golden chance had been allowed to slip away because collective talents had been so evenly balanced. Irritating, but no longer a disaster.

There are two reasons for this enormous shift in perceived attitudes towards the Volvo Tour and its players. Firstly, their quality is such that they have found other individual ways to assert themselves globally. Nick Faldo reigns supreme at the top of the Sony World Rankings. Bernhard Langer lifted his second US Masters title from the best company in the world. Other European names maintain their presence among the elite of international golf. Their prowess is not in doubt.

The other, perhaps more important reason is that the Volvo Tour has become an undisputed mecca for aspiring players from all over the world who seek to learn the art of winning, and also for established stars who know they must broaden their range of achievements against the searching challenge of a truly international circuit that allows the world's best players to meet in open conflict.

Curiously enough there was a time when any ambitious young professional would head west to the US Tour in order to sharpen his talents against proven opposition. Not anymore. The full examination is now to be found within Europe itself and those who succeed are well qualified to tackle any other arena in the world they might be allowed to enter.

The American professional Corey Pavin said as much after winning the Toyota World Match-Play Championship at Wentworth. During his early years he had toiled on the European Tour and acknowledged that it had taught him both technical and psychological skills that helped him to succeed. His judgement was endorsed by the venerable Arnold Palmer when he urged young American professionals to get out of their own cosy

Above, the champagne was on the Americans at The Belfry. Right, Nick Faldo was still cast as world number one.

backyard and travel to Europe and even beyond to learn the demands of winning as he had done in his day.

Perhaps the best illustration of the 'internationalisation' of the Volvo Tour was to be found in the diverse nationalities making up the Ryder Cup squad in 1993 — four Continental countries represented compared with three from the British Isles. Moreover the newcomers showed undisputed class and exuded a confidence beyond their years as they reached out for the great prizes.

Not too long into the season Costantino Rocca, a delightful Italian professional who came late to the sport after working in a factory, strengthened his claim for a team place when he scored his first Tour victory with the Open V33 du Grand Lyon and followed it with the Peugeot French Open. By coincidence no sooner had he acquired the glittering

prizes in France, than a Frenchman, Jean Van de Velde, was at work in Italy securing his first win on the main circuit by taking the Roma Masters.

Tony Jacklin's prophecy that a Swedish professional would eventually make the team was fulfilled when Joakim Haeggman, an exciting, intense young professional, captured the Peugeot Spanish Open in Madrid and so impressed skipper Bernard Gallacher that he was selected for duty. Indeed the

Swedish presence on Tour was further emphasised when fellow countryman Jesper Parnevik won the Bell's Scottish Open at Gleneagles.

The list of first-time winners included Jim Payne, the young Englishman who won the 1992 Rookie of the Year award and this year confirmed his potential with victory in the Turespana Iberian - Open de Baleares; and the powerful Darren Clarke from Northern Ireland who put together an impressive performance to win the Alfred

Dunhill Open at Royal Zoute in Belgium against a distinguished field that included Nick Faldo.

But first-time winners are not always freshed-faced newcomers and three maiden successes in 1993 offer hope to all those who struggle against the suspicion that glory has passed them by. Andrew Oldcorn sprang from the relative obscurity of the Condensed Biographies section of the Tour book to claim the Turespana Masters - Open de Andalucia. It was truly a double triumph because the former Walker Cup player who turned professional ten years earlier had battled against the debilitating ME illness and for a time had thought his career was over.

For Australian Peter Fowler there had been a different kind of frustration because his ability had already been proved with a variety of wins back home but the best he could manage in 11 years on the European Tour was a succession of second place finishes until he won the BMW International Open in Munich. And persistence paid off too for South African Wayne Westner when he won the Dubai Desert Classic to mark his first victory since joining the Tour in 1983.

For the most part, the backbone of the Volvo Tour remained firmly in place. Mark James was in commanding form with two wins and Sam Torrance went even better with three victories. And while Nick Faldo came away empty-handed from the major championships he maintained his leading position in the world rankings with wins in the Johnnie Walker Classic in Singapore and later in the Carrolls Irish Open at Mount Juliet.

Ian Woosnam left his return to form rather late in the season and was borderline material for an automatic Ryder Cup place when he scored his first win in the Murphy's English Open at the Forest of Arden with a few weeks to spare and then emphasised he was firmly back in form by taking the Trophée Lancôme.

Yet while Spain itself provided eight events for the Volvo Tour, it did not produce a winner in 1993. Both Jose Maria Olazabal and Seve Ballesteros endured a frustrating succession of near-misses which must still be regarded as mere vagaries of form. The point is that the great revival can happen at any time and without warning too and it is this prospect of changing fortunes that brings the troubled players back to try again and again.

For that reason, Greg Norman's relentless determination after so many cruel twists of luck, was rewarded when he laid hands on the Open Championship trophy at Royal St George's in July.

Equally significant was the comeback of Peter Baker who re-emerged after four years in the wilderness following his dramatic winning debut in 1988 when he beat Nick Faldo in a play-off for the Benson and Hedges International title. Faldo said at the time that Peter was 'the guy we've been looking for' but the full discovery process was to take a little longer until he burst through to win not only the Dunhill British Masters at Woburn but the Scandinavian Masters and later play a major role in Europe's Ryder Cup campaign at The Belfry.

In retrospect therefore, it was a season of great promise as more talent emerged from all over Europe with nine first-time winners and established itself as part of an even richer seam that offered the possibility of a high and long-term yield.

Indeed the next move for many of these new heroes is a place among the giants who have captured major titles.

The Volvo Tour has progressed dramatically with huge rewards of £19 million prize money spread throughout 38 tournaments in a pilgrimage that begins in the Far East and ends in Spain, and therein lies its strength. By its international character, it has bred a resilience and toughness of spirit that produced a generation of true champions who have dominated the sport for more than a decade.

Nick Faldo remains the role model against whom all others judge themselves. Bernhard Langer offers constant reminders of his rare ability not only at Augusta but also in the Volvo German Open in Dusseldorf. Indeed it is the mark of the truly great players that so long as they keep trying, they can never by written off. In other words Seve Ballesteros and Sandy Lyle are simply too good not to come back.

In any case their fame and fortune is secure. What Europe – and probably the world – now awaits is the new generation of champions to emerge to carry this success story into the next century. It is the next step and time is pressing. Come through when you're ready, gentlemen.

Left, Rodger Davis stooped to conquer in Cannes. Below, Mark Roe and new pro-am partner?

David Feherty stopped to smell the flowers at St Mellion.

One of those seasons for Seve.

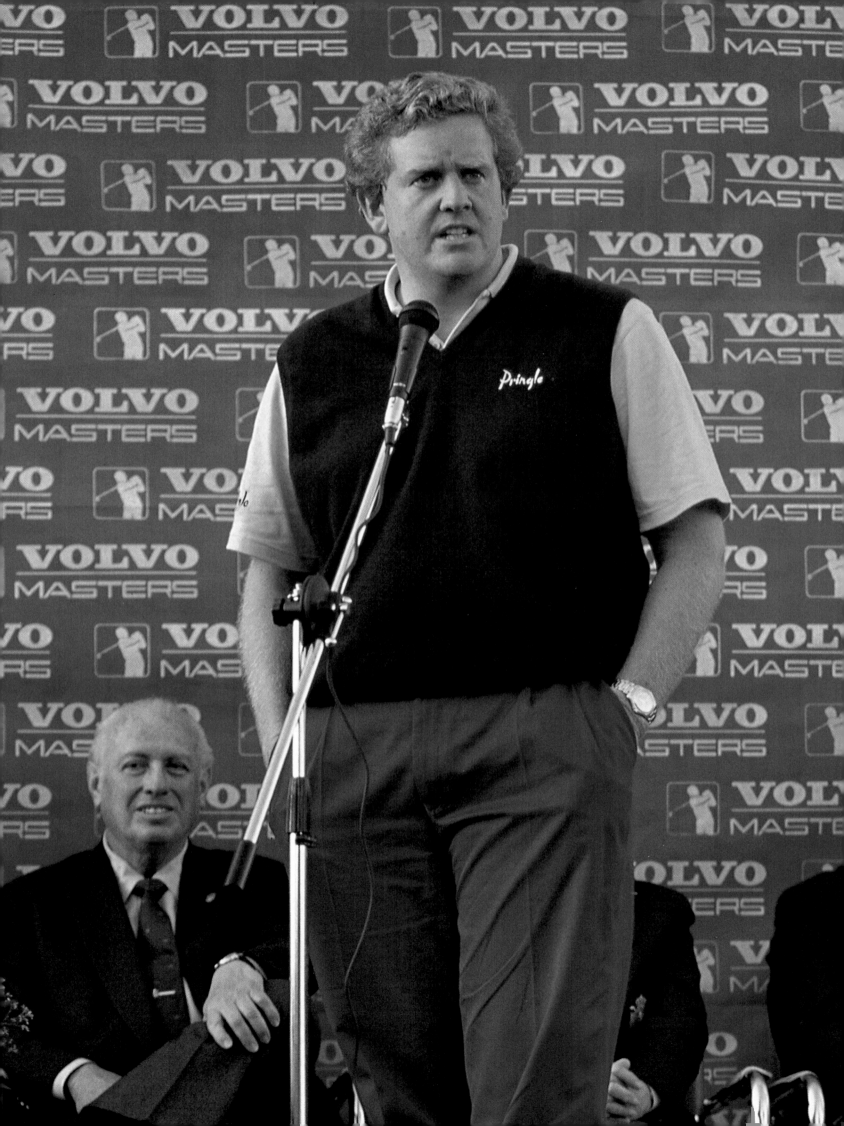

QUITE GOOD AT THE GAME

BY PETER CORRIGAN

Surely, no-one has shouldered his way through the field to win the Volvo Order of Merit quite as dramatically as Colin Montgomerie. If they have, then the quality of those who were shouldered would not bear comparison with the four players who stood between the Scot and the European title before the Volvo Masters began at Valderrama.

The pre-tournament pro-am having been rained off, Montgomerie had plenty of time to contemplate being fifth in the money list behind, in ascending order of fiscal shortcoming, Sam Torrance (£13,746), Ian Woosnam (£43,571), Bernhard Langer (£53,112) and Nick Faldo (£104,031). He didn't fancy his chances. But then he rarely does – or should we say didn't? We may now have a different man on our hands.

This is not to suggest that Montgomerie had been suffering from that well-known golf disease which goes by the rather appalling name of choking. He is not a player to back off when the pressure is applied. Quite the contrary. He has always had the bearing, and the haughty devil-may-care manner, of the cavalry officer. Courage has never been his problem.

It was just that he has an uncommon number of second places to his name, forever being called the bridesmaid by the mischievous press. This was not, however, a classic case of lack of self-belief. Montgomerie had plenty of belief – but he believed he was going to come second.

This theme was never stronger than when he began the 1993 Volvo Tour in earnest. He kicked off at the end of January in the Dubai Desert Classic where he finished joint 17th at the Emirates Course and then joined the trek east to the Singapore Island Country Club where the crowds were vast, the heat was close to unbearable and the golf course by no means a push-over.

The prospect was of another confrontation between Nick Faldo and Greg Norman after their taut battle a month or so earlier in the Johnnie Walker World Championship in Jamaica. Norman arrived in Singapore vowing that if the rest of the world was frightened of Faldo he wasn't. In the event he finished six shots behind him. There was only one player to disturb the world number one, and that was Montgomerie.

If Faldo ever took to writing books, one of them could be called 'I was Monty's trouble'. The Scotsman has never hidden his respect for Faldo and, although the two have been friends for some time, on the course the awe would always get in the way.

After the first two rounds when they were level pegging at the top of the leaderboard Montgomerie came into the cool of the press interview room, his face done medium rare, a towel around his neck and a bottle of water to his lips. And he talked about finishing second.

The year 1992 was not that distant he could forget that during it he had neglected to win a tournament. He finished a highly creditable third in the Volvo Order of Merit but hadn't put his hands on a trophy despite having been close enough to smell the Duraglit in six tournaments, seven if you count the US Open at Pebble Beach where he finished third to Tom Kite. He was placed second three times, the most notable being the Volvo Masters where had lost to Sandy Lyle in the play-off after hitting his drive into a tree on the first extra hole.

'I haven't been aggressive enough going into the final round,' he announced. 'I get to the top of the leaderboard and then I stop. If it is a 100 yard dash, I am running 98 yards and then stopping'.

After the third round, when he was three shots behind Faldo, Montgomerie was mouthing more familiar words: 'My first objective is to try to hold onto second,' he confided. 'The way Nick is playing I can't see him going over 67 tomorrow, which would mean I'd have to shoot 62'.

As it happened, Faldo scored 68 in the last round. Montgomerie shot 66, a brilliant round that almost earned him a play-off. There was no question of backing off. He knew he needed a birdie on the par five last, a dog-leg that bent the wrong way for his natural fade. He found the green with two metal woods and two putted for his birdie. Faldo needed to hole from 12 feet to match it and rolled it in to win by a shot. 'I have come second again,' said Monty, in case we hadn't noticed, 'I don't know what I am supposed to do'.

It is to his credit, and to the benefit of us who have to gather the crumbs from these great golfing achievers, that Montgomerie is honest in revealing his feelings. The habit often earns him rebuke and ridicule but it has its endearing quality.

I sympathised with him after his 1992 Pebble Beach disappointment. 'I don't think I was ready for it,' he said. 'It would have brought so much pressure when I wasn't expecting it. It would have been out of context in my career which has

been one of steady progress.'

Has there been a steadier one? His progress to the top of the Volvo Tour over his six years as a professional has been 52nd, 25th, 14th, 4th, 3rd, 1st.

Not the switchback ride that so many players take but the slow cable car to the stars. As smooth, in many ways, as his life thus far. He hasn't experienced following the Tour in a van and existing on cold baked beans. Son of the secretary at Royal Troon where he swung his first club at the age of four, public school, four years on a golf scholarship at a university the USA... hardly rags to riches stuff.

But a golf ball doesn't know who's hitting it and there weren't too many envying him when he missed the cut in The Open at Sandwich. His answer was to make a late entry into the Heineken Dutch Open the following week. In high winds he registered his first win in two years.

After the disappointments of the Ryder Cup, the Alfred Dunhill Cup and losing to Corey Pavin in the semi-final of the Toyota World Match-Play Championship, who would have dreamed he could have had anything left with which to knock Nick

Faldo, of all people, off his perch?

'I've now got to believe that I am actually quite good at this game whereas I have doubted it before,' he said after Valderrama.

Colin Montgomerie's doubts do not appear to have a rosy future.

Moments from a memorable season.

PROVIDING THE PERFECT PIPE-OPENER

For Canon, the big week comes each year in late summer, 5,000 feet above the Rhône Valley at the jet-setters' Alpine playground of Crans-sur-Sierre. Here in the shadow of the snow-capped Alps the holiday-makers ski and skate in the winter and in summer, play golf in arguably the most beautiful of all the many superbly scenic venues on the Volvo Tour.

Canon, internationally involved in many sports, has taken over the sponsorship of an event promoted vigorously by locals Gaston and Christian Barras. The tournament used to be known as the Swiss Open but is now more grandly titled the European Masters but that is only one part of Canon's Crans involvement.

The players that week have the chance to win the Canon Gold Putter which will go to the first player to shoot 59 at Crans where the record of 60 was matched just last year by tournament winner Jamie Spence and, in addition, there is the final of the supremely popular season-long Canon Shoot-Out series.

The first Shoot-Out was held in 1990 at Wentworth, prior to the Volvo PGA Championship. The object of this form of

The Canon Shoot-Out Series is an entertaining start to the tournament week

competition, where ten players tee up to play nine holes and, hole-by-hole, one player drops out, has strong commercial advantages. It's fast. It's fun. It's exciting. It's hassle-free for players and spectators and it is a perfect pipe-opener for the 72-hole tournament that follows.

Canon, aware of all those advantages, is involved in a five year contract with the PGA European Tour to stage, with the help of the ProServ Europe company based in Paris, the Shoot-Out series at various top venues each season and with the guaranteed involvement of most of the Volvo Tour's top players.

Forty-four players took part in the nine Shoot-Outs in 1993 including the final won by Swede Anders Forsbrand. Ten of the European Ryder Cup side teed up in the events throughout the season and so too did the US Open champion Lee Janzen. He played in the Shoot-Out which took place in driving rain and wind just before the Heineken Dutch Open at Noordwijk. Conditions were so bad that day that two players were eliminated at two of the holes and the competition, watched by only the hardiest of Dutch golf fans, was won by one of Europe's toughest competitors – Germany's iron-man Bernhard Langer.

Big-hitting American John Daly took part but for once lost out on the regular long-driving competition incorporated in each event along with a nearest-the-pin prize. Eduardo Romero from the Argentine surprised 'Wild Thing' by outdriving him by a few yards. Wind assisted Romero's drive which measured 340 yards!

Spectators also enjoyed watching players in less formal mood shoot it out in better weather at Cannes, in Madrid, at Modena in Italy, at Wentworth where the £30,000 prize-fund was donated by the ten contestants to charities of their choice, at Mount Juliet in Ireland, in Munich and in Vienna.

The nine events, which collectively were worth £146,000, provided six winners. Bernhard Langer won three and Barry Lane was twice 'left standing' at the end of golf's equivalent of ten green bottles – the rhyme which has one bottle accidentally fall off the wall with each verse.

Lane, who earned his first Ryder Cup cap during the season, won in Cannes where he was the long-drive winner and he also took the Shoot-Out first prize of £2,750 plus a Canon camera at Modena. Romero was once again the

longest driver of that week.

Appropriately in Madrid a Spaniard, Jose Maria Canizares, won the title, winning at the last hole from Jose Rivero. At the new Jack Nicklaus designed Mount Juliet course in County Kilkenny, Swede Per-Ulrik Johansson was successful in one of his six Shoot-Out appearances but Gordon J Brand edged out the Swede to win at Höhe Brücke in Vienna later in the year.

In addition to his success in Holland, Langer won at Nord-Eichenried in Munich having earlier given £12,000 first prize at Wentworth to the Diabetic Unit at Charing Cross Hospital. That week the PGA European Tour Benevolent Trust, the Great Ormond Street Hospital and Paul O'Gorman Foundation, Help a London Child, Projecto Hombre San Sebastian, MRI Appeal, the Robert Jones and Agnes

Hunt Hospital, The Golf Foundation and the Seve Ballesteros Charitable Trust all benefited.

The final at Crans, watched by 3,000 spectators involved world number one Nick Faldo, Lane, Johansson, Tony Johnstone, Jamie Spence, the 1992 Canon European Masters winner, Sandy Lyle, Ballesteros, the 1992 Shoot-Out final winner, Langer, Mark McNulty, and eventual winner Forsbrand.

That week the slim Swede picked up the £16,000 first prize with a last hole win over Ballesteros. Throughout the season the Shoot-Outs had earned him over £20,000 in prize-money and he, like the thousands of fans throughout Europe who had enjoyed the nine events, is delighted the Canon pre-tournament fun events are firmly placed on the 1994 schedule.

Left, Bernhard Langer beats Tony Johnstone at Wentworth. Below, star-studded line-up for charity at Volvo PGA Championship. Facing page, Ballesteros in full cry at Crans.

Sometimes Nick Faldo needs two caddies.

Canon

EUROPEAN MAST

CRANS MONTA

SUR SIERRE   SWITZE

4

460 m
503 yds

PAR

pm
cation

errier

PREPARING FOR THE WAY AHEAD

A welcome telephone call was made to the PGA European Tour office at Wentworth between Christmas and the New Year. Two time tournament winner and Ryder Cup player Paul Broadhurst was enquiring if there was a place available for him to attend the fifth Apollo Week at San Roque, the PGA European Tour's Andalusian Headquarters, during the first week of January 1993.

Broadhurst, who had attended the first two Apollo Weeks, ran into swing problems during 1992 and after closing his season with a second round 84 in the Volvo Masters decided that major surgery was required on his technique. He chose Bob Torrance as the surgeon and the two began work, initially on the leg action, during the final two months of 1992.

Torrance has been an ever-present feature of the five Apollo Weeks held so far, and Broadhurst saw the chance of a week's pre-season practice and fine tuning with Bob as the perfect way to begin his 1993 campaign. Not that practice and coaching is all that Apollo Week offers – far from it.

The principle of Apollo Week is to offer newly-qualified members of the Volvo Tour a week when they can focus their minds on all the elements that go into 'playing and living' on the Volvo Tour. As well as Torrance the impressive Apollo Week Teaching Panel included former

The Apollo Week at San Roque provided the perfect grounding for life on the Volvo Tour

Ryder Cup player Tommy Horton; Denis Pugh, the principal tutor at The Warren Golf Academy; Ted Pollard, regarded as one of the foremost fitness instructors in golf in Europe; Alan Fine, the respected sports psychologist; Guy Delacave, a senior physiotherapist who runs the PGA European Tour physio unit; and John O'Leary, the current Chairman of the PGA European Tour Tournament Committee.

Lectures started at 8.30am every day, group practice and instruction began at 9.30am and one-and-a-half hour lectures

resumed at 6.30pm. George O'Grady, Deputy Executive Director of the PGA European Tour, and Doug Billman, managing Director of PGA European Tour Productions gave a lecture on 'Television and Sponsorship on the Tour'; John Paramor, Director of Tour Operations and Chief Referee, and Guy Hunt, a PGA European Tour Referee, lectured on 'Rules and Refereeing' and Tommy Horton and John O'Leary gave an insight to 'Life on Tour'. Michael Lovett, Managing Director of Birchgrey, promoters of the GA European Open, and Guy Kinnings of The International Management Group, spoke on 'Event' and 'Client' management respectively, and Richard Hills, Managing Director of PGA European Tour Properties and Development, gave a lecture on 'Golf Course Design and Development'.

A group discussion on 'The Press' included a reconstruction of Broadhurst's winner's interview after the European Pro-Celebrity and involved Renton Laidlaw (*Evening Standard*), Mark Garrod (*The Press Association*), Richard Dodd (*The Yorkshire Post*), Alistair Tait (*Golf Monthly*), Bob Warters (*Today's Golfer*) and Mike Britten.

Andy Taylor, Managing Director of TI Apollo, said: 'This was our fifth year of organising the week, and I feel it was the best so far. The golfers who came along benefited enormously from all the professional advice, and we were blessed with

Above left, candidates line up at San Roque.

Above, rules discussions played an important part.

fantastic weather at San Roque, a venue which met all our requirements.'

The players also had ample time to work on their swings, and to play the excellent San Roque course. What is more, Jaime Patino, the owner of Valderrama, arranged for his course to be set up in a similar way to how it plays during the Volvo Masters, and the players enjoyed a fine round in hot sunshine.

Paul Affleck, who finished first on the 1992 PGA European Challenge Tour, was in attendance with five others who qualified from the Challenge Tour to play the Volvo Tour this year. Ian Garbutt, a former English amateur champion, was one of the 15 players from the PGA European Tour Qualifying School to attend Apollo Week. He said: 'It was an absolutely brilliant week for me. I learned so much, and not just about my game.

The early morning and evening lectures gave me an insight into life on the Tour, and what goes on behind the scenes to make the Tour work. It was interesting to hear what all the coaches had to say, and to see myself on the video machine.

'I learned an awful lot from Tommy Horton about the short game and about bunker play.'

Broadhurst said: 'I asked for an invitation and going to San Roque unquestionably helped me because I was able to work with Bob and benefit from the advice given to all the new faces. It is a refreshing week from which you can learn so much.'

Apollo have announced their continued sponsorship of Apollo Week for a further two years, providing 24 young qualifiers each year with the perfect springboard to their professional careers.

Paul Broadhurst discusses bunker tactics with Tommy Horton and Philip Talbot.

IT'S A PIECE OF CAKE FOR JAMES

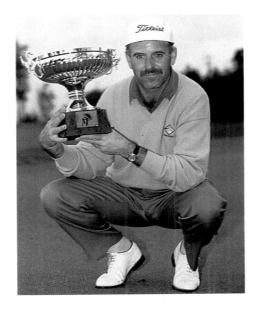

Early season specialist Mark James made the best possible start to the 1993 Volvo Tour with victory in Madeira

It seemed that golf had hardly been away when the Volvo Tour began the 1993 season, 2,000 feet up a mountain. Scarcely had Christmas ended than the Tour rolled into Funchal in the second week of January to provide plentiful examples of the unusual in the Madeira Island Open.

There was a white Caribbean arriving out of nowhere almost to win, a man pulling his own trolley to set a course record, an albatross six months ahead of schedule, probably the most brilliant start to a professional tournament career ever witnessed, and a Yorkshire gardener emerging as champion.

The Tour had come to Madeira as part of a campaign to promote the island 500 miles south-west of Lisbon as a destination for golf holidaymakers. The Campo de Golfe de Madeira had opened two years earlier having been redesigned by Robert Trent Jones on the site of a nine-hole course which had existed since 1937. A second course, Quinta do Palheiro, set alongside botanical gardens dating from 1800, was also under construction.

Maybe, it was the holiday atmosphere that inspired Jeff Hall. On the first day of the season the 35-year-old from Bristol produced a story which had even the veteran inhabitants of the press tent rubbing their hands.

Called from the beach in Marbella, where he and his family were getting away from it all, Hall came back to it all with a vengeance. He lost his Tour card in 1988 and for two years been head teaching pro at Ponta Ala in Southern Italy. After failing at the PGA European Tour Qualifying School two months earlier by a single shot he required a late call-up as reserve to even take part. After one practice round, and without a caddie, he negotiated his way around the ravines and hills of the 6,606-yard course, cut through a eucalyptus forest, in just 65 strokes. It was the outstanding round of the week.

The undulating greens were a constant mystery to all the competitors. A successful long putt was a rarity. By common consensus it was an achievement to get down in two from as near as 20 feet. Some players solved the problems by outrageously holing out from the fairway. Germany's Thomas Goegele potted a four-iron from 210 yards for an albatross at the 523-yards 12th on Friday. Last year it was June before such a bird was sighted on the Volvo Tour so this was like hearing the first cuckoo on Boxing Day. By comparison Glenn Ralph's nine iron straight into the hole from 124 yards at the 18th on Thursday and John

Top three in perspective: joint runners-up Paul Broadhurst, right, and Gordon J.Brand, below right, had to give best to Mark James, centre.

McHenry's nine iron from 129 yards at the ninth on Saturday were relatively routine as were the sand-wedge eagles of David R Jones and David Curry at the tenth on Saturday.

Hall simply hit the ball stiff. His eight birdies included five putts inside four feet and left him two shots ahead of Roger Chapman, with the eventual winner, Mark James a distant six shots back. In the circumstances the grateful press corps might have been expected to be kind to Hall. But what did they do? Provide him with a caddie from among their number. His numbers, meanwhile, went up – from 65 to 77. A last round 79 sent him tumbling to 32nd place and a moderate cheque of £1,975. 'I think', said the journalist, who was not retained after the second round, 'the trolley must have given him better yardages than me.'

Meanwhile, Stephen Ames, a white West Indian from Trinidad and Tobago who had finished fifth at the PGA European Tour Qualifying School, threatened to win at his very first attempt. After rounds of 70, 72, and 70 he was within a shot of playing companion James as they stood on the 71st tee. Glory beckoned but Ames tugged his tee shot left of the 144-yard par-three 17th and took five more to get down, eventually finishing ninth. As he trudged the steep, heartbreak hill of the 18th his caddie-wife was in tears. That's the thing about caddies (and wives), they have been known on occasion to become over-emotional. It was, nonetheless, a brave effort by the newcomer of whom more will be heard.

So James, the doughty fighter, claimed the main prize. The 39-year-old from Ilkley proved that consistency pays – to the tune of £41,660 – with four sub-par rounds of 71, 69, 70, 71. He liked the greens no better than anyone else but stuck doggedly to his task to gain his first victory for two and a half years by a three shot margin from Paul Broadhurst and Gordon Brand.

The joint runners-up were both pleased. Broadhurst had reconstructed his swing only five weeks earlier under the guidance of Bob Torrance and was not expecting such immediate returns. Brand, of the two-piece backswing, had worked hard on his strength during the winter to counter a troublesome back injury.

And what about the man who made professional golf's greatest ever start? Take a bow Ian Garbutt. Immediately after attending Apollo Week, the 20-year old former English amateur champion launched his Volvo Tour career with four straight birdies. Piece of Madeira cake, this game. On the seventh he drove into a hazard, took a penalty drop, returned a double-bogey seven and finished with a 73. That's the reality of life on Tour, something that the experienced Mark James knows only too well.

COURSE: CAMPO DE GOLFE DA MADEIRA						YARDAGE: 6504	PAR: 72

POS	NAME	CTY	1	2	3	4	TOTAL	PRIZE MONEY
1	Mark JAMES	Eng	71	69	70	71	281	£41660
2	Paul BROADHURST	Eng	72	71	70	71	284	21710
	Gordon J BRAND	Eng	71	72	70	71	284	21710
4	Jamie SPENCE	Eng	72	69	73	71	285	11550
	Ronan RAFFERTY	N.Ire	73	73	67	72	285	11550
6	Gordon BRAND Jnr	Scot	69	75	72	70	286	7500
	David GILFORD	Eng	73	73	70	70	286	7500
	Glenn RALPH	Eng	72	74	69	71	286	7500
9	Peter MITCHELL	Eng	71	73	72	71	287	4872
	Steven RICHARDSON	Eng	71	73	73	70	287	4872
	David WILLIAMS	Eng	72	72	73	70	287	4872
	Stephen AMES	T&T	70	72	70	75	287	4872
13	Roger CHAPMAN	Eng	67	75	73	73	288	3532
	Ole ESKILDSEN	Den	68	76	71	73	288	3532
	Ricky WILLISON	Eng	73	70	76	69	288	3532
	Alberto BINAGHI	It	72	70	74	72	288	3532
	Jeremy ROBINSON	Eng	74	70	71	73	288	3532
	Andrew HARE	Eng	76	70	69	73	288	3532
	Sam TORRANCE	Scot	70	77	70	71	288	3532
20	De Wet BASSON	SA	73	71	71	74	289	2887
	Adam HUNTER	Scot	70	73	72	74	289	2887
	Jim PAYNE	Eng	71	71	74	73	289	2887
	Paul McGINLEY	Ire	70	77	69	73	289	2887
24	Carl MASON	Eng	72	72	71	75	290	2662
	Olle KARLSSON	Swe	73	72	71	74	290	2662
	David CURRY	Eng	73	74	72	72	291	2362
	Richard BOXALL	Eng	72	72	71	76	291	2362
	Mark DAVIS	Eng	70	71	79	71	291	2362
	Steen TINNING	Den	72	77	68	74	291	2362
	David R JONES	Eng	71	76	73	71	291	2362
	Patrick HALL	Eng	72	72	76	71	291	2362
32	Jeff HALL	Eng	65	77	71	79	292	1975
	Andrew SHERBORNE	Eng	74	71	71	76	292	1975
	Des SMYTH	Ire	70	74	72	76	292	1975
	Phillip PRICE	Wal	73	75	73	71	292	1975
	Peter BAKER	Eng	75	73	73	71	292	1975
	Martin GATES	Eng	72	72	81	67	292	1975
38	John McHENRY	Ire	72	72	76	73	293	1700
	Nick GODIN	Eng	69	77	74	73	293	1700
	Jonathan SEWELL	Eng	76	72	76	69	293	1700
	Christian HéRDIN	Swe	73	69	76	75	293	1700
	Sven STRöVER	Ger	72	76	73	72	293	1700
43	Stephen McALLISTER	Scot	74	72	75	73	294	1550
44	Eric GIRAUD	Fr	73	72	76	74	295	1400
	Gary ORR	Scot	73	71	77	74	295	1400
	John COE	Eng	72	74	78	71	295	1400
	Mike MILLER	Scot	74	75	73	73	295	1400
	Robert LEE	Eng	74	70	74	77	295	1400
49	David RAY	Eng	74	73	76	73	296	1200
	Antoine LEBOUC	Fr	78	71	74	73	296	1200
	John HAWKSWORTH	Eng	72	77	77	70	296	1200
52	Grant TURNER	Eng	78	71	79	69	297	1025
	Ian GARBUTT	Eng	73	74	77	73	297	1025
	Mikael KRANTZ	Swe	72	75	78	72	297	1025
	Stuart LITTLE	Eng	73	76	77	71	297	1025
56	Paul MAYO	Wal	75	73	77	73	298	875
	Brian MARCHBANK	Scot	75	74	72	77	298	875
58	Mike MCLEAN	Eng	72	76	75	76	299	775
	Ignacio GERVAS	Sp	75	73	76	75	299	775
	Daniel SILVA	Port	75	72	74	78	299	775
61	Thomas GöEGELE	Ger	80	69	77	74	300	700
	Bill LONGMUIR	Scot	74	74	78	74	300	700
	Tony CHARNLEY	Eng	71	76	77	76	300	700
64	Björn SVEDIN	Swe	74	74	84	71	303	650
65	Stuart SMITH	Eng	75	73	77	79	304	512
	Brian BARNES	Scot	76	72	77	79	304	512
67	Ralf BERHORST	Ger	73	74	77	83	307	398
68	Michel BESANCENEY	Fr	79	70	80	80	309	396

WESTNER CRUISES TO DESERT VICTORY

Dubai is a wonderful place to be in the middle of a European winter. It is warm, its people are welcoming and friendly, and the course at the Emirates Golf Club is one of the wonders of the modern sporting world. It was enough in the dying days of January to tempt a couple of the Volvo Tour's aristocrats out of their redoubts to grace the merely mortal with their lordly company.

Nick Faldo and Severiano Ballesteros played in Dubai, and the tournament was the better for their presence. Ballesteros, the defending champion, was to finish in a tie for third place at the end of four days in the Arabian sun. Even he, though, had to bow in the end to the power and precision of Wayne Westner of South Africa, who after four days of immense hitting and straight-as-a-die putting won the tournament with a total of 274, 14 under par. So it was that Westner, once an unheralded and unrated journeyman on the brink of giving up the game, had the biggest triumph of his career with Retief Goossen, his young compatriot, birdieing the last two holes to take second place, a shot in front of Ballesteros and Barry Lane. Westner had led since he birdied the tenth hole of the third round, and never looked in the remotest danger of letting the £66,660 first prize slip out of his hands on a blistering day.

Westner, a self-contained 31-year-old who pilots his own plane and likes nothing better than to fly off to the veldt to commune with nature for anything up to three weeks at a time, came to Dubai after a successful campaign in Europe the previous season.

Long-hitting Wayne Westner demonstrated great poise and control in capturing his first Volvo Tour title

It was not ever thus. He played, unsuccessfully, in Europe from 1983 to 1988 and discovered that he lagged far behind the standard that was being set on the burgeoning European Tour. In addition, sanctions that were being imposed against South African sportsmen at the time by several European countries were leaving him too often with nowhere to go, nowhere to turn to make his living.

His solution was that of so many peo-

ple when they are confused and isolated – he went home. It was then that he seriously contemplated pulling out of the game he loved, but he was pulled back from that decision by two things – he discovered God and he discovered Bob Torrance. His faith had made him a new person; Torrance, one of the great coaches of modern times, had made him a new golfer.

Encouraged by the twin influences that had entered his life, he changed dramatically from failure to achiever. He was in the top three on the South African money list for four years running, he won two South African Opens and four other events on his domestic circuit. He was ready, he felt, to take on the best in Europe, and within weeks of his arrival was taking Faldo to a play-off in the Carrolls Irish Open. He went on to claim three other top ten finishes, and won nearly £123,000. Yes, he was ready.

He was never really out of the frame in Dubai for the entire four days, but it was not until the third day that the long, slow swing that is so often the trademark of the exceptional player, thrust him to the top of the leaderboard. Up until then others had stepped into the arc light of celebrity, played their tune or danced their dance and retired back into the crowd.

The one exception was Ballesteros. After a season of travails in 1992, he was talking of himself as a champion before the tournament started and patiently, like a schoolmaster lecturing a room full of recalcitrent children, he maintained the theme throughout the four days. If it seemed at times as though he was trying to convince

himself as much as his audience, it was no less understandable for all that. Great sportsmen have many facets to their characters – what they all share is pride.

In any event, he was never out of contention, even surviving a brush with the law on the first day. The magisterial eye of Andy McFee, one of the Tour's senior Rules men, caught the Spaniard falling behind the clock. Ballesteros had, he said, committed two breaches of the slow play code; Ballesteros obviously liked the sound of the word, rolling it reflectively

round his palate like a vintage Rioja.

'He said I had two breaches,' he said. 'I thought I played quite fast, but I don't like to have these breaches. I am worried about Bernhard Langer – I think he is going to have a lot of breaches this year.' A short silence. 'And Nick Faldo. Breaches for him, too.'

Ballesteros was six shots off the pace after the first day, and a hot pace it was. The lead was held by Paul McGinley, the young former Walker cup player from Ireland, with a 65, a shot in front of

Above, desert sunset over the clubhouse. Right, Wayne Westner steps forward to receive the trophy. Far right, South African Retief Goosen found himself back in the bush.

Above, Severiano Ballesteros finds sand in the desert.

Russell Claydon with ten players, including Westner, three strokes further back.

McGinley shared the lead with Ronan Rafferty and Westner at the halfway point but on day three Westner came through on the rails to take up the running. He had four birdies and a solitary bogey in his 69, and the precocious McGinley stayed in the hunt with a mature and soundly constructed 70.

Westner, meanwhile, used his great power to reduce the par fives to matchwood – on the 530-yard third he needed only a six-iron to put himself well within birdie range, and on the 547-yard home hole another six-iron second shot just short of the water that fronts the green, a little lobbing sand-wedge and a single putt from 12 feet took him into the clubhouse a stroke in front of McGinley.

For all his new-found belief in himself, Westner must have wondered how he would stand up to the pressure on the final day. Would he crack? He would not. He birdied the third hole and he birdied the tenth. Before, between and beyond he played flawless, safety-first golf of which even Faldo, master of the defensive winning round, would have been proud. It was the biggest test of Wayne Westner's sporting life. He passed, gloriously, with flying colours.

Left, first round leader Paul McGinley faded to fifth place.

POS	NAME	CTY	1	2	3	4	TOTAL	PRIZE MONEY
	COURSE: EMIRATES GOLF CLUB, DUBAI			YARDAGE: 7100			PAR: 72	
1	Wayne WESTNER	SA	69	66	69	70	274	£66660
2	Retief GOOSEN	SA	70	66	72	68	276	44440
3	Barry LANE	Eng	70	69	68	70	277	22520
	Seve BALLESTEROS	Sp	71	68	69	69	277	22520
5	Mark DAVIS	Eng	72	65	70	71	278	14313
	Paul McGINLEY	Ire	65	70	70	73	278	14313
	Anders FORSBRAND	Swe	73	66	68	71	278	14313
8	Ernie ELS	SA	71	72	67	71	281	10000
9	Sven STRUVER	Ger	69	70	69	74	282	6905
	Costantino ROCCA	It	73	69	67	73	282	6905
	Joakim HAEGGMAN	Swe	69	71	71	71	282	6905
	Peter BAKER	Eng	70	72	69	71	282	6905
	David GILFORD	Eng	71	72	69	70	282	6905
	Ronan RAFFERTY	N.Ire	69	66	73	74	282	6905
	Mats LANNER	Swe	73	69	69	71	282	6905
	Patrick HALL	Eng	69	73	71	69	282	6905
17	Gordon BRAND JNR.	Scot	72	72	71	68	283	5173
	Paul WAY	Eng	70	69	74	70	283	5173
	Colin MONTGOMERIE	Scot	73	70	67	73	283	5173
20	Jim PAYNE	Eng	69	73	71	71	284	4500
	Carl MASON	Eng	71	73	68	72	284	4500
	Jeff HAWKES	SA	70	75	69	70	284	4500
	Russell CLAYDON	Eng	66	73	71	74	284	4500
	Paul BROADHURST	Eng	72	70	70	72	284	4500
	Peter MITCHELL	Eng	71	70	74	69	284	4500
26	Bill MALLEY	USA	72	72	73	68	285	3665
	Paul AFFLECK	Wal	69	73	70	73	285	3665
	Ruben ALVAREZ	Arg	72	71	71	71	285	3665
	Martin POXON	Eng	72	71	72	70	285	3665
	Nick FALDO	Eng	70	71	74	70	285	366
	Glen DAY	USA	74	70	69	72	285	3665
	Heinz P THUL	Ger	69	72	70	74	285	3665
	Roger CHAPMAN	Eng	69	70	75	71	285	3665
34	Glenn RALPH	Eng	69	69	75	73	286	2960
	Justin HOBDAY	SA	72	72	72	70	286	2960
	Isao AOKI	Jap	76	67	71	72	286	2960
	Danny MIJOVIC	Can	71	73	69	73	286	2960
	Anders GILLNER	Swe	71	73	70	72	286	2960
	Brian MARCHBANK	Scot	72	69	74	71	286	2960
	Steven RICHARDSON	Eng	70	72	71	73	286	2960
41	Martin GATES	Eng	74	70	70	73	287	2560
	Mark ROE	Eng	72	70	74	71	287	2560
	Phillip PRICE	Wal	73	72	73	69	287	2560
44	Mike McLEAN	Eng	72	71	71	74	288	2320
	Miguel Angel JIMENEZ	Sp	75	68	68	77	288	2320
	Robert KARLSSON	Swe	71	70	72	75	288	2320
47	Mark JAMES	Eng	73	70	74	72	289	2000
	Jamie SPENCE	Eng	70	71	71	77	289	2000
	Silvio GRAPPASONNI	It	74	69	72	74	289	2000
	Ross McFARLANE	Eng	74	71	69	75	289	2000
	Eoghan O'CONNELL	Ire	71	73	73	72	289	2000
52	Paul LAWRIE	Scot	71	73	72	74	290	1680
	Michel BESANCENEY	Fr	74	69	71	76	290	1680
	Anders SORENSEN	Den	71	74	73	72	290	1680
55	David WILLIAMS	Eng	74	70	73	74	291	1290
	Craig McCLELLAN	USA	73	72	73	73	291	1290
	Daniel SILVA	Port	73	71	74	73	291	1290
	Mike HARWOOD	Aus	71	74	71	75	291	1290
	Vijay SINGH	Fij	71	74	73	73	291	1290
	Jeremy ROBINSON	Eng	74	70	73	74	291	1290
	Stephen AMES	T&T	71	70	72	78	291	1290
	Gary EVANS	Eng	72	71	74	74	291	1290
63	Marc FARRY	Fr	74	71	75	72	292	930
	Andrew SHERBORNE	Eng	73	71	72	76	292	930
	Adam HUNTER	Scot	76	69	75	72	292	930
	Ian GARBUTT	Eng	75	70	71	76	292	930
67	Steen TINNING	Den	71	72	75	75	293	598
68	Antoine LEBOUC	Fr	72	73	70	80	295	596
69	Ricky WILLISON	Eng	73	70	76	79	298	594
70	Jon ROBSON	Eng	73	71	75	81	300	592

ANOTHER CLASSIC
FROM FALDO

Singapore was the site of another immaculate performance from Nick Faldo

For centuries Singapore has been a meeting and trading place for East and West, a dot on the map where a score of peoples live and work together in perfect harmony. The tiny island state could have been made for golf, a game that itself crosses the cultural divide more successfully than most. The travellers of the Volvo Tour dropped in for a few days in early February to contest the Johnnie Walker Classic, and immediately felt completely at home.

At home, perhaps, but not always totally comfortable. For some it was too hot (in the 90s) and too humid (80 per cent) for playing golf. For others it was too hot and too humid for even standing dead still and not moving a muscle; Noel Coward, a frequent visitor to the island, might have had the Singapore Island Country Club in mind when he penned his famous ditty about mad dogs, Englishmen and midday suns.

Not that there was anything even faintly hot and humid about Nick Faldo, who in four days of majestic golf strode regally around the Bukit course to win the tournament with a total of 269, 11 under par. Until the final few holes, he scarcely broke sweat.

That he was forced to worry just a little as that Sunday afternoon progressed was due almost entirely to the efforts of Colin Montgomerie. The burly Scot had spoken earlier in the week of his 1992 record – no wins, four seconds, four thirds and nearly £550,000 in the bank – and what he planned to do about it 1993. 'I've

been running 98 yards and stopping,' he said. 'I've got to dip for the line a little earlier. If it's there this year I'm going to go for it.'

This time he kept going for the full distance, and no argument; his 66 was jointly the best score of the fourth day. In the end, though, the three-shot cushion that Faldo carried into the final round was the decisive factor as his 68 took him to a one-shot victory.

Faldo collected £91,660 and Montgomerie £61,100, but the abiding feeling was that Montgomerie would cheerfully have torn up his cheque into small pieces and thrown the lot into the South China Sea for the sake of a rare and precious victory. He had regret tinged with admiration afterwards.

'I played the best I could, and I think I would have beaten any other player,' he said, a touch wistfully. 'But Nick's not any other player.'

He could not have summed it up better. Faldo was remorseless in his efficiency on the final day as no other golfer in the world can be. He had 14 pars, three birdies and a bogey – but those who knew the game could see that at one or two key moments in what had long since become a match-play situation Faldo was the coolest and most controlled man on the course.

He three-putted the 14th for a bogey, Montgomerie birdied it from 15 feet to trail by only one. A Faldo par to the third and a Montgomerie birdie in succession at the next put them level at ten under par. If Faldo was going to crack, as even he had once or twice the previous year, this was the time.

He did not, of course. Instead, it was his mere massive presence that assuredly caused his opponent to bogey the 16th when he hit his second shot edgily into a greenside bunker, blasted out nervously to 15 feet and missed by a foot with his first putt. It was there that the tournament was effectively won and lost. No matter that

both men birdied the last, Montgomerie's eagle putt stopping an agonising six inches short, while Faldo's birdie putt crept in, as he said, 'by the skin of its balata'. Faldo was among the silverware again.

It was no less than he deserved. His had been the dominant influence on the tournament from first to last. His 67 on the opening day gave him a share of the lead, he shared it again after 36 holes with Montgomerie, and by Saturday evening he was three shots clear. He never allowed anybody to forget who was playing in this tournament and who was going to win it. All manner of people, some likely, others less so, had a dash at him as the week went on, but none of them had the game or the endurance to stay with him.

Darren Clarke, Peter Senior, and one Boonchu Ruangkit were audacious enough to equal Faldo's score on day one. Boonchu who? Ruangkit, who had been 16th in the tournament the year

before, was one of the more fascinating characters to emerge during the week. A 37-year-old former Thai kick-boxing champion, he came into the tournament on the crest of a small Oriental wave, but the fact that he had just won two tournaments running in his native land did not protect him from becoming the victim of a small joke by Greg Norman. 'He'll be here on Saturday,' said the Great White Shark. 'Sixty five and Thais make the cut, don't they?'

Faldo, who bogeyed the first two holes he played but followed it with five birdies, was one of only 11 players who broke par in the opening round, and one of a mere 14 who were up on the card at the halfway stage, which he reached with a 68. Montgomerie, meanwhile, added a 67 to his first-round 68 to stand alongside Faldo on the top of the pile.

Faldo had his best round of the week in round three, a 66 which contained four birdies and not a semblance of a mistake.

Enthusiastic crowds, left, turned out in huge numbers to watch Fred Couples, below, and Greg Norman, below left.

Montgomerie shot a 69, which left him temporarily ratty and in second place. Mike McLean, meanwhile, had a course-record 63, which was to win him a £4,000 bonus from Johnnie Walker.

So the scene was set for a showdown between two of the Tour's heavyweights on the final day. It turned into quite a battle, but in the end Faldo, with a sort of relentless inevitability, was the man, and Sunday afternoon was the moment. And Colin Montgomerie, once again, was left just short of the line.

Colin Montgomerie, above, was thwarted by Nick Faldo's winning birdie putt on the final green, below.

COURSE: SINGAPORE ISLAND COUNTRY CLUB							YARDAGE: 6642	PAR: 70
POS	NAME	CTY	1	2	3	4	TOTAL	PRIZE MONEY
1	Nick FALDO	Eng	67	68	66	68	269	£91660
2	Colin MONTGOMERIE	Scot	68	67	69	66	270	61100
3	Sang Ho CHOI	Kor	69	67	71	67	274	34430
4	Steven RICHARDSON	Eng	70	70	66	69	275	25400
	Greg NORMAN	Aus	71	68	68	68	275	25400
6	Boonchu RUANGKIT	Thai	67	72	68	69	276	19250
7	Frankie MINOZA	Phil	70	69	71	67	277	15125
	Fred COUPLES	USA	73	65	70	69	277	15125
9	Ernie ELS	SA	71	65	72	70	278	10339
	Miguel Angel JIMENEZ	Sp	69	72	69	68	278	10339
	Mike McLEAN	Eng	76	69	63	70	278	10339
	Vijay SINGH	Fij	72	69	69	68	278	10339
	Gordon BRAND Jnr	Scot	72	67	71	68	278	10339
14	Wayne RILEY	Aus	72	69	68	70	279	7920
	Robert ALLENBY	Aus	71	70	70	68	279	7920
	Tony JOHNSTONE	Zim	70	73	71	65	279	7920
	Ian WOOSNAM	Wal	71	69	69	70	279	7920
18	Rodger DAVIS	Aus	70	69	70	71	280	6838
	Mats LANNER	Swe	73	71	68	68	280	6838
	Todd HAMILTON	USA	69	72	69	70	280	6838
21	Jeff HAWKES	SA	68	71	72	70	281	6435
22	Derrick COOPER	Eng	71	71	67	73	282	6105
	Carl MASON	Eng	71	74	66	71	282	6105
	Wayne WESTNER	SA	71	70	72	69	282	6105
25	Frank NOBILO	NZ	76	69	68	70	283	5362
	Peter BAKER	Eng	72	71	70	70	283	5362
	Ian PALMER	SA	72	72	69	70	283	5362
	Tze-Chung CHEN	Tai	68	74	70	71	283	5362
	Tze Ming CHEN	Tai	74	69	74	66	283	5362
	Barry LANE	Eng	70	69	74	70	283	5362
31	Anders FORSBRAND	Swe	71	70	71	72	284	4407
	Retief GOOSEN	SA	74	69	70	71	284	4407
	Chie-Hsiang LIN	Tai	74	68	72	70	284	4407
	Yoshinori MIZUMAKI	Jap	77	68	71	68	284	4407
	Ricky WILLISON	Eng	74	70	68	72	284	4407
	Isao AOKI	Jap	71	73	70	70	284	4407
	Craig PARRY	Aus	71	73	70	70	284	4407
38	Sam TORRANCE	Scot	73	64	73	75	285	3630
	Costantino ROCCA	It	70	73	74	68	285	3630
	Ronan RAFFERTY	N.Ire	73	70	72	70	285	3630
	Mike CLAYTON	Aus	72	72	69	72	285	3630
	Peter SENIOR	Aus	67	71	71	76	285	3630
	Tsukasa WATANABE	Jap	75	69	70	71	285	3630
	John McHENRY	Ire	73	72	68	72	285	3630
45	Thomas HARDING	USA	71	72	71	72	286	2805
	Eric MEEKS	USA	73	70	73	70	286	2805
	Peter TERAVAINEN	USA	72	72	70	72	286	2805
	Jim PAYNE	Eng	74	71	72	69	286	2805
	David FEHERTY	N.Ire	75	69	72	70	286	2805
	Roy MACKENZIE	Chil	69	73	68	76	286	2805
	Perry PARKER	USA	75	69	70	72	286	2805
	Martin POXON	Eng	74	70	71	71	286	2805
53	Magnus SUNESSON	Swe	73	72	73	69	287	2035
	Peter FOWLER	Aus	74	71	71	71	287	2035
	Darren CLARKE	N.Ire	67	78	66	76	287	2035
	Joakim HAEGGMAN	Swe	75	70	67	75	287	2035
	Mike HARWOOD	Aus	74	69	73	71	287	2035
	Stewart GINN	Aus	70	75	70	72	287	2035
59	Richard BACKWELL	Aus	77	68	73	70	288	1650
	Jorge BERENDT	Arg	76	69	70	73	288	1650
	Bradley KING	Aus	71	72	72	73	288	1650
62	Silvio GRAPPASONNI	It	70	75	71	73	289	1540
63	Bob MAY	USA	73	72	75	70	290	1430
	Anders SORENSEN	Den	74	71	70	75	290	1430
	Greg TURNER	NZ	71	74	74	71	290	1430
66	Peter O'MALLEY	Aus	73	69	73	76	291	823
	Liang-Hsi CHEN	Tai	73	72	75	71	291	823
	Mark AEBLI	USA	72	73	73	73	291	823
69	Glen DAY	USA	72	73	71	76	292	819
70	Aki OMACHI	Jap	76	69	75	74	294	817
71	Roger CHAPMAN	Eng	71	74	76	74	295	814

Radio communications is our business

MOTOROLA

Radio Communications

For decades the world's emergency services have depended on the reliability and performance of Motorola products and services for their mobile communications capability.

Today all kinds of businesses are realising the benefits of mobile communications, and are turning to the quality systems and equipment from the world's leading manufacturer. Motorola is providing leading-edge solutions for private and public mobile networks, fixed and mobile data networks, cordless telephone and paging networks, cellular services and satellite communications. Whether your organisation is aiming for local, regional or pan-European operations, choose the mobile communications solutions of the world's leading innovator and supplier of radio communications.

Motorola Ltd., Victory House, 3 Fleetwood Park, Barley Way, Fleet, Hants., GU13 8US. Tel: 0252 801801

Official Communication Sponsors to the PGA

JAMES IS KING OF THE ISLANDS

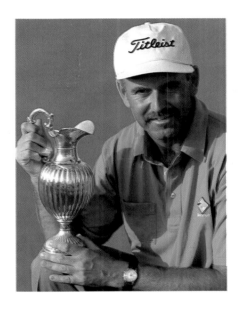

Following his victory in Madeira Mark James made it an early season double in Tenerife

Mark James likes to keep his hands warm, but he can never be accused of cold feet when he scents a Volvo Tour title. So when the weather turned hot and sunny in Tenerife that was the signal for the Lancastrian from Yorkshire to surge to his second victory in the first month of his 1993 campaign.

James added the Turespana Iberia – Open de Canarias to the Madeira Island Open he won at Santa Cruz and proved the enduring quality of a game that had already earned him five previous Ryder Cup appearances.

The margin was a commanding six strokes over South African newcomer De Wet Basson after defending champion Jose Maria Olazabal had put himself out of the running for a third win in four attempts by only just surviving the cut.

The consistency of James' golf at such an early stage of the season took him by surprise. He had put away his clubs after the Volvo Masters which had brought down the curtain on a 1992 programme that had been his least successful since 1987. Although he had won more than £115,000, he had failed to add to his Dunhill British Masters and NM English Open victories of 1990. 'I tried to keep my game in shape during the winter at Ilkley,' he said, 'but it was too cold to practise. I cannot grip the club properly and play golf when my hands are cold, so I just did a little bit of chipping before I went to Madeira.'

Throughout the week at Golf de Sur his sometimes uncertain short game was never put under pressure because his driving and iron play were so accurate. That became evident on the first day after he had been reunited with his clubs which had been 'lost' en route, forcing him to withdraw from the pro-am. James shot 71 in a swirling wind that permitted only three players to break 70 – Kent's Michael McLean, and the Irishmen Eamonn Darcy and Christy O'Connor Junior.

McLean gave the credit for his pace-setting 68, which contained six birdies, to American Fred Couples whom he had partnered the previous week in the Johnnie Walker Classic in Singapore. 'Golf has always taken every ounce of my effort,' said the former Portuguese Open champion, 'and he showed me that being laid back and relaxed could also pay dividends.' Darcy and O'Connor both had 69 to show the value of experience and local knowledge in charting a safe path through the outcrops of volcanic rock. They stayed in contention to the final afternoon.

But James was the man in front at the halfway point after a second day of brisk sea breezes in which his 69 was not bettered. As Olazabal began with scores of 76 and 75 he trailed James by eleven shots, while McLean (77) and Darcy (76) had fallen victims to the quickening greens and difficult pin positions.

Basson had played for South Africa in the World Cup in Madrid the previous November and gone on to win his Volvo Tour card at the PGA European Tour Qualifying School. His unusual forename derives from a Boer general whom his grandfather greatly admired. 'I got named after him when my elder brothers and sister were given all the family names,' he explained. But his golf is of the very modern kind – long and accurate driving backed up by a deft short game which put him into a share of second place after 36 holes. Basson then went on to secure second place with a last day 68 that put him three shots ahead of Darcy. 'I did not expect to do so well so soon,' he said, 'but I have not had a bad tournament for over a year now. The standard of golf in South Africa is improving and it can only get better because players of the quality of Mark McNulty, Nick Price and Tony Johnstone are now competing there on a regular basis.'

Darcy has tried almost every putting method to revive his fortunes on the greens in recent years and for the third round he opted for a left-hand-below-right style, with spectacular results. He had six birdies and an eagle in a 65, also returned by Spain's Jose Rozadilla, to rekindle his interest in a first prize of more than £58,000. The Irishman had been forced to withdraw from the opening event in Madeira because of back trouble so, like James, he appreciated the spring sunshine. He later had another 69, four birdies in the first ten holes, ensuring a one stroke advantage for the last lap.

O'Connor, who had recovered with a 69, former European Open champion Andrew Murray, David Gilford and Barry Lane, and Argentina's formidable Eduardo Romero were all within striking distance, but James left them all behind with a breakneck start to his fourth round. Within six holes he had extended his lead to five shots and few can give the Englishman that kind of lead and hope to catch him.

O'Connor put himself out of the running by three-putting four of those opening six holes, taking 43 to the turn and an eventual 80. Darcy covered them in level par but was a helpless bystander as James produced four birdies without needing to hole from more than ten feet, to waltz to eleven under par. A near-perfect three iron to the short second, an accurate pitch to the fourth, a drive and one iron to be home at the long fifth, and a six iron only five feet from the next flag were the strokes that made James 'Lord of the Atlantic Isles'.

When he turned in 32 and was still five shots clear only his winning margin remained to be established. The rest were left to scrap for the not inconsiderable £38,880 runners-up prize, and Basson was the man who wanted it most. Despite starting with a bogey he produced a pair of outward twos to turn in 34 and claimed further birdies at the 14th and 16th to overhaul Darcy, who took 74.

Caribbean newcomer Stephen Ames had two closing rounds of 67 to share fourth place with Romero and Murray.

After adding birdie fours at the tenth and 14th to underline his command James was cock-a-hoop at his re-run of the early days of 1989 when he also won twice in four weeks by capturing the Dubai Desert Classic and the AGF Open. 'I cannot remember putting together four better rounds. I ripped it at the pin all the way and I enjoyed every minute of it,' he enthused. He had taken a significant step towards another Johnnie Walker Ryder Cup appearance, perhaps places in the US Open and Open Championships, and a possible European number one spot.

Mark is too wise an owl to make public his goals. 'I don't believe in setting myself targets,' he said. 'If you don't achieve them you get disappointed, and if you do, you only have to set new ones. The limit of my ambition is not to lose my balance on the next backswing!'

Newcomer De Wet Basson, left, finished runner-up. Above, blue haze over Tenerife for Eamonn Darcy and Mark James, who drove to victory, right.

POS	NAME	CTY	1	2	3	4	TOTAL	PRIZE MONEY
1	Mark JAMES	Eng	71	69	69	66	275	£58330
2	De Wet BASSON	SA	71	70	72	68	281	38880
3	Eamonn DARCY	Ire	69	76	65	74	284	21910
4	Stephen AMES	T&T	77	74	67	67	285	14860
	Eduardo ROMERO	Arg	72	73	71	69	285	14860
	Andrew MURRAY	Eng	74	71	68	72	285	14860
7	Wayne RILEY	Aus	74	72	73	67	286	10500
8	Andre BOSSERT	Swi	77	74	69	67	287	8285
	David A RUSSELL	Eng	73	74	72	68	287	8285
10	Peter MITCHELL	Eng	74	74	70	70	288	5930
	Barry LANE	Eng	75	72	69	72	288	5930
	Juan QUIROS	Sp	75	72	71	70	288	5930
	David RAY	Eng	74	72	70	72	288	5930
	David GILFORD	Eng	71	73	70	74	288	5930
	Jose ROZADILLA	Sp	72	78	65	73	288	5930
16	Sven STRUVER	Ger	71	74	72	72	289	4542
	David CURRY	Eng	77	72	69	71	289	4542
	Pierre FULKE	Swe	75	73	70	71	289	4542
	Santiago LUNA	Sp	74	74	69	72	289	4542
	Mike McLEAN	Eng	68	77	75	69	289	4542
21	Jeff HALL	Eng	77	72	75	66	290	3937
	Jose COCERES	Arg	72	74	79	65	290	3937
	Derrick COOPER	Eng	73	71	74	72	290	3937
	Jean VAN DER VELDE	Fr	72	78	74	66	290	3937
25	Paul MAYO	Wal	73	77	71	70	291	3169
	Christy O'CONNOR Jnr	Ire	69	73	69	80	291	3169
	Peter SMITH	Scot	77	74	70	70	291	3169
	Diego BORREGO	Sp	77	69	77	68	291	3169
	Miguel Angel JIMENEZ	Sp	73	75	70	73	291	3169
	Giuseppe CALI	It	77	73	68	73	291	3169
	Bill MALLEY	USA	74	75	72	70	291	3169
	Stephen BENNETT	Eng	75	73	73	70	291	3169
	Eoghan O'CONNELL	Ire	80	70	73	68	291	3169
	Chris VAN DER VELDE	Hol	72	69	77	73	291	3169
	Eric GIRAUD	Fr	76	75	71	69	291	3169
36	Jose Maria OLAZABAL	Sp	76	75	72	69	292	2555
	Mikael KRANTZ	Swe	72	76	73	71	292	2555
	Craig CASSELLS	Eng	73	75	71	73	292	2555
40	Bill LONGMUIR	Scot	75	72	74	72	293	2205
	Miguel GUZMAN	Arg	73	75	71	74	293	2205
	Alberto BINAGHI	It	74	72	77	70	293	2205
	Jose RIVERO	Sp	72	75	76	70	293	2205
	Gordon J BRAND	Eng	72	74	73	74	293	2205
	Jon ROBSON	Eng	79	70	68	76	293	2205
46	Gary ORR	Scot	78	73	72	71	294	1785
	Des SMYTH	Ire	75	73	74	72	294	1785
	John HAWKSWORTH	Eng	78	73	70	73	294	1785
	Jeremy ROBINSON	Eng	73	75	72	74	294	1785
	Russell CLAYDON	Eng	71	76	75	72	294	1785
	Gary EVANS	Eng	74	75	74	71	294	1785
52	Heinz P THUL	Ger	73	76	72	74	295	1330
	Paolo QUIRICI	Swi	75	74	73	73	295	1330
	Roy MACKENZIE	Chil	76	75	72	72	295	1330
	Paul AFFLECK	Wal	70	74	75	76	295	1330
	Alfonso PINERO	Sp	75	73	78	69	295	1330
	David WILLIAMS	Eng	74	75	77	69	295	1330
	Jamie SPENCE	Eng	73	77	76	69	295	1330
59	Paul Richard SIMPSON	Eng	72	79	78	67	296	1050
	Mats HALLBERG	Swe	73	72	77	74	296	1050
	Jorge BERENDT	Arg	77	73	74	72	296	1050
62	Stephen FIELD	Eng	77	72	72	76	297	927
	Glenn RALPH	Eng	73	73	72	79	297	927
	Ross DRUMMOND	Scot	78	71	76	72	297	927
	Patrick HALL	Eng	76	75	75	71	297	927
66	Philip TALBOT	Eng	77	71	79	71	298	523
	Martin SLUDDS	Ire	77	73	72	76	298	523
	Jonathan SEWELL	Eng	76	72	77	73	298	523
69	Thomas LEVET	Fr	77	73	75	74	299	519
70	Ignacio FELIU	Sp	72	76	75	78	301	517
71	Rick HARTMANN	USA	78	73	75	79	305	515

COURSE: GOLF DEL SUR **YARDAGE: 6384** **PAR: 72**

GILFORD IS KING OF MOROCCO AGAIN

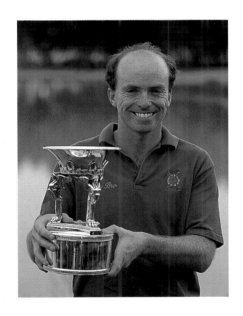

David Gilford retained his Moroccan Open title in the regal setting of the King's own private course

David Gilford is the strong, silent type. He likes to let his golf do the talking. While others speak of technicalities and the power of positive thinking, Gilford pulls the brim of his baseball cap down low over his eyes, smiles a secretive, don't-mind-me smile, and sets off round the golf course in a quiet, undemonstrative way. Seventy-two holes later, the potency of his method becomes clear. While the collective gaze of players, press and public is fixed on golfers more loquacious, more famous, or more extrovert than he, the man from Crewe steals up and wins the tournament.

Thus did it happen at the Moroccan Open, where Gilford was defending champion. This time however the venue was not Dar-es-Salaam but Royal Agadir, a Robert Trent Jones designed course belonging to King Hassan II and previously only played by royalty. Built within the shadow of the castle walls, it wends its way through eucalyptus forests and bulrushes, almost as far as the ocean. Tight fairways and small, wickedly sloping greens place a high premium on accuracy.

One round of the tournament was enough to convince any sceptics of its difficulty; gale force winds transformed it into a monster. Among the walking wounded were Jonathan Sewell (82), Johan Rystrom (82) and a Moroccan amateur by the name of Bendiab, who achieved the unparalleled score of 102.

Gilford and Jamie Spence were alone in relishing the black side of Royal Agadir's Jekyll and Hyde persona. 'I think you have to treat it as a bit of a challenge,' said the former blithely, having sauntered to a four under par 68, which almost included an albatross at the 17th. 'Look forward to it, rather than be afraid of it. And I think you've got to be patient.'

Spence, who led Gilford by a stroke after a near-miraculous course record 67, felt much the same way. He liked the fact that it was a links-like course, which suited his style of play. 'I don't think this is a smasher's course,' he commented, 'because here, if you miss the fairway, you lose your ball. I think someone who can keep the ball under control will win.' His score was all the more remarkable due to the fact that his regular caddie had to return home and Spence had been left to do the best he could with a yardage book and a local bag carrier known as Abdil Kadir, who spoke no English.

The language barrier did not prove a hindrance to Spence the following day either. In swirling, unpredictable winds, which sent the cut soaring to 151, seven over par, he recorded a 69. That was when luck – or rather, that intangible combination of fortune and the mysterious workings of fate which has affected the eventual outcome of golf tournaments since time immemorial – brought its influence to bear. Spence had played in the morning when, because of the horrendous conditions, he was the only player under par in his half of the draw. By midday the wind had dropped and, by the time the other leaders teed off, there was a virtual flat calm.

At sundown five men shared the leaderboard with him. Gilford was on six under par, Wayne Westner on three, and Robert Karlsson, Jay Townsend and Stephen Ames on two under. Seve Ballesteros, who had captained the European side in their match against Africa at the start of the week (result: Europe 3, Africa 0), and who had come close to withdrawing because of chronic backache and exhaustion, was on 150.

Saturday was dominated by Ames, a gifted rookie from Trinidad and Tobago, who owed his presence in Morocco to the vigilance of US customs officials. Having been temporarily denied access to the United States after failing to meet visa requirements, Ames had resolved to put heart and soul into the Moroccan Open. He did this by shooting a course record 66 and moving boldly through the field to share a three-way tie on 208 with Spence and Gilford. Their nearest rivals, Vicente Fernandez and Westner, were six strokes behind.

'I'll be nervous if I've got a chance to win,' said Gilford in his softly spoken, reticent way. 'I think you have to be. I think if you weren't nervous it would mean that it didn't mean very much and you wouldn't play well.'

Nevertheless, though Gilford might have quaked inwardly as he teed off in the final round, outwardly he was the epitome of calm. Accuracy is his forte, and he used it to his advantage. By the time he reached the 17th, where he was unlucky to three-putt for a par, he was on nine under par and level with Ames, who had birdied three of the last four holes.

A play-off loomed. Both men drove down the centre of the last fairway, but Gilford found the heart of the green, while Ames over-flew it with a nine-iron. Then all eyes were on Spence, the fallen favourite, and the potential star from Trinidad and Tobago. Ames failed to match the Englishman's two-putt from 18 feet having chipped back too strongly and missed his putt. So the prize went to lion-hearted David Gilford.

COURSE: GOLF ROYAL DE AGADIR							YARDAGE: 6657		PAR: 72

POS	NAME	CTY	1	2	3	4	TOTAL	PRIZE MONEY
1	David GILFORD	Eng	68	70	70	71	279	£62500
2	Jamie SPENCE	Eng	67	69	72	72	280	32550
	Stephen AMES	T&T	70	72	66	72	280	32550
4	Robert KARLSSON	Swe	75	67	73	69	284	19000
5	Vicente FERNANDEZ	Arg	77	67	70	72	286	16000
6	Wayne WESTNER	SA	70	71	73	73	287	12000
	Magnus SUNESSON	Swe	75	72	69	71	287	12000
8	Frank NOBILO	NZ	73	74	69	72	288	8433
	Carl MASON	Eng	76	69	71	72	288	8433
	Tony JOHNSTONE	Zim	78	71	72	67	288	8433
11	Mark MOULAND	Wal	72	79	71	67	289	7000
12	Des SMYTH	Ire	75	73	71	71	290	6500
13	Roger CHAPMAN	Eng	75	73	73	70	291	5783
	Adam HUNTER	Scot	75	73	71	72	291	5783
	Darren CLARKE	N.Ire	76	67	76	72	291	5783
16	Mark JAMES	Eng	74	76	69	73	292	5050
	David CURRY	Eng	72	74	74	72	292	5050
	Ian PALMER	SA	75	74	74	69	292	5050
	Paul MAYO	Wal	71	74	71	76	292	5050
20	Jeff HAWKES	SA	77	72	71	73	293	3877
	Miguel Angel MARTIN	Sp	70	75	73	75	293	3877
	Gordon BRAND Jnr	Scot	73	77	74	69	293	3877
	Nick GODIN	Eng	76	73	73	71	293	3877
	Jesper PARNEVIK	Swe	76	72	69	76	293	3877
	Steven RICHARDSON	Eng	73	75	74	71	293	3877
	Philip WALTON	Ire	77	72	70	74	293	3877
	Sam TORRANCE	Scot	74	72	75	72	293	3877
	Sven STRUVER	Ger	77	71	72	73	293	3877
	Colin MONTGOMERIE	Scot	73	77	73	70	293	3877
	Jay TOWNSEND	USA	72	70	78	73	293	3877
31	Jean VAN DE VELDE	Fr	75	76	68	75	294	3158
	Mike McLEAN	Eng	74	72	73	75	294	3158
	Andrew SHERBORNE	Eng	74	73	74	73	294	3158
34	Anders FORSBRAND	Swe	76	74	75	70	295	2737
	Per-Ulrik JOHANSSON	Swe	76	75	71	73	295	2737
	Eduardo ROMERO	Arg	76	72	74	73	295	2737
	Antoine LEBOUC	Fr	72	77	70	76	295	2737
	Ross McFARLANE	Eng	74	71	74	76	295	2737
	Seve BALLESTEROS	Sp	73	77	74	71	295	2737
	Chris MOODY	Eng	77	74	72	72	295	2737
	Silvio GRAPPASONNI	It	72	72	78	73	295	2737
42	Mikael KRANTZ	Swe	76	71	76	73	296	2362
	Russell CLAYDON	Eng	78	72	71	75	296	2362
44	Mark ROE	Eng	75	76	72	74	297	2062
	Pierre FULKE	Swe	76	72	77	72	297	2062
	Ross DRUMMOND	Scot	74	75	76	72	297	2062
	Miguel GUZMAN	Arg	72	75	74	76	297	2062
	Tom PERNICE	USA	75	75	70	77	297	2062
	Paul McGINLEY	Ire	74	77	75	71	297	2062
50	Gary ORR	Scot	77	73	74	74	298	1725
	Paul BROADHURST	Eng	76	73	78	71	298	1725
	Eamonn DARCY	Ire	71	76	74	77	298	1725
53	Ronan RAFFERTY	N.Ire	77	72	78	72	299	1500
	John McHENRY	Ire	78	71	77	73	299	1500
	Ian GARBUTT	Eng	77	74	76	72	299	1500
56	Paul EALES	Eng	75	73	79	73	300	1350
57	Jim PAYNE	Eng	71	79	75	76	301	1250
	Craig McCLELLAN	USA	74	77	77	73	301	1250
	Marc FARRY	Fr	73	75	73	80	301	1250
60	Ruben ALVAREZ	Arg	80	70	76	76	302	1100
	Mats LANNER	Swe	77	73	72	80	302	1100
	Costantino ROCCA	It	74	75	71	82	302	1100
63	David RAY	Eng	74	76	77	76	303	950
	Alberto BINAGHI	It	74	77	76	76	303	950
	David R JONES	Eng	76	74	73	80	303	950
66	Anders GILLNER	Swe	72	77	83	73	305	560
	Brian MARCHBANK	Scot	80	71	75	79	305	560
	Martin POXON	Eng	71	77	80	77	305	560
69	Paolo QUIRICI	Swi	75	76	76	82	309	556
70	Rick HARTMANN	USA	77	74	81	78	310	554

Above, runner-up Stephen Ames made a bold bid for the title. Left, the Moroccan guard of honour was on parade. Far left, Jay Townsend made a splash.

David Gilford putts, watched by main challenger Ames.

OLDCORN FINDS THE WINNING CURE

Andrew Oldcorn's recovery from a career-threatening illness was completed with his first Volvo Tour title

The course that Seve Ballesteros built on the windswept shores of the Bay of Cadiz is no place for the faint-hearted. Whether it is the *levante* sweeping through the straits of Gibraltar, or the Atlantic gales that bring the heavy spring showers, Novo Sancti Petri is a fearsome ordeal, even for the longest hitters.

When the flagsticks are rattling in their sockets as they were for most of the Turespana Masters – Open de Andalucia the sages pointed to the credentials of power men like Steven Richardson, Anders Forsbrand, and Eduardo Romero, and no-one gave a second thought to Andrew Oldcorn. To be fair, the 32-year old former English Amateur champion and Walker Cup golfer who was raised in Lancashire but now lives in Edinburgh, had given little advance warning that he was about to transform his fortunes after

ten moderate seasons as a professional.

He had finished 181st in the Volvo Order of Merit for 1992 and had to return to the PGA European Tour Qualifying School which he had won in 1983. Then having regained his 'card' by taking 12th place he failed to survive the cut in his first event of the new season, the Madeira Island Open. His best performance as a professional remained his third place in the now defunct Lawrence Batley International at Royal Birkdale in 1987. Yet Oldcorn not only mastered a formidable field and everything that architect Ballesteros had devised, he also showed he had beaten the debilitating virus which had almost put him out of the game.

Oldcorn contracted the stamina-sapping illness, erroneously dubbed 'Yuppie flu' in 1989. 'A walk to the corner shop left me

— 45 —

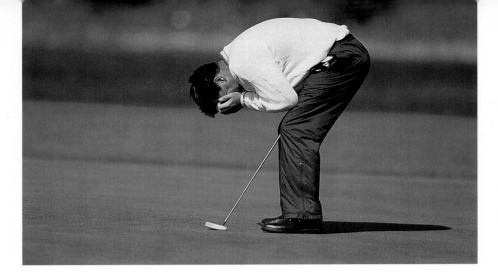

Steven Richardson, above, can't look as putt slips by. Right, backed by the Atlantic Peter Mitchell putts up close.

Andrew Oldcorn and Eduardo Romera, left, shadowed each other until the final hole.

exhausted and even getting up the stairs required a major effort,' he said. 'If I practised on the golf range for 30 minutes I had to rest for three hours. It was so bad I thought I would never play again. I had to push myself to the limit, drag my mind out of the mire and think positively to keep going.'

His condition was eventually diagnosed as myalgic encephalomyelitis or post-viral fatigue syndrome, and it took Oldcorn three years to rid himself of the torpor. Because of exhaustion he had to cut back on overseas travel and confine his activities to his domestic 'Tartan Tour', but encouraged by his family and girlfriend he never lost faith in his ability to one day become a Volvo Tour champion. Amidst the fierce competition of a flagship Volvo Tour event Andrew was to achieve his ambition sooner than he thought possible.

Ballesteros, who had aggravated his long-standing back problems through excessive practice in Morocco the previous week, had suggested after seeing only six players better or equal par in the pro-am that his course was hard but fair. 'It is not one on which a competent professional should take a triple bogey,' he declared. The gods of golf have a way of punishing those who tempt fate, and Seve, wearing a protective belt for his sore back, immediately marked a seven on his card when he started his first round at the par four tenth and hooked out of bounds. Ballesteros handed in a 77, ten shots behind Ireland's Des Smyth whose first sight of the 7100-yard course came when he stepped on to the first tee.

In 1993 Smyth had celebrated his entry to the Tour's 'Millionaires' Club' by taking his prize money into seven figures,

and also celebrated his 40th birthday. He had preferred an extra day with his family to a practice round. Two eagles arising from a 15-yard bunker shot at the eighth and a 15-yard putt at the 11th showed that after two years in the doldrums the former Ryder Cup golfer has rediscovered his appetite. He suffered for his slightly cavalier approach the next day when he took 79 despite sharing the rarest of double eagles with 1992 Rookie of the Year, Jim Payne. Both sank nine iron shots at the par four 15th, Payne from 134 yards and Smyth from 117 yards. Sadly for Smyth he had taken seven at the 12th and dropped five more shots on his inward half.

He survived to finish eighth, but Ballesteros did not after a 73 on the second day which ended as most suspected, with Richardson and Romero at the head

of the field and Bernhard Langer and Jose Maria Olazabal two shots behind. In between were Oldcorn and the immensely promising Swede, Joakim Haeggman.

There was little change on a wild third day when no-one broke 70 and almost a quarter of the 68 survivors failed to beat 80, among them former European number one Ronan Rafferty and Volvo Tour champions Chris Moody, Richard Boxall and Gavin Levenson.

Oldcorn's battling 73 enabled him to tuck in between leader Richardson and third man Romero and this trio comprised the only men under par for 54 holes. A 70 from South African Ian Palmer moved him up to fourth place on 216, just ahead of Olazabal and Forsbrand. 'Everyone expected me to blow up in those conditions but I am used to seaside golf and I just stuck in there,' commented Oldcorn.

The Englishman with the broad Scots accent and his caddy-manager Alan Maxwell were thus surrounded by a formidable array of talent and his winning prospects receded when he fell two shots behind Richardson after five holes of the final round. Then the Ryder Cup golfer handed Oldcorn a two stroke cushion and a leadership he never relinquished. Richardson overshot the sixth green from where he fluffed a recovery chip and a double bogey was marked on his card. Three putts followed at the short seventh where he was lured into a conservative stroke because of the wind blowing towards the lake. Oldcorn holed there from 12 yards for a birdie two, then turned with a three shot lead over Romero after Richardson missed the green with his pitch to the eighth and took another six, then failed from four feet to match

Oldcorn's three at the ninth.

Further birdies at the 13th and 14th kept Oldcorn in command before he made the mistake that kept the outcome in doubt until the last putt on the last green. He went through the drive and pitch 15th where his ball finished close to a boundary fence. A penalty shot, two chips and a putt were required before he holed out for six.

All three contenders bogeyed the 225-yard 16th into the wind over water before Richardson birdied the long uphill 17th. Oldcorn arrived on the final tee standing three under par, one ahead of Romero, with Richardson a further stroke behind.

That was how they finished but the drama lingered to the last because Oldcorn again went through the green at the 200 yard par three finale. His return chip left him four feet from the flag, and consigned him to an anxious few minutes. After Richardson had missed the birdie he had to make from 30 feet it was the Argentinian's turn. But his uphill putt from 20 feet did not have enough pace, and Oldcorn's task was clear. He calmly rolled his victory putt into the centre of the hole, and ten years of frustration had ended.

'My desire to win gave me the edge,' he declared, 'although when I looked at the opposition it was scary. But I never lost my belief that I could win, and the Volvo Tour is the stage I want to be on.'

Oldcorn's maiden victory made him the 22nd new winner of the 1990s and now as the proud owner of a three-year exemption he can choose where and when he plays. 'I hope I have inspired all those other sufferers of ME to never lose hope,' he added. 'Winning is also a great cure.'

The champion exults after winning putt.

COURSE: NOVO SANCTI PETRI							YARDAGE: 7020	PAR: 72
POS	NAME	CTY	1	2	3	4	TOTAL	PRIZE MONEY
1	Andrew OLDCORN	Eng	70	71	73	71	285	£58330
2	Eduardo ROMERO	Arg	68	72	75	71	286	38880
3	Steven RICHARDSON	Eng	69	71	73	74	287	21910
4	De Wet BASSON	SA	75	71	73	72	291	16165
	Ian PALMER	SA	69	77	70	75	291	16165
6	Wayne WESTNER	SA	71	73	75	73	292	11375
	Costantino ROCCA	It	77	69	75	71	292	11375
8	Joakim HAEGGMAN	Swe	69	72	77	75	293	7856
	Jose Maria OLAZABAL	Sp	71	71	75	76	293	7856
	Des SMYTH	Ire	67	79	73	74	293	7856
11	Brian MARCHBANK	Scot	73	73	75	73	294	6440
12	Anders FORSBRAND	Swe	75	71	71	78	295	5187
	Paul BROADHURST	Eng	76	72	77	70	295	5187
	Darren CLARKE	N.Ire	75	69	78	73	295	5187
	Colin MONTGOMERIE	Scot	72	74	75	74	295	5187
	Bernhard LANGER	Ger	70	72	78	75	295	5187
	Sam TORRANCE	Scot	74	73	76	72	295	5187
	Eoghan O'CONNELL	Ire	71	72	75	77	295	5187
19	Jose RIVERO	Sp	71	74	77	74	296	4048
	Gary ORR	Scot	70	76	78	72	296	4048
	Jean VAN DE VELDE	Fr	75	72	75	74	296	4048
	Olle KARLSSON	Swe	74	72	76	74	296	4048
	Magnus SUNESSON	Swe	72	71	79	74	296	4048
	Russell CLAYDON	Eng	75	72	73	76	296	4048
25	Craig CASSELLS	Eng	74	73	77	73	297	3570
	Phillip PRICE	Wal	77	71	74	75	297	3570
	Vicente FERNANDEZ	Arg	72	72	79	74	297	3570
28	Jose Maria CANIZARES	Sp	73	72	76	77	298	3307
	Peter MITCHELL	Eng	73	70	77	78	298	3307
30	David WILLIAMS	Eng	73	73	77	76	299	2848
	Glenn RALPH	Eng	75	72	79	73	299	2848
	Jorge BERENDT	Arg	75	72	78	74	299	2848
	Jesper PARNEVIK	Swe	73	73	76	77	299	2848
	Jose ROZADILLA	Sp	70	75	77	77	299	2848
	Stuart LITTLE	Eng	73	73	78	75	299	2848
	Ronan RAFFERTY	N.Ire	72	72	82	73	299	2848
	Danny MIJOVIC	Can	71	74	76	78	299	2848
38	Greg TURNER	NZ	72	71	77	80	300	2345
	Per-Ulrik JOHANSSON	Swe	75	73	74	78	300	2345
	Marc FARRY	Fr	77	71	77	75	300	2345
	Antoine LEBOUC	Fr	74	74	74	78	300	2345
	Antonio GARRIDO	Sp	70	72	80	78	300	2345
	Jim PAYNE	Eng	72	73	77	78	300	2345
44	Paul WAY	Eng	70	76	79	76	301	2030
	Miguel Angel MARTIN	Sp	68	75	78	80	301	2030
	Stephen McALLISTER	Scot	74	73	77	77	301	2030
47	Michel BESANCENEY	Fr	72	74	81	75	302	1785
	Richard BOXALL	Eng	74	73	82	73	302	1785
	Pierre FULKE	Swe	70	75	77	80	302	1785
	Justin HOBDAY	SA	73	72	80	77	302	1785
51	Ove SELLBERG	Swe	73	70	81	79	303	1505
	Silvio GRAPPASONNI	It	75	72	79	77	303	1505
	Alfonso PINERO	Sp	76	71	82	74	303	1505
	Mats LANNER	Swe	74	73	77	79	303	1505
55	Paul MAYO	Wal	71	73	81	79	304	1260
	Miguel Angel JIMENEZ	Sp	72	74	79	79	304	1260
	Craig McCLELLAN	USA	76	71	77	80	304	1260
58	Heinz P THUL	Ger	78	69	77	81	305	1120
59	Anders GILLNER	Swe	68	76	83	80	307	1067
	Diego BORREGO	Sp	75	73	80	79	307	1067
61	Steve REY	Swi	72	74	82	81	309	945
	Ignacio GERVAS	Sp	73	74	81	81	309	945
	Tom PERNICE	USA	73	71	78	87	309	945
	Andrew COLTART	Scot	76	71	82	80	309	945
	Chris MOODY	Eng	72	71	85	81	309	945
66	Roger CHAPMAN	Eng	74	73	84	79	310	525
67	Gavin LEVENSON	SA	72	76	81	82	311	523

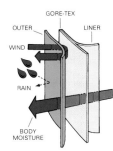

Making a golf suit that is both 100% waterproof, windproof and has total breathability requires two things. Skill and a ruthless eye for perfection. Thankfully, our Production Director has both of these qualities in abundance. A fact that has not gone unnoticed by current European and US Ryder Cup Teams, who gladly suit up in ProQuip weatherwear when the storm clouds gather.

Nor need rain necessarily stop play on the PGA European Tour, thanks again to our weatherwear. Indeed, in recognition of the high standards we continue to apply to rainwear manufacturing, ProQuip are the only company to receive the PGA European Tour's 'Tournament Quality' Award.

So when we say that our suits are waterproof, windproof and have total breathability, the professionals are in total agreement.

All our Gore-Tex lined rainsuits come with a fully comprehensive 3 year guarantee, so when you buy your rainsuit you can do so with the knowledge that you are guaranteed the very best protection against the elements.

PROQUIP

MASTERS OF WEATHERWEAR

ProQuip International Ltd. U.K. Head Office, Wisloe Road, Cambridge, Gloucestershire. GL2 7AF. England. Tel: (0453) 890707 Fax: (0453) 890826.

NOBILO'S DETERMINATION SEES HIM THROUGH

This is the tale of two of golf's good guys – 'Gentleman' Jim Payne and 'Friendly' Frank Nobilo – and their contrasting adventures over the weekend of the Turespana Open Mediterrania – The Land of Valencia.

The small differences between the young Englishman and the New Zealander are the obvious ones. Nobilo is tall, but Payne, at 6'4", is taller. Nobilo speaks at a speed which only the most experienced of shorthand merchants can reproduce verbatim, while Payne, though no less open to questioning, is more considered, allowing his listeners ample time for their notations.

The big difference, though, is the decade that separates the thirtysomething from the twentysomething and the gulf in golfing experience that implies. Nobilo, aged 32, leaning on past triumphs and failures, recorded rounds of 67 and 72 over the weekend for his third Volvo Tour win. The 22-year old Payne, who had gone into the last two days five strokes ahead of Nobilo, ended three behind after scores of 78 and 69.

Over the sand dunes of El Saler, to the south of Valencia and rated one of the best courses on Tour, Payne, who learned his golf on the Lincolnshire links of Sandilands, took possession of the halfway lead at nine under par, three in front of the field. 'I have never been in this

Frank Nobilo drew on all his experience to record his third Volvo Tour victory

position before,' said last year's Rookie of the Year on being asked if he was a good frontrunner, 'but it will be interesting. I am looking forward to finding out how I cope. You can find out a bit more about yourself.'

And so he did. 'I learnt,' he said the following evening having aged in golfing terms far more than the time his third round took to play, 'that if I keep getting into the lead after two rounds then one day I'll shoot better than a 78.'

Level par to the 11th, he bogeyed the 12th and 14th, then lost a ball from the tee at the 15th and racked up a double bogey seven. 'I found that difficult to

take,' he said. 'It looked good from the tee but must have hit a tree.' Bogeys at the 16th followed. 'It was a disappointing finish but I tried on every shot and I'll do the same tomorrow.'

Later that night Payne phoned his coach, Eric Sharp, who told him: 'To have a three shot lead is the hardest position from which to play. You have still done well. Just go out and finish in the top ten.' Payne is a quick learner and that is just what he did.

Nobilo, who is of Italian descent, has a great-grandfather who pirated his way around the Mediterranean, and the Kiwi has decided to follow suit by basing himself full-time in Europe. 'I think it is the best move for my family and golf,' he said. 'European Tour players are respected all over the world. Playing on a different course with good competition makes you better and at 32 I hope my best golf is still ahead of me.'

Nobilo, with his London-born wife Gaynor and their three-year old daughter, joined a host of other Down Under golfers in 'Ramsey Street' in Bagshot, Surrey. 'I think Britain is a great place to live and maybe one day I'll become a resident,' Nobilo said. It also means being near his British coach Denis Pugh, with whom he has been working for four years.

On Sunday, all that hard work was

Above, Mike Harwood enveloped in a swirl of sand. Left, Mediterranean backdrop as Jim Payne drives off.

paying off. But while no challenge materialised from his immediate playing companions, Sam Torrance and Mark Roe, ahead Glenn Ralph was making an unexpected appearance. When Ralph, aged 36, from Sussex, failed to retain his card at the PGA European Tour Qualifying School, he didn't bother to shave. By March, he was sporting the shaggiest of beards but, giving good money for the sponsor's invitation, he was out in a three-under-par 33 to tie Nobilo at nine under par at the turn. 'That is the best I have ever played in that position,' he said. But it couldn't last. He came home in 40, one too many even to earn a top ten place and an unexpected start in the following week's tournament.

Elsewhere, Jose Maria Olazabal was sounding an echo of Bernhard Langer's

62 to win the Spanish Open in 1984. But he was running from too far back and a 66 took him only to 281, seven under par. Two other Ryder Cup men, Gordon Brand Junior and David Feherty, then had long putts on the final green but neither dropped so they stuck at eight under.

Nobilo had had one birdie and one bogey on the front nine and was still level par as the Scotsman and the Irishman watched him play El Saler's sting-in-the-tail final three holes on television. At the par four 16th he chipped to ten feet and holed the putt. At the 213-yard 17th he two-putted from 50 feet and then at the last he bunkered his approach behind the green, splashed out to four feet and holed that too.

'It was tough, but it was there to be won,' Nobilo said after finishing on 279,

nine under par, for a one-stroke victory. 'I made nine of the best pars of my life. I was really proud of the way I played the closing holes. I was patient and I never gave up.'

Here endeth today's lesson. Was that Jim Payne paying close attention?

Mark Davis drives through a funnel of trees.

COURSE: EL SALER		YARDAGE: 7091				PAR: 72	
POS	NAME	CTY	1	2	3	4	TOTAL	PRIZE MONEY

POS	NAME	CTY	1	2	3	4	TOTAL	PRIZE MONEY
1	Frank NOBILO	NZ	71	69	67	72	279	£66660
2	David FEHERTY	N.Ire	70	69	72	69	280	34740
	Gordon BRAND Jnr	Scot	70	72	70	68	280	34740
4	Thomas LEVET	Fr	71	70	69	71	281	15735
	Santiago LUNA	Sp	67	72	72	70	281	15735
	Costantino ROCCA	It	70	72	71	68	281	15735
	Jose Maria OLAZABAL	Sp	71	69	75	66	281	15735
8	Mark ROE	Eng	69	70	70	73	282	8232
	David GILFORD	Eng	70	73	70	69	282	8232
	Jim PAYNE	Eng	68	67	78	69	282	8232
	Jesper PARNEVIK	Swe	71	67	73	71	282	8232
	Mats LANNER	Swe	73	69	69	71	282	8232
13	Mark DAVIS	Eng	68	72	74	69	283	5896
	Roger CHAPMAN	Eng	72	71	67	73	283	5896
	Sam TORRANCE	Scot	71	70	68	74	283	5896
	Colin MONTGOMERIE	Scot	69	72	70	72	283	5896
	Glenn RALPH	Eng	74	68	68	73	283	5896
18	Jose Maria CANIZARES	Sp	71	70	75	68	284	4973
	Eduardo ROMERO	Arg	68	73	75	68	284	4973
	Fredrik LINDGREN	Swe	71	73	67	73	284	4973
21	Eoghan O'CONNELL	Ire	75	68	70	72	285	4620
	Bernhard LANGER	Ger	72	74	69	70	285	4620
23	Magnus SUNESSON	Swe	74	70	72	70	286	4140
	Justin HOBDAY	SA	74	68	74	70	286	4140
	Adam HUNTER	Scot	72	69	74	71	286	4140
	Vijay SINGH	Fij	69	74	73	70	286	4140
	De Wet BASSON	SA	72	71	72	71	286	4140
	Paul LAWRIE	Scot	77	67	71	71	286	4140
29	Johan RYSTROM	Swe	69	76	68	74	287	3488
	Peter BAKER	Eng	70	71	71	75	287	3488
	John McHENRY	Ire	72	69	76	70	287	3488
	Gary EVANS	Eng	73	68	72	74	287	3488
	Paul WAY	Eng	75	68	70	74	287	3488
34	Paul BROADHURST	Eng	72	69	73	74	288	3040
	Danny MIJOVIC	Can	73	72	73	70	288	3040
	Joakim HAEGGMAN	Swe	69	75	70	74	288	3040
	Russell CLAYDON	Eng	72	70	74	72	288	3040
	Phillip PRICE	Wal	73	71	74	70	288	3040
39	Mike HARWOOD	Aus	69	70	76	74	289	2680
	Philip WALTON	Ire	72	74	72	71	289	2680
	Chris MOODY	Eng	73	72	71	73	289	2680
	Stephen FIELD	Eng	71	74	72	72	289	2680
43	Patrick HALL	Eng	71	74	73	72	290	2360
	Heinz P THUL	Ger	69	73	75	73	290	2360
	Craig CASSELLS	Eng	72	73	75	70	290	2360
	Ian PALMER	SA	72	73	73	72	290	2360
47	Antonio GARRIDO	Sp	72	74	73	72	291	2120
	Barry LANE	Eng	72	73	74	72	291	2120
49	Vicente FERNANDEZ	Arg	72	73	75	72	292	1800
	Jose RIVERO	Sp	73	73	72	74	292	1800
	Keith WATERS	Eng	72	71	75	74	292	1800
	David J RUSSELL	Eng	73	73	70	76	292	1800
	Giuseppe CALI	It	73	73	76	70	292	1800
	Domingo HOSPITAL	Sp	72	72	74	74	292	1800
55	Jeremy ROBINSON	Eng	72	71	76	75	294	1368
	Richard BOXALL	Eng	73	72	75	74	294	1368
	Greg TURNER	NZ	72	68	76	78	294	1368
	Gordon J BRAND	Eng	72	73	72	77	294	1368
	Ruben ALVAREZ	Arg	71	68	74	81	294	1368
60	Roger WINCHESTER	Eng	72	73	73	77	295	1200
61	David R JONES	Eng	72	73	75	76	296	1140
	Ole ESKILDSEN	Den	72	74	75	75	296	1140
63	Craig McCLELLAN	USA	70	72	80	75	297	1040
	Bill MALLEY	USA	73	71	76	77	297	1040
	Andrew HARE	Eng	77	68	79	73	297	1040
66	Robert LEE	Eng	71	74	81	72	298	600
67	Mats HALLBERG	Swe	76	69	78	76	299	597
	Mike McLEAN	Eng	76	70	75	78	299	597
69	Roy MACKENZIE	Chil	75	71	79	75	300	593
	Antoine LEBOUC	Fr	75	71	75	79	300	593
71	Alberto BINAGHI	It	73	71	79	80	303	590

PAYNE MAKES IMMEDIATE AMENDS

The young man rated most likely to succeed took another step up the ladder to stardom in Majorca, even though he took a helping hand from another of Europe's brightest golf prospects. For Lincolnshire's Jim Payne, early days on the Volvo Tour have mirrored his outstanding amateur career. PGA European Tour Rookie of the Year honours in 1992 duly followed his Walker Cup achievements and the Open championship silver medal at Royal Birkdale in 1991.

The Turespana Iberia – Open de Baleares at Santa Ponça saw Payne become the third new champion in the first eight weeks of the 1993 Volvo Tour as he grabbed his chance in a sudden-death decider with Sweden's young hopeful, Anders Gillner.

The maiden victory which came just a few days before his 23rd birthday had almost arrived the previous week in Valencia where Payne had led by three shots at the halfway stage but took 78 in the third round and eventually finished eighth. That could so easily have resulted in another case of a promising new talent succumbing to the crushing pressure of the most competitive of golf tours, and quietly settling for a period of anonymity to lick his wounds.

But lanky Jim is a resilient character with an enviably unflappable temperament, and he is also a very quick learner.

Having lost a lead the previous week, Jim Payne redeemed himself in Majorca with his maiden Volvo Tour victory

Jack Nicklaus recognised these qualities when they played together in that 1991 Open, forecasting that he had the capacity to reach the very top. After Majorca Payne accordingly raised his sights.

'I learnt an awful lot from my failure in Valencia,' he said, 'and it made it much easier for me the second time I got into

contention.' He also appreciated the irony of succeeding the incomparable Seve Ballesteros as Open de Baleares champion only a few months after the Spaniard had taken the rookie aside to deliver some 'fatherly' advice.

Payne listened intently to that breakfast-time pep talk in a Spanish hotel and can now look back and laugh at his initial feelings of indignation. 'For a little while I wondered if my game was good enough,' he smiled.

Majorca 1993 proved that it was, even though it was Gillner's inability on the final day to play the last two par fours in a total of nine strokes that presented Payne with his place on the season's roll of honour.

The 25-year old Swedish golfer, also aiming for a maiden victory, led by two strokes when he stood on the 17th tee, only to take three putts at the drive and pitch hole. Then, needing a four at the uphill last, he found sand with his second shot and bladed his recovery right across the green.

That signalled a play-off for the second year running and when they returned to the 17th Anders again made a mess of the gentle dog-leg, missing the green with his pitch and chipping well short of the flag so that he could not match Payne's solid par four.

Jim Payne had forced himself into contention with a second round 66 and

on the last day had closed with a 67 for 277, eleven under par after starting out three shots adrift of PGA European Challenge Tour graduate Gillner.

Essex golfer David R Jones was third after closing with a course record 64 in which he had four birdies and an eagle in the first six holes of an outward 30. Jones had another eagle at the long 13th and birdied the last too in a bold attempt to score his first Volvo Tour success.

With two more Scandinavians, Steen Tinning and Joakim Haeggman, in the top ten the Open de Baleares once again proved a happy hunting ground for the northern Europeans. Gillner was the third Swedish runner-up in the event which his countryman Ove Sellberg won in 1989.

Three times champion Ballesteros had to withdraw after the first round, a victim of the back problems that had troubled him in Morocco and Cadiz in the previous fortnight. 'The problem is at the

Third place finish for David R Jones after final round course record.

bottom of the spine near the sacroiliac joint,' said Seve before taking a month's rest to prepare for Augusta. He said it hurt so much that he was not even able to pick up his children, and that his spirits were at the lowest they had been for many years. 'I have to wait for the rain to stop,' he added. 'I had my umbrella up but the water was still coming through.'

But it was all sunshine for Payne as he savoured the satisfaction of a victory that put him right in the running for a Johnnie Walker Ryder Cup place. 'It was a big relief to win my first professional tournament,' he said modestly. 'It has helped me raise my targets and now I know that when I get into contention I have the ability to win.'

Those who have charted his progress have known that all along, and that when the big occasion does arrive the quiet man from the east coast of England will not let himself or his supporters down.

Winning style from Jim Payne.

The winner is driven off to meet the press.

								PRIZE
POS	NAME	CTY	1	2	3	4	TOTAL	MONEY
1	Jim PAYNE	Eng	73	66	71	67	277	£50000
2	Anders GILLNER	Swe	71	69	67	70	277	33330
3	David R JONES	Eng	76	68	70	64	278	18780
4	Andrew SHERBORNE	Eng	72	70	66	71	279	15000
5	Steen TINNING	Den	69	69	70	72	280	11600
	Greg TURNER	NZ	70	70	73	67	280	11600
7	Ronan RAFFERTY	N.Ire	70	70	70	71	281	9000
8	Joakim HAEGGMAN	Swe	72	67	73	70	282	6730
	Ian PALMER	SA	71	68	72	71	282	6730
	Derrick COOPER	Eng	70	72	70	70	282	6730
11	Jose Maria OLAZABAL	Sp	71	71	72	69	283	5340
	Colin MONTGOMERIE	Scot	76	69	68	70	283	5340
13	Jesper PARNEVIK	Swe	70	72	70	72	284	4610
	Wayne RILEY	Aus	74	70	73	67	284	4610
	Frank NOBILO	NZ	72	69	74	69	284	4610
16	Costantino ROCCA	It	73	70	71	71	285	4230
17	Paul BROADHURST	Eng	72	72	70	72	286	3880
	Roger CHAPMAN	Eng	72	70	73	71	286	3880
	Jean VAN DE VELDE	Fr	72	72	70	72	286	3880
20	Ruben ALVAREZ	Arg	69	74	74	70	287	3420
	Fredrik LINDGREN	Swe	70	72	74	71	287	3420
	Steven RICHARDSON	Eng	72	69	70	76	287	3420
	Olle KARLSSON	Swe	73	68	73	73	287	3420
	Ove SELLBERG	Swe	70	76	71	70	287	3420
25	Yago BEAMONTE	Sp	73	73	69	73	288	2925
	Paul LAWRIE	Scot	71	73	74	70	288	2925
	Mark MOULAND	Wal	74	69	73	72	288	2925
	Mark DAVIS	Eng	71	72	72	73	288	2925
	Robert KARLSSON	Swe	73	73	70	72	288	2925
	Jamie SPENCE	Eng	71	71	72	74	288	2925
31	Adam HUNTER	Scot	73	72	72	72	289	2343
	Eduardo ROMERO	Arg	71	71	76	71	289	2343
	Paul McGINLEY	Ire	72	73	73	71	289	2343
	Heinz P THUL	Ger	73	72	71	73	289	2343
	Howard CLARK	Eng	72	73	72	72	289	2343
	Stephen McALLISTER	Scot	70	70	75	74	289	2343
	Michel BESANCENEY	Fr	74	68	73	74	289	2343
	Jose RIVERO	Sp	73	73	71	72	289	2343
	David RAY	Eng	74	71	74	70	289	2343
40	Roy MACKENZIE	Chil	74	69	74	73	290	1890
	Gary EVANS	Eng	70	73	72	75	290	1890
	Giuseppe CALI	It	73	72	75	70	290	1890
	Des SMYTH	Ire	72	72	73	73	290	1890
	Peter FOWLER	Aus	74	72	74	70	290	1890
	Retief GOOSEN	SA	71	71	74	74	290	1890
46	Miguel Angel JIMENEZ	Sp	73	69	77	72	291	1470
	Ian GARBUTT	Eng	72	71	74	74	291	1470
	Johan RYSTROM	Swe	70	73	77	71	291	1470
	Chris MOODY	Eng	77	66	78	70	291	1470
	Jon ROBSON	Eng	74	72	74	71	291	1470
	Peter MITCHELL	Eng	72	74	74	71	291	1470
	Magnus SUNESSON	Swe	72	72	75	72	291	1470
	David A RUSSELL	Eng	73	73	70	75	291	1470
54	Stephen FIELD	Eng	71	72	78	71	292	1055
	Peter TERAVAINEN	USA	74	71	76	71	292	1055
	Silvio GRAPPASONNI	It	70	75	71	76	292	1055
	Peter BAKER	Eng	70	73	71	78	292	1055
	Gary ORR	Scot	75	71	76	70	292	1055
	Eoghan O'CONNELL	Ire	69	75	76	72	292	1055
60	Antonio GARRIDO	Sp	72	74	76	71	293	· 885
	Jose Manuel CARRILES	Sp	73	72	74	74	293	885
62	Mike CLAYTON	Aus	71	72	77	74	294	825
	Malcolm MACKENZIE	Eng	72	74	75	73	294	825
64	Justin HOBDAY	SA	73	73	72	78	296	607
	Gordon J BRAND	Eng	74	72	76	74	296	607
	De Wet BASSON	SA	71	74	72	79	296	607
	Miguel GUZMAN	Arg	71	71	80	74	296	607
68	Haydn SELBY-GREEN	Eng	72	73	77	75	297	445
	Glen DAY	USA	73	73	72	79	297	445
70	David CURRY	Eng	69	77	76	77	299	441
	Ross DRUMMOND	Scot	75	70	77	77	299	441

COURSE: GOLF SANTA PONÇA, MAJORCA   YARDAGE: 7157   PAR: 72

GILFORD AT THE PINNACLE

At the start of the 1993 Volvo Tour David Gilford set himself a goal – to win one tournament and to gain at least six top ten finishes.

By the time he left Portugal after the ninth event of the year, the man from Crewe had chalked up two victories in his six starts and hadn't been out of the top ten in the others. It was, he admitted, 'time for a rethink'.

As he returned to his Midland farm with the Portuguese Open title, a first prize of £41,660, and the equivalent number of Johnnie Walker Ryder Cup points in his pocket, Gilford put a smile on the faces of Bernard Gallacher and his friendly building society manager. Gallacher's joy was manifest because Gilford, the man he had to omit from the Ryder Cup singles in Kiawah Island 18 months earlier to balance the teams when American Steve Pate pulled out through injury, had continued his climb up the points table and put himself well on the road to securing a place in the 1993 team. The building society chief was equally as happy because Gilford invests his winnings with him and another large cheque was on the way. 'It goes into the building society because I haven't room to

David Gilford's second title of the season took him to the top of the Volvo Order of Merit

buy any more cows,' explained Gilford.

Wearing less of a smile and with cows furthest from his thoughts was the former caddie from Argentina, Jorge Berendt, who was denied his first Tour victory by Gilford in a first hole play-off for the title at Vila Sol after both had finished on 13-under-par 275.

The 28-year-old family man from Formosa, 800 miles north of Buenos Aires, was the surprise package. Coming into the tournament, his best performances were two fourth places while in his previous seven outings of 1993, he had missed four cuts and finished no higher than 30th. He hardly rated a second

glance, but after opening up with a ten-birdie 63, just one outside the course record set by Jose Maria Canizares the previous year, Berendt was the focus of all attention.

He revealed that although he had won several times back home and was rated number three in Argentina behind Eduardo Romero and Vicente Fernandez, his poor form in Europe had been traced to a five-year-old wrist injury sustained on the hard surfaces in South America. With surgery unlikely to afford a cure, it forced him to change his swing and his grip so that it was so strong now that he showed four knuckles at address. It may have defied all the textbooks but it worked as he led by one from Sweden's Jesper Parnevik with Gilford and Kiwi Frank Nobilo, another 1993 winner, on 65, gleaned in such pleasant conditions that 56 players broke par.

The weather was just as kind on the second day when Gilford continued in his calm, collected way with a 66 to lead on 13-under-par 131, opening a three-stroke lead over Nobilo and Berendt who could do no better than 71. As Parnevik slipped back, the victim of a suspect Chinese meal the previous evening, the Swedish

**Runner-up Jorge Berendt,
right**

**Far right, David Gilford was only
occasionally off the rails**

challenge was taken up by Olle Karlsson, a shot further back with Britain's Jeremy Robinson, who had trimmed three strokes off his previous best Tour round with a stunning 64.

The 27-year-old who won the Zambia Open title last year by holing a 75 yard pitch shot after driving into trees in a three-way play-off, was due a break-through. He had earned his card in the previous two years by finishing in the top ten on the PGA European Challenge Tour but put his poor Volvo Tour form down to the after-effects of salmonella poisoning and his poor putting. 'But I just holed everything today,' he admitted.

Scoring was more difficult on a breezier third day but the spotlight remained on Gilford with a 70 – including an eagle two at the 16th when he holed a 150-yard seven iron – for 201, 15 under par, but Berendt nipped back into the frame with a 69 for 203 while Parnevik was back on song with a 67 for 204. However, lurking menacingly were Nobilo, five shots back, and Ryder Cup men Steven Richardson and Mark James, who both found form with 66s.

With Gilford and Berendt paired together, the final round turned into a head-to-head struggle that saw the lead change hands several times. Whether it was the pressure of the occasion or the less favourable conditions is open to debate, but both chose to produce their worst rounds of the week although Berendt made a perfect start with two birdies in the opening five holes to edge in front as Gilford double-bogeyed the third after tangling with a ditch.

However, he was ahead again after six holes as the Argentinian double-bogeyed the same hole and by the turn Gilford was two in front again, both being out in level par 36. With five holes to play, Gilford retained that cushion and seemed home and dry. But a momentary

lapse saw him drive into the trees on the long 14th for bogey and with Berendt gaining a birdie, they were level again.

When Gilford also bogeyed the 194-yard 15th to slip behind, thoughts turned to an Argentinian victory. But there was still a tale to tell. Berendt missed the green at the 16th to drop a shot. Level yet again. On the par four 18th, Gilford looked to have the title in his grasp after just missing his birdie while Berendt was still six feet away in three. But the gutsy South American coolly knocked it in to force the play-off.

Back to the 18th tee. Both reached the green in two, but Gilford was easily the

closer. Berendt putted from 25 feet and the ball shaved the hole. A safe par. Gilford wasn't going to let the chance slip again and from seven feet he knocked it in without fear or fuss.

Clearly disappointed, Berendt said: 'I was hitting the ball well, and felt I could win. I was nervous in the play-off, but now I know I can win on the Volvo Tour.' Although allowing himself a broad smile, Gilford was the epitome of modesty: 'I'm delighted but I didn't play well today until the play-off hole. In fact, I didn't play as well in the last two rounds as I had been, but it's hard to do so when you're in front.'

COURSE: VILA SOL GOLF CLUB, VILLAMOURA							YARDAGE: 6828	PAR: 72
POS	NAME	CTY	1	2	3	4	TOTAL	PRIZE MONEY
1	David GILFORD	Eng	65	66	70	74	275	£41660
2	Jorge BERENDT	Arg	63	71	69	72	275	27770
3	Mark JAMES	Eng	69	73	66	69	277	12916
	Frank NOBILO	NZ	66	68	72	71	277	12916
	Gordon J BRAND	Eng	68	72	70	67	277	12916
6	Martin POXON	Eng	66	70	74	68	278	8750
7	Sam TORRANCE	Scot	70	72	70	68	280	6450
	Ricky WILLISON	Eng	68	69	71	72	280	6450
	Fredrik LINDGREN	Swe	74	66	69	71	280	6450
10	Miguel Angel JIMENEZ	Sp	72	68	68	73	281	5000
11	Bill MALLEY	USA	70	66	70	76	282	4303
	Jesper PARNEVIK	Swe	64	73	67	78	282	4303
	Eduardo ROMERO	Arg	67	71	71	73	282	4303
14	Jose RIVERO	Sp	72	71	69	71	283	3387
	Steven RICHARDSON	Eng	70	71	66	76	283	3387
	John MCHENRY	Ire	71	72	68	72	283	3387
	Carl MASON	Eng	68	73	72	70	283	3387
	Johan RYSTROM	Swe	71	71	70	71	283	3387
	Mark ROE	Eng	70	67	76	70	283	3387
	Paul EALES	Eng	70	69	72	72	283	3387
21	Barry LANE	Eng	70	73	67	74	284	2850
	Des SMYTH	Ire	71	70	74	69	284	2850
	Jeremy ROBINSON	Eng	71	64	71	78	284	2850
24	Mike CLAYTON	Aus	73	71	73	68	285	2437
	Brian MARCHBANK	Scot	69	72	71	73	285	2437
	Jim PAYNE	Eng	70	74	71	70	285	2437
	Jonathan SEWELL	Eng	72	68	72	73	285	2437
	Marc FARRY	Fr	73	71	71	70	285	2437
	Howard CLARK	Eng	68	75	70	72	285	2437
	Roger CHAPMAN	Eng	75	69	73	68	285	2437
	Pierre FULKE	Swe	72	71	71	71	285	2437
32	Jose Manuel CARRILES	Sp	72	68	76	70	286	2100
33	Olle KARLSSON	Swe	69	66	77	75	287	1900
	Robert KARLSSON	Swe	72	71	69	75	287	1900
	Ronan RAFFERTY	N.Ire	67	76	72	72	287	1900
	Miguel Angel MARTIN	Sp	72	72	71	72	287	1900
	Andrew OLDCORN	Eng	72	70	72	73	287	1900
	Steen TINNING	Den	70	68	73	76	287	1900
	David CURRY	Eng	72	72	71	72	287	1900
40	Jon ROBSON	Eng	74	69	73	72	288	1650
	Steven BOWMAN	USA	75	69	72	72	288	1650
	Retief GOOSEN	SA	73	70	68	77	288	1650
43	Eamonn DARCY	Ire	71	72	70	76	289	1475
	Paul LAWRIE	Scot	68	74	76	71	289	1475
	Peter TERAVAINEN	USA	71	73	73	72	289	1475
	Stephen McALLISTER	Scot	68	75	74	72	289	1475
47	Mark MOULAND	Wal	71	72	71	76	290	1275
	Stephen BENNETT	Eng	72	71	76	71	290	1275
	Vicente FERNANDEZ	Arg	75	69	70	76	290	1275
	Ross DRUMMOND	Scot	70	71	73	76	290	1275
51	Phillip PRICE	Wal	70	72	75	74	291	1025
	Chris MOODY	Eng	72	70	70	79	291	1025
	Peter FOWLER	Aus	71	71	77	72	291	1025
	Anders SORENSEN	Den	70	72	73	76	291	1025
	David WILLIAMS	Eng	70	70	75	76	291	1025
	Jose ROZADILLA	Sp	68	75	76	72	291	1025
57	Roger WINCHESTER	Eng	72	71	73	76	292	825
	Gary EVANS	Eng	68	76	70	78	292	825
59	Santiago LUNA	Sp	71	72	77	74	294	775
60	Russell CLAYDON	Eng	75	68	75	77	295	737
	Mike McLEAN	Eng	69	73	77	76	295	737
62	Peter BAKER	Eng	71	73	76	76	296	687
	Glenn RALPH	Eng	74	70	71	81	296	687
64	Keith WATERS	Eng	68	71	74	85	298	650
65	Ruben ALVAREZ	Arg	71	71	72	85	299	625

No-one seriously threatened the leading two although James with 69, Gordon J Brand, 67, and Nobilo, 71, had high hopes but finished in joint third place two strokes back, while Parnevik and Robinson slipped down the field with closing 78s.

Even in his exalted position at the top of the Volvo Order of Merit, Gilford found time to play down his achievement. 'The people you'd expect to be challenging for the Volvo Order of Merit, people like Faldo and Woosnam, haven't played that much yet. I've had a fantastic start but there's still a long way to go.' With that he went off to set those new goals.

Husband and wife combination, Ricky and Alex Willison.

TORRANCE BACK IN THE RECKONING

Victory in Italy put Sam Torrance in the hunt for a place in the European Ryder Cup team

Remember Sam Torrance? Yes, of course you do: he's the cheery Scot who hits the ball a long way, putts with one of those broomhandle things and whose triumphal pose on the 18th green at The Belfry in the 1985 Ryder Cup is an image which hangs in practically every clubhouse in the land.

You could however, be forgiven if Torrance wasn't uppermost in your mind in tournament victory terms because it had been nearly two years since he mounted the winner's rostrum when he captured the Jersey European Airways Open in 1991. Domestic upheaval in the shape of moving house and the arrival of a new baby were the factors in Torrance's temporary absenteeism from the victory rolls.

In the Kronenbourg Open, played over the 7,114 yard Gardagolf Country Club at Salo, the Italian resort in the hills above Lake Garda, Torrance put his distractions behind him with a four-under-par total of 284 to take the title by one shot from fellow Scot Mike Miller and two from home hope Costantino Rocca.

Perhaps another motivating force was the Ryder Cup by Johnnie Walker. Torrance, an ever-present Ryder Cup player since 1981, had set his heart on a seventh appearance and his victory, worth £33,330, moved him from 31st to 21st in the Cup rankings, as well as boosting his confidence.

After an opening 69 which left him two strokes behind Andrew Sherborne and one behind Paolo Quirici, Torrance took charge in the second round with a 68. This put him two ahead of Rocca with Craig Cassells handily placed on 140. David Gilford, already a double winner in 1993, and Thomas Goegele were on 141 but Miller lay eight strokes off the pace which enabled Torrance to win his

own weight in Italian champagne as halfway leader.

Gusting winds and slick greens made scoring tricky on the third day but Torrance remained rock solid. He turned in level par and kept to the card all the way to the final hole. At this stage he was five shots clear of Rocca and Stephen McAllister. After a good drive which left him just 80 yards from the flag, Torrance put his sand-wedge approach shot into a bunker, splashed out and two-putted for a five. Worse still, Rocca with whom Torrance was playing, pitched on with his

second shot and holed the putt to cut the margin to three strokes.

Torrance was inconsolable. 'I couldn't believe I could miss the green from 80 yards,' he said. On the other hand, Rocca was delighted: 'My final birdie might make a big difference. You can't give a man like Sam five shots but three is another matter.' Meanwhile, Miller with a 71 had crept up into sixth place, six shots behind.

After three holes of the final round, Rocca's words were proving prophetic. Two birdies by the Italian and a bogey from Torrance and the two were tied. Then disaster struck Rocca. Two drives out of bounds on the fourth and fifth sank his challenge and by the turn Torrance was five strokes ahead.

Miller began with bogies at the first and third but redressed matters with a birdie at the fifth and a holed sand-wedge at the seventh for an eagle two. Even so, he also stood five behind the leader as they turned for home.

Then things started to go wrong for Torrance and began to go right for Miller. Three birdies on the inward half from Miller and two bogies from Torrance saw the lead down to one after Miller hit a four iron to 12 feet on the short 17th and holed the putt. Torrance came to the last needing a par four for victory and made sure there was no repeat of his third day aberration by pitching to five feet and two-putting. Miller's final round of 69 won him £22,220, the largest cheque of his career to date.

It was Torrance's 16th victory in Europe and his third in Italy but more importantly, it put him back in the Ryder Cup reckoning and another chance perhaps to repeat that victory salute at The Belfry in September.

**Costantino Rocca lined up
for third place.**

**Sam Torrance was worth his
weight in champagne.**

POS	NAME	CTY	1	2	3	4	TOTAL	PRIZE MONEY
	COURSE: GARDAGOLF COUNTRY CLUB				**YARDAGE: 7114**			**PAR: 72**
1	Sam TORRANCE	Scot	69	68	73	74	284	£33330
2	Mike MILLER	Scot	74	71	71	69	285	22220
3	Costantino ROCCA	It	69	70	74	73	286	12520
4	Antoine LEBOUC	Fr	73	76	71	68	288	7294
	Craig CASSELLS	Eng	71	69	75	73	288	7294
	Stephen McALLISTER	Scot	70	73	71	74	288	7294
	Brian MARCHBANK	Scot	72	72	74	70	288	7294
	Paul McGINLEY	Ire	72	72	73	71	288	7294
9	David GILFORD	Eng	72	69	76	72	289	4460
10	Thomas GOEGELE	Ger	70	71	78	71	290	3706
	Glenn RALPH	Eng	73	73	75	69	290	3706
	David RAY	Eng	75	68	75	72	290	3706
13	Richard BOXALL	Eng	72	73	74	72	291	3073
	Ian GARBUTT	Eng	74	70	75	72	291	3073
	Gabriel HJERTSTEDT	Swe	72	72	71	76	291	3073
16	Miguel GUZMAN	Arg	73	72	75	72	292	2700
	Marc PENDARIES	Fr	72	74	73	73	292	2700
	David CURRY	Eng	75	70	73	74	292	2700
19	Grant TURNER	Eng	75	72	73	73	293	2406
	Andrea CANESSA	It	74	73	71	75	293	2406
	Retief GOOSEN	SA	76	72	72	73	293	2406
22	Jim PAYNE	Eng	75	72	76	71	294	2160
	Ross DRUMMOND	Scot	73	73	75	73	294	2160
	David WILLIAMS	Eng	72	75	74	73	294	2160
	Jeremy ROBINSON	Eng	75	70	79	70	294	2160
	Domingo HOSPITAL	Sp	69	75	76	74	294	2160
27	Peter SMITH	Scot	70	78	75	72	295	1777
	Paul EALES	Eng	75	72	72	76	295	1777
	Peter MITCHELL	Eng	75	73	72	75	295	1777
	Jonathan SEWELL	Eng	70	78	77	70	295	1777
	Manuel MORENO	Sp	70	73	73	79	295	1777
	Jorge BERENDT	Arg	71	76	77	71	295	1777
	Giuseppe CALI	It	74	72	77	72	295	1777
	Gary ORR	Scot	71	74	74	76	295	1777
35	Russell CLAYDON	Eng	69	74	76	77	296	1480
	Ricky WILLISON	Eng	72	73	79	72	296	1480
	Alexander CEJKA	Ger	72	75	77	72	296	1480
	Joakim HAEGGMAN	Swe	70	74	76	76	296	1480
	Alberto BINAGHI	It	71	77	76	72	296	1480
40	John BICKERTON	Eng	69	75	73	80	297	1300
	Steven BOWMAN	USA	71	71	78	77	297	1300
	Jon ROBSON	Eng	74	73	76	74	297	1300
	Yago BEAMONTE	Sp	70	79	73	75	297	1300
44	Mike McLEAN	Eng	71	77	72	78	298	1080
	Andrew SHERBORNE	Eng	67	77	76	78	298	1080
	Tom PERNICE	USA	73	75	76	74	298	1080
	Lee JONES	Eng	71	73	75	79	298	1080
	Paul MAYO	Wal	75	74	73	76	298	1080
	Andrew COLTART	Scot	74	75	75	74	298	1080
	Miguel Angel MARTIN	Sp	74	70	75	79	298	1080
51	Adam HUNTER	Scot	72	73	78	76	299	860
	Clinton WHITELAW	SA	72	75	78	74	299	860
	Paul Richard SIMPSON	Eng	76	73	72	78	299	860
	John HAWKSWORTH	Eng	75	74	75	75	299	860
55	Mike CLAYTON	Aus	74	72	83	71	300	700
	Martin SLUDDS	Ire	71	75	76	78	300	700
	Scott WATSON	Eng	72	77	77	74	300	700
	Silvio GRAPPASONNI	It	74	73	78	75	300	700
59	Philip TALBOT	Eng	72	75	79	75	301	600
	Lee VANNET	Scot	75	74	78	74	301	600
	Dennis EDLUND	Swe	73	74	77	77	301	600
62	Ulrich ZILG	Ger	75	73	79	75	302	540
	David R JONES	Eng	75	74	79	74	302	540
	Paul CURRY	Eng	74	75	79	74	302	540
65	Ross McFARLANE	Eng	73	73	83	74	303	500
66	Massimo FLORIOLI	It	73	73	79	80	305	400
67	Kenny WALKER	Scot	75	72	86	77	310	398

ROCCA ON A ROLL

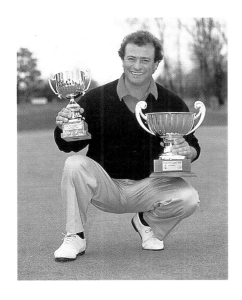

*A final round of 63
gave Costantino Rocca
his maiden Volvo Tour
victory*

He came from a poor family. No-one at home played golf. He began caddieing as a little lad of seven. He taught himself to play the game with a solitary two iron. By the time he was 35 he would be the best golfer in his country.

If Costantino Rocca's story sounds familiar it is only because a certain Severiano Ballesteros has already written the script. The Rocca Story, however, has twists of its own.

Ballesteros was a teenage prodigy, Rocca a late developer. While the Spaniard was winning his first Open title at Royal Lytham St Annes, the Italian had already spent six years working in a polystyrene factory in his home town of Bergamo. When Seve was winning his second US Masters Rocca had left the production line to become a caddie master. And while Ballesteros was performing Ryder Cup heroics the Italian was making unsuccessful visits to the PGA European Tour Qualifying School.

However, ten years after he hopefully turned professional with a four handicap, Rocca confirmed at the relatively mature golfing age of 36 what many have known for a while: he is the best Italian golfer in the world.

In gaining his maiden Volvo Tour victory at the Open V33 du Grand Lyon the amiable Rocca became the first of his countrymen to win on Tour since Massimo Mannelli took the Italian Open in 1980.

That Rocca possessed the ability to win on Tour was not in dispute. Since 1990 the dashing Italian had become a regular fixture among the top 50 money winners in Europe. He had threatened victory on a number of occasions – not least the week before Lyon at the Kronenbourg Open when, having tied for the lead after three holes of the final round, Rocca

went out of bounds twice at the fourth and fifth.

But there were many, including it must be said Rocca himself, who doubted his temperament. 'The head is difficult,' said Rocca in his stumbling English, after victory in France. 'I did not feel my concentration before was good. Other players more strong than me.' Far from demoralising him, Rocca's disappointment the week before had given him the little extra confidence. 'Last week I play good. After five holes I hit two out-of-bounds and still finish third,' he said. 'Today I am playing against the course, not the player – and this, a 63.'

It was a victory born of gritty resolve and a liberal dose of Latin style and

panache. Tied for the lead at 12 under par going into the final round, Rocca's closing 63 not only obliterated the challenge from the rest of the field, it also secured him a bonus of £10,000 from Johnnie Walker for setting a new course record at Villette D'Anthon. Laser-like iron play gained the Italian nine birdies and not a single bogey. His two longest birdie putts were 12 and 15 feet, and for six of the other seven birdies Rocca was not more than five feet from the hole.

It was a demoralising experience for Rocca's closest final day challenger, 26-year old Paul McGinley. While the Italian's flashing blade produced birdie after birdie, McGinley, playing in the group ahead, struggled to stay with him. Both players went to the turn in a four under par 32, but with Rocca firing a hat-trick of birdies from the tenth McGinley, who had drawn level at one stage thanks to a putt of 30 feet for an eagle at the sixth, found himself three strokes adrift with four holes to play. 'I lost momentum when I saw him birdie hole after hole,' said the former Walker Cup golfer. 'I felt I was playing well, but what can you do if someone goes out and shoots 63?'

What you do is play aggressively. At the 540-yard, par-five 15th the Irishman decided to go for the green in two in search of an eagle. But with 257 yards to the pin, off an uneven lie, McGinley pushed his three wood right, into a small copse short of the green. The Irishman's escape caught more branches and dropped short of the green where, from a horrible lie, he chipped onto the edge of the green, before two-putting for bogey.

For good measure, Rocca, who had been watching the drama unfold from the middle of the fairway, unleashed a glorious wedge from 110 yards to two feet. The resulting birdie, and another at the following hole, completed a comprehensive display.

McGinley eventually settled for a share of second place, his best finish on Tour thus far, thanks to a slippery putt he holed at the last for par and a closing 68 for a total of 273. Also on the 273 mark were England's Barry Lane, and a pair of Swedes – Joakim Haeggman and Gabriel Hjertstedt. The 21-year old Hjertstedt, who emigrated to Australia when he was 11, and whose father owns a textile factory there, was the halfway leader in France at 11 under par. The youngster was asked what it felt like to see his name on the leaderboard. 'I don't know,' said the Swede, 'they haven't spelt it right yet.'

If the experience was unusual for Hjertstedt, it was becoming something of a welcome habit for Mike Miller. The previous week the 41-year old, who finished 148th on the 1992 Volvo Order of Merit and lost his Tour card, had finished second in the Kronenbourg Open without the aid of a caddie. In France he opened with 64 to be first-round leader, followed with a 71 and 69, then found himself out last with Rocca on Sunday. 'It's nice to be playing at this end of the field for a change,' said the Scot, who pulled his own trolley for the first two rounds in France. 'Everybody keeps asking me what has happened. And I keep saying I don't know. I hadn't played for five weeks before Italy. I hadn't practised for five weeks, the weather was dreadful,' said Miller who eventually settled for a tie for seventh place.

In Italy it was Miller who had been unable to find a caddie for the weekend. In France it was a similar story, although this time it was the entire field who found themselves chasing after an Italian ex-caddie master. But no-one could catch Costantino Rocca.

Rough times for joint runner-up Paul McGinley.

POS	NAME	CTY	1	2	3	4	TOTAL	PRIZE MONEY
1	Costantino ROCCA	It	67	71	66	63	267	£41660
2	Joakim HAEGGMAN	Swe	69	72	66	66	273	16630
	Gabriel HJERTSTEDT	Swe	67	67	72	67	273	16630
	Paul McGINLEY	Ire	67	69	69	68	273	16630
	Barry LANE	Eng	70	69	70	64	273	16630
6	Antoine LEBOUC	Fr	70	72	67	66	275	8750
7	Mike MILLER	Scot	64	71	69	72	276	6087
	Steven RICHARDSON	Eng	67	73	70	66	276	6087
	Frank NOBILO	NZ	69	67	70	70	276	6087
	Gary ORR	Scot	68	69	72	67	276	6087
11	Mark DAVIS	Eng	72	69	69	67	277	4445
	Gordon J BRAND	Eng	69	73	68	67	277	4445
13	Gordon BRAND Jnr	Scot	68	71	70	69	278	3757
	Jean Ignace MOUHICA	Fr	69	70	66	73	278	3757
	Santiago LUNA	Sp	71	71	70	66	278	3757
	Per-Ulrik JOHANSSON	Swe	71	70	70	67	278	3757
17	Andrew SHERBORNE	Eng	70	73	71	65	279	3233
	Michel BESANCENEY	Fr	72	72	71	64	279	3233
	Martin GATES	Eng	75	69	67	68	279	3233
20	Jamie SPENCE	Eng	70	68	73	69	280	2812
	Ian GARBUTT	Eng	73	70	69	68	280	2812
	Anders SORENSEN	Den	71	69	69	71	280	2812
	Ricky WILLISON	Eng	70	72	68	70	280	2812
	Jose RIVERO	Sp	70	69	72	69	280	2812
	Peter TERAVAINEN	USA	67	70	75	68	280	2812
26	Andre BOSSERT	Swi	69	71	72	69	281	2325
	Peter MITCHELL	Eng	72	72	66	71	281	2325
	Lee VANNET	Scot	71	71	67	72	281	2325
	David R JONES	Eng	71	70	73	67	281	2325
	Miguel GUZMAN	Arg	75	67	70	69	281	2325
	Wayne RILEY	Aus	69	72	73	67	281	2325
	Roger CHAPMAN	Eng	70	70	72	69	281	2325
33	Ross DRUMMOND	Scot	70	70	73	69	282	1875
	Ronan RAFFERTY	N.Ire	75	69	70	68	282	1875
	Mark ROE	Eng	74	70	69	69	282	1875
	Alfonso PINERO	Sp	68	72	73	69	282	1875
	Andrew HARE	Eng	69	73	72	68	282	1875
	David CURRY	Eng	71	73	70	68	282	1875
	Stephen McALLISTER	Scot	69	70	70	73	282	1875
	Johan RYSTROM	Swe	71	71	68	72	282	1875
41	Anders GILLNER	Swe	71	69	71	72	283	1550
	Andrew MURRAY	Eng	69	70	74	70	283	1550
	Nick GODIN	Eng	71	69	69	74	283	1550
	Lee JONES	Eng	71	71	72	69	283	1550
	Gavin LEVENSON	SA	75	68	72	68	283	1550
46	Thomas LEVET	Fr	71	73	71	69	284	1300
	Clinton WHITELAW	SA	71	69	74	70	284	1300
	Paul EALES	Eng	70	72	73	69	284	1300
	David GILFORD	Eng	72	71	71	70	284	1300
	Domingo HOSPITAL	Sp	71	72	73	68	284	1300
51	Paul BROADHURST	Eng	71	72	71	71	285	1000
	Steve REY	Swi	70	70	74	71	285	1000
	Marc PENDARIES	Fr	71	73	70	71	285	1000
	Paul CURRY	Eng	73	69	74	69	285	1000
	Philip TALBOT	Eng	70	73	71	71	285	1000
	John McHENRY	Ire	72	71	71	71	285	1000
	Adam HUNTER	Scot	73	71	69	72	285	1000
58	Giuseppe CALI	It	70	73	70	73	286	750
	Mike CLAYTON	Aus	70	71	70	75	286	750
	Eric GIRAUD	Fr	74	70	73	69	286	750
	Paolo QUIRICI	Swi	72	71	72	71	286	750
	Haydn SELBY-GREEN	Eng	76	68	72	70	286	750
63	Eoghan O'CONNELL	Ire	73	68	72	74	287	650
	Ignacio GERVAS	Sp	69	74	71	73	287	650
	Darren CLARKE	N.Ire	69	72	76	70	287	650
66	Stephen BENNETT	Eng	72	70	72	74	288	399
	Paul MAYO	Wal	70	74	73	71	288	399
68	Marc FARRY	Fr	75	68	75	71	289	396
69	Andrew COLTART	Scot	72	72	73	73	290	394
70	Nicolas KALOUGUINE	Fr	72	69	74	76	291	391
	Steen TINNING	Den	71	71	75	74	291	391
72	Derrick COOPER	Eng	69	72	77	74	292	388
73	Fabrice TARNAUD	Fr	72	70	76	75	293	385
	Mats HALLBERG	Swe	70	70	77	76	293	385

COURSE: GOLF CLUB DE LYON   YARDAGE: 6764   PAR: 72

VIVE VAN DE VELDE

Jean Van de Velde became the first Frenchman to win in Europe for 23 years

The last time a Frenchman won a European tour event, the hippies from the 1960s had started to surface from a euphoric haze, Edward Heath was preparing the nation for a Tory comeback and Jack Nicklaus was busy at St Andrews securing his second Open title. That was in 1970 and Jean Van de Velde, France's top golfer today, was just four years old.

At such a tender age, Van de Velde could not have known that fellow countryman Jean Garialde was the man to beat then. He was his country's golfing hero, the only Frenchman ever to win on the professional European circuit. He was crowned 1970 German Open champion the year after he had won the French, German and Spanish titles. France has been waiting ever since for another tournament winner – now she has one in Van de Velde.

Van de Velde, who comes from Mont de Marsan, defeated Greg Turner of New Zealand in a play-off for the Roma Masters title and proved that victory on today's Volvo Tour is within a Frenchman's reach.

Van de Velde has been the highest-placed Frenchman on the Volvo Order of Merit for the past four years, reaching 42nd in 1991, but until his victory in Rome his greatest achievement was as a member of his country's Alfred Dunhill Cup team which stunned the favourites, the US, in 1990. Van de Velde played a crucial role in that upset, halving his match with Curtis Strange, twice US Open champion.

He didn't need two team members and the atmosphere of St Andrews to produce inspired results at the Robert Trent Jones-designed Castelgandolfo Country Club near Rome. He opened with a 66 and then appeared to lose his head at the start of the second round. He had three bogeys in the first four holes and the result was a 76. On Saturday afternoon,

however, Van de Velde had a 67 and was back at the top of the leaderboard sharing it, albeit briefly, with England's Jamie Spence on seven under par.

Spence missed his chance of a second Volvo Tour title – and valuable Johnnie Walker Ryder Cup points – after taking an incorrect drop at the 15th. The two-shot penalty imposed by tournament officials resulted in disqualification for the 1992 Canon European Masters champion. 'It was my fault and I was absolutely devastated,' he said, adding, 'They say you learn the game the hard way.'

Van de Velde took a lead of one stroke into Sunday's final round and was still ahead by three strokes when he came to grief at the 514-yard 15th hole where he took a seven. Two holes later, Turner, his playing companion, chipped in for a birdie to tie for the lead. Van de Velde finished with a 72 to Turner's 71 and only squeezed into a play-off by holing a putt of 20 feet on the final hole.

It was nearly a three-way tie. De Wet Basson, the promising 24-year old from South Africa, finished strongly with rounds of 68 and 69. The problem was that the 69 on Sunday included a double bogey on the last green when a par would have sent him back to the 16th with the other two. So, level on 281, seven under par, the Frenchman and the Kiwi strode to the 366-yard 16th to settle the score.

Following flawless golf at the first two extra holes, it was on to the small, kidney-shaped 18th green for a third time.

Then, Turner executed a clumsy chip from off the green and, obviously unsettled, missed his par putt of eight feet. After Van de Velde had chipped beautifully to seven feet, he confidently rolled in his putt to the centre of the hole and punched the air in triumphant fashion

'For me this feels good. It was only a question of time,' said the man who believes that his breakthrough should prove a spur for future French success. 'For the past 20 years there have been only two or three French golfers on the circuit. This year there are six. Now that I have won the others will know that winning is not impossible.'

Meanwhile, the local hero Costantino Rocca was still acknowledging familiar but frenzied calls of 'bravo' for his first victory on the Volvo Tour in the Open V33 de Grand Lyon two weeks earlier. An even par final round in Rome helped him to finish third. It was his sixth finish in the top ten this season.

For Rocca victory was not meant to be. And perhaps that is right. Rocca, the Italian, had won in France so it was only appropriate that Van de Velde, the Frenchman, should triumph in Italy.

Exultation from Jean Van de Velde as winning putt drops.

Van de Velde climbed to the top at Castelgandolfo.

COURSE: CASTELGANDOLFO, ROME			YARDAGE: 6786				PAR: 72	
POS	NAME	CTY	1	2	3	4	TOTAL	PRIZE MONEY
1	Jean VAN DE VELDE	Fr	66	76	67	72	281	£50000
2	Greg TURNER	NZ	72	68	70	71	281	33330
3	Costantino ROCCA	It	68	68	74	72	282	18780
4	De Wet BASSON	SA	75	71	68	69	283	15000
5	Barry LANE	Eng	69	71	72	72	284	10733
	Frank NOBILO	NZ	68	73	73	70	284	10733
	Des SMYTH	Ire	74	67	73	70	284	10733
8	David GILFORD	Eng	73	73	70	69	285	7095
	Gary ORR	Scot	73	72	68	72	285	7095
10	Peter FOWLER	Aus	71	74	70	71	286	5220
	Ulrich ZILG	Ger	76	67	71	72	286	5220
	Alberto BINAGHI	It	70	71	75	70	286	5220
	Jeremy ROBINSON	Eng	70	71	69	76	286	5220
	Michel BESANCENEY	Fr	69	73	71	73	286	5220
15	Santiago LUNA	Sp	75	71	69	72	287	3793
	Adam HUNTER	Scot	68	71	77	71	287	3793
	Domingo HOSPITAL	Sp	71	69	71	76	287	3793
	Martin GATES	Eng	72	71	74	70	287	3793
	Paul CURRY	Eng	74	68	71	74	287	3793
	Silvio GRAPPASONNI	It	69	75	73	70	287	3793
	Paul MAYO	Wal	73	72	75	67	287	3793
	Glenn RALPH	Eng	73	69	74	71	287	3793
	John McHENRY	Ire	74	71	70	72	287	3793
24	Jay TOWNSEND	USA	68	73	73	74	288	3105
	Sam TORRANCE	Scot	73	72	75	68	288	3105
	Mats LANNER	Swe	74	70	72	72	288	3105
	Jim PAYNE	Eng	70	72	72	74	288	3105
28	Roger WINCHESTER	Eng	75	70	70	74	289	2700
	Stephen McALLISTER	Scot	71	72	78	68	289	2700
	Gordon J BRAND	Eng	71	69	72	77	289	2700
	Gordon BRAND Jnr	Scot	72	73	69	75	289	2700
	Paolo QUIRICI	Swi	72	71	75	71	289	2700
33	Giuseppe CALI	It	70	72	74	74	290	2280
	Mike McLEAN	Eng	72	72	73	73	290	2280
	Sven STRUVER	Ger	70	76	72	72	290	2280
	Jonathan SEWELL	Eng	70	75	73	72	290	2280
	Mark JAMES	Eng	72	71	71	76	290	2280
	Retief GOOSEN	SA	76	71	69	74	290	2280
	Charles RAULERSON	USA	74	72	73	71	290	2280
40	Bill MALLEY	USA	74	73	73	71	291	2040
41	Steve REY	Swi	76	71	74	71	292	1890
	Fredrik LINDGREN	Swe	74	69	74	75	292	1890
	David A RUSSELL	Eng	72	69	72	79	292	1890
	Peter BAKER	Eng	71	72	73	76	292	1890
45	Darren CLARKE	N.Ire	71	76	71	75	293	1680
	Jeff HALL	Eng	74	72	71	76	293	1680
	Paul WAY	Eng	72	71	73	77	293	1680
48	Jose ROZADILLA	Sp	76	71	72	75	294	1410
	Tim PLANCHIN	Fr	74	73	71	76	294	1410
	Andre BOSSERT	Swi	75	72	75	72	294	1410
	Howard CLARK	Eng	71	74	76	73	294	1410
	Carl MASON	Eng	73	71	77	73	294	1410
54	Haydn SELBY-GREEN	Eng	72	72	78	73	295	1140
	Stephen BENNETT	Eng	72	72	74	77	295	1140
	David WILLIAMS	Eng	71	75	74	75	295	1140
57	Alexander CEJKA	Ger	74	73	77	72	296	970
	Russell CLAYDON	Eng	76	71	74	75	296	970
	Eoghan O'CONNELL	Ire	76	71	75	74	296	970
60	Heinz P THUL	Ger	71	72	75	79	297	885
	Gabriel HJERTSTEDT	Swe	76	71	74	76	297	885
62	Lee JONES	Eng	71	75	76	76	298	810
	Lee VANNET	Scot	75	71	75	77	298	810
	Ole ESKILDSEN	Den	72	75	76	75	298	810
65	Jose Manuel CARRILES	Sp	76	70	76	77	299	750
66	Paul EALES	Eng	72	73	75	80	300	447
	Baldovino DASSU	It	79	68	77	76	300	447
	Paul LAWRIE	Scot	72	74	74	80	300	447
	Philip WALTON	Ire	71	76	75	78	300	447
70	Antoine LEBOUC	Fr	69	77	77	78	301	442
71	Emanuele CANONICA	It	72	69	78	83	302	440
72	Jon EVANS	Eng	74	73	79	77	303	438
73	Ian GARBUTT	Eng	75	71	81	77	304	436

Greg Turner was play-off victim on the third extra hole.

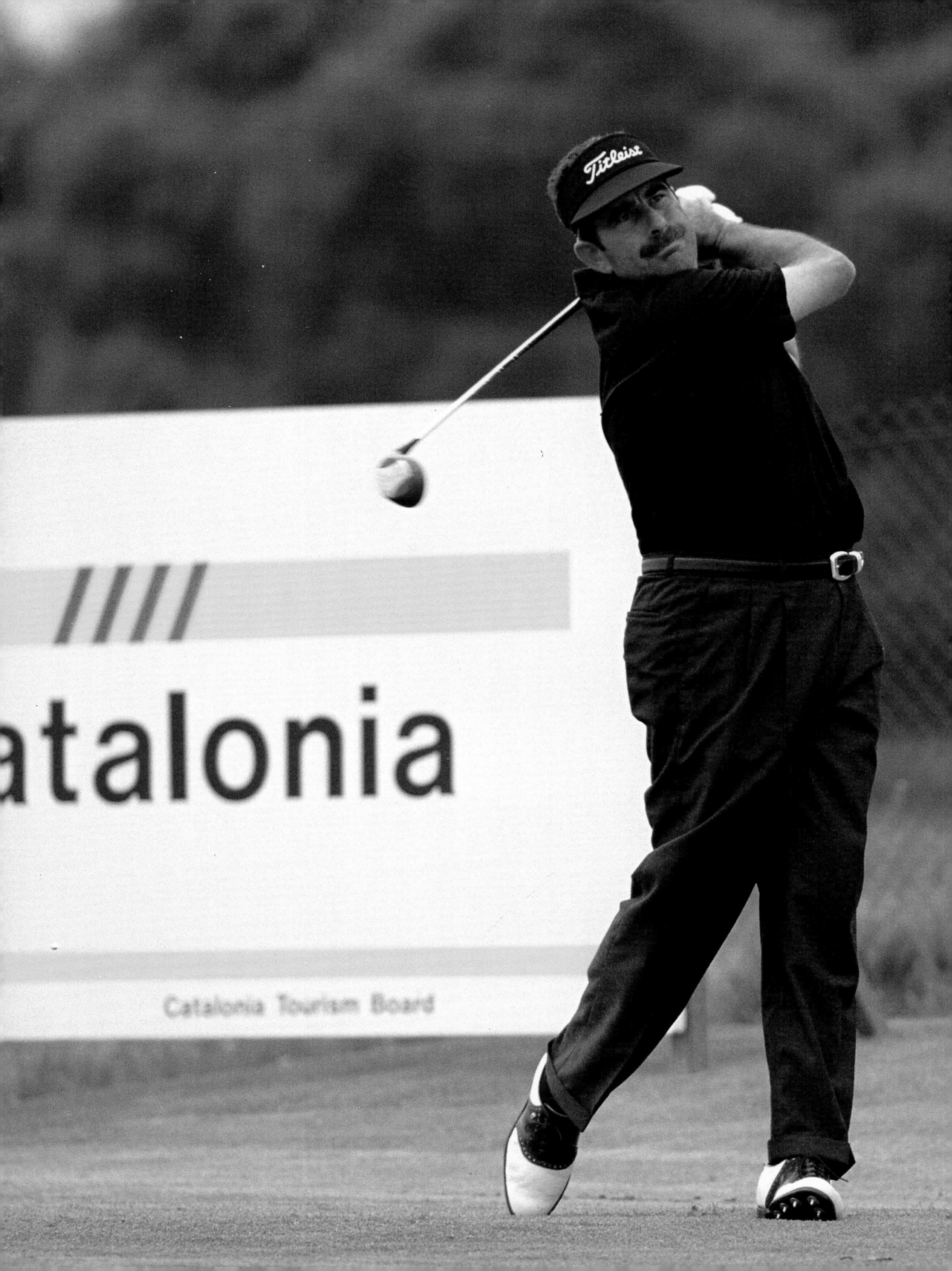
Titleist
atalonia
Catalonia Tourism Board

TORRANCE BENEFITS FROM THE TORRENT

The Ryder Cup was in everyone's mind by the time the Volvo Tour reached the Olympic town of Barcelona in late April – for no-one more than Sam Torrance, the player who sank the putt at The Belfry on that memorable afternoon in 1985 which finally ended nearly a quarter of a century of American dominance.

Having missed his chance of totting up points in late 1992 by playing so poorly until the last few tournaments, Torrance was anxious to start 1993 with a bang. If he did, he reasoned, he would put himself well in contention for his seventh successive appearance in the Ryder Cup.

He did that with a battling victory in the Kronenbourg Open. By the time the Heineken Open Catalonia was over – rain, hail, lightning *et al* – Torrance had given himself hope that he would be in Europe's team at The Belfry in September.

What the affable Scot called his 'alcohol double' was completed when he did not have to strike a ball on the final day at Osona Montanya. The last round was abandoned as rain and hail made the mountain-top course unplayable apart from 50 minutes around mid-day. At times it resembled a ski run. The £50,000 and points collected for his 17th European success enabled Torrance to zoom up to 14th place in the points table and left him saying: 'Now I've got half the work done. I'm not going to let the Ryder Cup put me under pressure, but at the same time I'm desperate to play. Sinking the putt in 1985 was and is the highlight of my

Sam Torrance secured his second Volvo Tour title of the season when rain caused the final round to be abandoned

career. I wouldn't mind if it all happened to me again. In fact, I'd love it.'

The foundations for his triumph at Osona Montanya were laid when he scored a glorious nine-under-par 63 in the second round, a course record which earned him another £2,000 for the Johnnie Walker Course Record Award. Just behind Torrance came the man from

Jupiter (in Florida that is) Jay Townsend, who moved into second place with Barry Lane after two rounds. Townsend was to push Torrance all the way until late on Saturday when a sudden collapse on the greens halted him in his tracks. Even so Townsend chalked up his best finish, coming second to Torrance and earning a healthy £33,330.

Osona Montanya was the home for the equestrian event at the Olympics and the eventing water hazard yawned between the 17th and 18th fairways. The undulating, winding course had been more used to hooves than spikes; Dave Thomas licked it into shape though, and scorching sunshine gave no hint of the rainy blasts to come. A field containing several appearing for the first time in Europe after their forays at Augusta – Ian Woosnam, Jose Maria Olazabal, Colin Montgomerie and Anders Forsbrand – tackled a layout that often required more of a subtly-placed iron off the tee than a booming drive.

What Costantino Rocca could do, his touring friend and fellow countryman Alberto Binaghi, fired by his room-mate's success in Lyon, could do too, he felt. He had a first round of 65 to give him a share of the lead with Andrew Sherborne. The Bristolian was trying for a Spanish hat-trick in as many years after wining the 1991 Madrid Open and the 1992 Peugeot Spanish Open.

They reckoned without Torrance though. The Scot was lucky to be able to play at all after he had displaced a rib while lifting his luggage the week before. He had it manipulated by a Sunningdale physiotherapist just in time for him to think about flying to Spain. Then he charged into the lead on Friday morning. He began with seven successive threes, among them an eagle and four birdies. The three-ball in which he was playing recorded a spectacular 17 under par with a best-ball score of 57. Lane posted a 67 and Gary Evans a 69.

Woosnam threatened and another Scot, Ross Drummond, was just two off the pace. Woosnam reckoned he was beginning to see signs of benefit from 'standing taller to the ball and stretching myself from 5ft 1in to 5ft 5in again.'

In the end though, no-one could stand as tall as Torrance, not even Jose Rivero who made a fine defence of his title for 12th place and not Townsend who dropped three shots in two holes in a flurry of missed putts.

The downpour left everyone whiling away hours in the locker room and club-house. Torrance lost £80 playing cards with Jamie Spence before he was declared the winner. 'It was my longest day,' Torrance said. 'I was as much on edge as I've been in my life. But I did it on Saturday really and that's fitting. It was my parents' 40th wedding anniversary so this was a nice little present for them.'

Torrance had another couple of nice presents to hand out. He gave five per cent of his winnings to his caddie, Billy Foster, Seve's caddie, who was standing in for Malcolm Mason. Mason also got five per cent. Sam had promised it to his faithful bagman who had been on honeymoon the week the boss came up with his alcohol double. No small beer for the caddies either!

The hail in Spain stayed mainly on the golf course.

Sam Torrance finishes his third round for what was ultimately victory.

Welcome refreshment for the winner.

COURSE: OSONA MONTANYA GOLF CLUB, BRULL						YARDAGE: 6727	PAR: 72
POS	NAME	CTY	1	2	3	4	TOTAL	PRIZE MONEY
1	Sam TORRANCE	Scot	71	63	67		201	£50000
2	Jay TOWNSEND	USA	66	69	69		204	33330
3	Andrew SHERBORNE	Eng	65	72	68		205	16890
	Paul WAY	Eng	66	73	66		205	16890
5	Jesper PARNEVIK	Swe	69	68	69		206	10733
	David CURRY	Eng	69	73	64		206	10733
	Eamonn DARCY	Ire	69	68	69		206	10733
8	Gary EVANS	Eng	68	69	70		207	6427
	Ian WOOSNAM	Wal	69	67	71		207	6427
	Jose Maria OLAZABAL	Sp	68	73	66		207	6427
	Ross DRUMMOND	Scot	66	70	71		207	6427
12	Barry LANE	Eng	68	67	73		208	4644
	Darren CLARKE	N.Ire	66	73	69		208	4644
	Jose RIVERO	Sp	70	68	70		208	4644
	Martin GATES	Eng	67	70	71		208	4644
	Frank NOBILO	NZ	68	71	69		208	4644
17	Steen TINNING	Den	67	70	72		209	4050
18	Fredrik LINDGREN	Swe	69	69	72		210	3624
	De Wet BASSON	SA	69	69	72		210	3624
	Malcolm MACKENZIE	Eng	70	69	71		210	3624
	Alberto BINAGHI	It	65	72	73		210	3624
	Chris MOODY	Eng	72	71	67		210	3624
23	Jeremy ROBINSON	Eng	69	70	72		211	2882
	Per-Ulrik JOHANSSON	Swe	71	69	71		211	2882
	Ole ESKILDSEN	Den	71	72	68		211	2882
	Heinz P THUL	Ger	68	74	69		211	2882
	Steven BOWMAN	USA	70	72	69		211	2882
	Miguel Angel MARTIN	Sp	69	73	69		211	2882
	Andrew HARE	Eng	68	71	72		211	2882
	Jose DAVILA	Sp	70	73	68		211	2882
	Anders GILLNER	Swe	69	72	70		211	2882
	Gordon J BRAND	Eng	70	72	69		211	2882
	Jim PAYNE	Eng	68	72	71		211	2882
34	Brian MARCHBANK	Scot	68	75	69		212	2220
	Jean VAN DE VELDE	Fr	70	73	69		212	2220
	Retief GOOSEN	SA	73	69	70		212	2220
	Jamie SPENCE	Eng	68	75	69		212	2220
	Jose COCERES	Arg	72	69	71		212	2220
	Greg TURNER	NZ	67	72	73		212	2220
	Jose Manuel CARRILES	Sp	69	71	72		212	2220
41	Stephen AMES	T&T	68	76	69		213	1950
	Peter FOWLER	Aus	73	69	71		213	1950
43	Paul CURRY	Eng	68	75	71		214	1680
	Paul EALES	Eng	71	71	72		214	1680
	Andre BOSSERT	Swi	69	71	74		214	1680
	Jose Maria CANIZARES	Sp	69	72	73		214	1680
	Anders FORSBRAND	Swe	70	73	71		214	1680
	Stephen McALLISTER	Scot	70	70	74		214	1680
	Roy MACKENZIE	Chil	72	71	71		214	1680
50	David J RUSSELL	Eng	70	69	76		215	1320
	Silvio GRAPPASONNI	It	67	73	75		215	1320
	Domingo HOSPITAL	Sp	69	72	74		215	1320
	Jose ROZADILLA	Sp	73	70	72		215	1320
	Paul McGINLEY	Ire	70	74	71		215	1320
55	Richard BOXALL	Eng	71	72	73		216	1080
	Robin MANN	Eng	70	74	72		216	1080
	Derrick COOPER	Eng	70	73	73		216	1080
58	Mike HARWOOD	Aus	72	70	75		217	930
	Wayne RILEY	Aus	71	73	73		217	930
	Philip WALTON	Ire	70	74	73		217	930
61	David RAY	Eng	72	72	74		218	840
	Magnus SUNESSON	Swe	70	73	75		218	840
	Ove SELLBERG	Swe	72	71	75		218	840
64	Adam HUNTER	Scot	72	71	76		219	607
	Ronan RAFFERTY	N.Ire	71	70	78		219	607
	Bill MALLEY	USA	70	74	75		219	607
	Anders SORENSEN	Den	73	71	75		219	607
68	Olle KARLSSON	Swe	74	70	76		220	445
	Ignacio GERVAS	Sp	71	72	77		220	445
70	Martin POXON	Eng	72	69	80		221	442

Home hope

Jose Maria

Olazabal.

DAVIS WINS IN FAMILIAR STRIDES

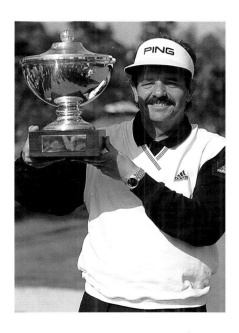

Ken Schofield, Executive Director of the PGA European Tour, made a point when looking back over the 1992 Volvo Tour season of singling out for special praise the three over-40s who had enjoyed victories: Jose Maria Canizares in the Roma Masters, Christy O'Connor Junior in the Dunhill British Masters and Vicente Fernandez in the Murphy's English Open. 'Their performances indicated that given dedication and discipline careers can remain successful over two or more decades,' said Schofield. 'I feel their experiences can and will benefit our new generation of players.'

If 40 is the age when one takes on 'elder statesman' status on Tour – 50 being the age when one officially becomes a senior and eligible for pastures new – then the Air France Cannes Open brought the first such victory of 1993, with Australian Rodger Davis as the player in question.

Two weeks away from his 42nd birthday Davis, a Tour regular since 1977, was looking and feeling not old, but like his old self. First there was his return to plus-two trousers and monogrammed socks, last seen at the 1990 Open, and secondly there was the rejuvenation effect of almost four months at home. 'I hadn't planned to take so long off,' he explained. 'I was hoping to be given a place in the US Masters, but when that

Resplendent in his famous plus two trousers, Rodger Davis was back on the victory trail

didn't come I just decided to extend my break. My family got to know me again and even the dog stopped barking when I came in. I needed the lay-off and it's done me the world of good. I'm ready to play again and I want to get back in the top ten on the Sony World Ranking.' He had fallen to 33rd.

Davis's return to Europe had actually been at the previous week's Heineken

Open Catalonia, but the less said about that the better. He missed the cut by nine strokes, finishing off his second round 82 with a quadruple bogey nine. Rodger and out in a big way.

After a week of rust removing on the practice range, however, the Sydney golfer followed up an opening 68 with a sparkling 64. It was Jolly Rodger now. Whereas he had trouble staying on the course at Osona Montanya – that nine included two out-of-bounds drives – here he had difficulty straying from the flag. Of his nine birdies seven came with putts of five feet or less. Putts all made using the increasingly popular Bernhard Langer method.

His 132 halfway total represented not 12 under par, as would normally be the case at Cannes Mougins, but ten under. The rain which had prevented play the previous Sunday in northern Spain had followed the Volvo Tour to the French Riviera and it was decided to take the saturated first fairway out of action and reduce the opening hole from a 448-yard par four (the toughest on the course) to a 182-yard par three.

That the rest of the course was playable – albeit with preferred lies in operation – was thanks to sterling work by the greenkeeping staff. The pro-am had been called off, but despite the fact that it continued to rain overnight and virtually all of Thursday there was not a single

Jamie Spence misses his putt to get into the play-off.

hold-up once the first tee shot was struck.

Scotland's Brian Marchbank and 22-year old Swede Pierre Fulke set the pace on the opening day with 66s and Fulke, a PGA European Challenge Tour graduate who had never before broken 70 on the main circuit, added another in the second round to be alongside Davis out in front. For the third time in four tournaments the cut came on level par and among those who bowed out early was – again – Seve Ballesteros, just three weeks after he had raised his spirits by finishing 11th in the US Masters.

Davis and Fulke found themselves being overtaken by Jamie Spence during the third round. Spence, putting the shock of his disqualification from the Roma Masters behind him, collected seven birdies, but allowed Davis to regain a share of the lead by hitting his four-iron approach to the 17th into the lake in front of the green for a double bogey six.

A similar error cost him the title the following day. Out in 32, Spence led by two, but he bogeyed the short 11th and then saw a five iron drift into water on the 545-yard 14th. With three putts as well a seven went on the Kent player's card and he dropped to joint third.

The man who looked like taking advantage was twice former winner Mark McNulty. A closing 64 had put the Zimbabwean in the clubhouse with a 13-under-par total of 271 and when Davis bogeyed the 17th he and Spence were 12 under. However, the Australian's pitch to the last spun back over the cup and stopped only 18 inches away.

The birdie putt was a formality and so back he and McNulty went to the 17th. It was the only hole needed to settle the issue. McNulty, 50 feet from the flag in two and six feet away in three, bogeyed to give Davis his seventh Tour victory 12 years after the first.

In 1990 Davis became only the second non-European to join the Tour Millionaires' Club. McNulty had become the first just a few months earlier, but in Cannes it was Davis who did the pipping.

Pierre Fulke finished one stroke out of the play-off.

Rodger Davis

signals the

'arm ball'.

COURSE: CANNES MOUGINS COUNTRY CLUB						YARDAGE: 6700	PAR: 71

POS	NAME	CTY	1	2	3	4	TOTAL	PRIZE MONEY
1	Rodger DAVIS	Aus	68	64	69	70	271	£66660
2	Mark McNULTY	Zim	69	70	68	64	271	44440
3	Jamie SPENCE	Eng	68	67	66	71	272	22520
	Pierre FULKE	Swe	66	66	72	68	272	22520
5	Anders FORSBRAND	Swe	68	68	68	69	273	16940
6	Mike HARWOOD	Aus	69	71	68	66	274	13000
	Jose COCERES	Arg	69	69	66	70	274	13000
8	Barry LANE	Eng	68	68	68	71	275	8973
	Brian MARCHBANK	Scot	66	70	71	68	275	8973
	Carl MASON	Eng	68	70	68	69	275	8973
11	Andrew MURRAY	Eng	70	68	71	67	276	7120
	Manuel PINERO	Sp	69	66	70	71	276	7120
13	Malcolm MACKENZIE	Eng	70	70	67	70	277	6280
	Paul WAY	Eng	72	68	67	70	277	6280
15	Giuseppe CALI	It	68	70	72	68	278	5408
	Stephen McALLISTER	Scot	72	68	68	70	278	5408
	Jesper PARNEVIK	Swe	70	69	70	69	278	5408
	Justin HOBDAY	SA	70	69	71	68	278	5408
	Tony JOHNSTONE	Zim	73	66	70	69	278	5408
20	Jose RIVERO	Sp	70	66	72	71	279	4560
	Steen TINNING	Den	69	71	65	74	279	4560
	Peter FOWLER	Aus	71	70	66	72	279	4560
	Per-Ulrik JOHANSSON	Swe	70	69	70	70	279	4560
	Stephen FIELD	Eng	71	66	73	69	279	4560
25	Marc PENDARIES	Fr	69	73	71	67	280	3840
	Silvio GRAPPASONNI	It	67	72	67	74	280	3840
	Ian PALMER	SA	68	72	67	73	280	3840
	Darren CLARKE	N.Ire	71	70	68	71	280	3840
	Wayne WESTNER	SA	71	69	67	73	280	3840
	Alberto BINAGHI	It	71	71	69	69	280	3840
	Des SMYTH	Ire	72	70	69	69	280	3840
32	Ross McFARLANE	Eng	67	71	68	75	281	3240
	Mark ROE	Eng	73	67	70	71	281	3240
	Jose Manuel CARRILES	Sp	74	68	70	69	281	3240
	Gordon J BRAND	Eng	71	70	70	70	281	3240
36	Lucas PARSONS	Aus	72	68	68	74	282	2600
	Sam TORRANCE	Scot	68	69	75	70	282	2600
	Eamonn DARCY	Ire	71	71	71	69	282	2600
	Peter O'MALLEY	Aus	69	67	72	74	282	2600
	Howard CLARK	Eng	68	74	70	70	282	2600
	Colin MONTGOMERIE	Scot	67	70	73	72	282	2600
	Roger WINCHESTER	Eng	74	67	67	74	282	2600
	Domingo HOSPITAL	Sp	70	66	73	73	282	2600
	David A RUSSELL	Eng	73	69	68	72	282	2600
	Anders SORENSEN	Den	69	71	66	76	282	2600
	Paul BROADHURST	Eng	68	71	70	73	282	2600
	Andrew SHERBORNE	Eng	72	70	72	68	282	2600
48	Andrew OLDCORN	Eng	71	70	72	70	283	1920
	Jamie TAYLOR	Aus	68	66	72	77	283	1920
	Ian GARBUTT	Eng	69	71	71	72	283	1920
	Roy MACKENZIE	Chil	67	73	68	75	283	1920
	Peter MITCHELL	Eng	69	68	71	75	283	1920
53	David R JONES	Eng	69	70	74	71	284	1560
	Robert KARLSSON	Swe	70	69	73	72	284	1560
	Anders GILLNER	Swe	69	73	71	71	284	1560
	Martin POXON	Eng	68	71	69	76	284	1560
57	Martin GATES	Eng	69	72	74	70	285	1185
	Richard BOXALL	Eng	71	70	71	73	285	1185
	Craig CASSELLS	Eng	70	71	73	71	285	1185
	Roger CHAPMAN	Eng	69	67	76	73	285	1185
	Eoghan O'CONNELL	Ire	71	69	71	74	285	1185
	Michel BESANCENEY	Fr	68	71	75	71	285	1185
	Tim PLANCHIN	Fr	70	71	72	72	285	1185
	Bill LONGMUIR	Scot	71	70	72	72	285	1185
65	Juan QUIROS	Sp	69	73	70	74	286	677
	Sven STRUVER	Ger	70	67	71	78	286	677
	Charles RAULERSON	USA	69	70	74	73	286	677
	De Wet BASSON	SA	70	71	72	73	286	677
	Tom PERNICE	USA	69	72	71	74	286	677
70	Daniel SILVA	Port	70	72	73	72	287	592
71	Jon ROBSON	Eng	71	71	75	71	288	590
72	Bill MALLEY	USA	68	72	71	78	289	587
	Marc FARRY	Fr	72	67	77	73	289	587
74	Paul McGINLEY	Ire	71	70	74	75	290	584
75	Paul AFFLECK	Wal	72	68	78	74	292	582
76	Gary EVANS	Eng	71	69	78	75	293	580
77	Ove SELLBERG	Swe	70	72	75	77	294	578

BENSON and HEDGES
INTERNATIONAL OPEN

15 PAR 4
YARDS 442

BROADHURST

BENSON
and
HEDGES

THANK
AMPTON
STEWARDING
THIS HOLE

BROADHURST IS ALIGHT AGAIN

After two years without a victory on the Volvo Tour, Paul Broadhurst found something to smile about at St Mellion

Paul Broadhurst was a star of the 1991 Ryder Cup. The rookie's record was played two, won two. But two weeks afterwards his game began to creak and groan. It was the start of an 18-month slump during which he got so depressed that he didn't want to pick up a golf club, let alone play.

Even when he arrived at St Mellion for the Benson and Hedges International Open he dismissed his chances. Taking on the Jack Nicklaus course, one of the toughest on the Volvo Tour, was no recipe for confidence. But a week in golf is a long time and Broadhurst's renaissance over the hills and dales of Cornwall bore testimony to the swing changes he had developed under the guiding hand of coach Bob Torrance.

Coming into the tournament,

Broadhurst was being offered at 50-1 by the bookies. Few took the bait. Those who did cleaned up as the 27-year old from Atherstone produced rounds of 69, 69, 67 and 71 for a 12-under-par 276 and a one-shot victory over Mark James and Jose Maria Olazabal, three ahead of Gordon Brand Junior and Sweden's Joakim Haeggman.

Broadhurst's manager Andrew 'Chubby' Chandler was kicking himself for not getting some money on his man, but at least he had the satisfaction that the win justified the broadside he delivered to Broadhurst during the winter. 'I got into such a pit of depression over my game that Chubby said to me: "It's about time you got off your backside and did something". It was then that I went to see Bob Torrance and basically what he did was

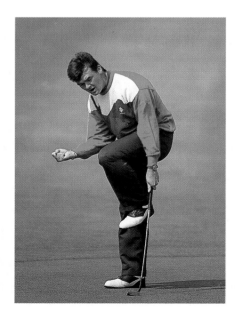

try to take my hands out of the swing. I've always been a bit wristy, so it was a case of getting rid of the wild shots.'

The medicine worked. Despite his doubts, Broadhurst opened with a 69 to be two behind joint leaders Brand Junior, Olazabal and Germany's Sven Struver. 'To be honest, the signs were there in Cannes last week that my form was coming back,' Broadhurst admitted. How right he was.

Another 69 followed but he was still two back of Brand Junior at halfway, sharing second spot with Haeggman, a stroke ahead of Olazabal and James, while Nick Faldo, making only his third European start of the year, was on 140, four off the lead. 'It's a test of character

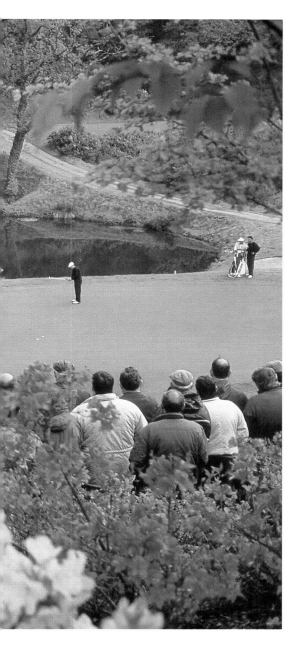

**Most of the time Paul Broadhurst
kept both feet on the ground.**

Roger Chapman pitches to the 12th.

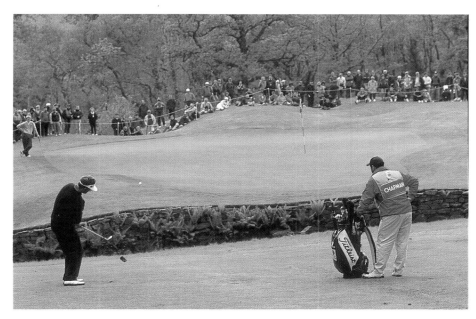

now whether I have the bottle to stick with what I'm trying to achieve,' said Broadhurst. It was test he was to pass with flying colours.

The bright, sunny weather which blessed the tournament after two years of bleak conditions was reflected in the scoring, none more so than on day three when the course record of 65 was twice threatened. First, young Scot Paul Lawrie, another who had been remodelling his swing and who had just survived the cut, went out in 30 with six birdies. Coming home, he scored another two as well as his only bogey. On the par four 18th he needed another birdie for a 64 and a handsome payout from Johnnie Walker's course record pool. He reached the

green in two and his long putt threatened the hole until it veered away at the last moment. Another 65.

Then Roger Chapman, so often so close to a tournament win but still seeking, was eight under par after 14 holes, bogeyed the 15th, and needed a last hole birdie for 64. He also had to settle for 65 but at least it hoisted him into joint second spot with Olazabal (68) and Brand Junior (71) on nine under par, but two adrift of Broadhurst who carded a 67 for 205. Faldo, on the other hand, had, he admitted, put himself out of contention with 74 to drop back to two under, the same mark as the fast-rising Lawrie.

While Faldo was having trouble – 'I'm turning my shoulders 110 degrees, far

too much for someone my height' – Broadhurst was doing very nicely. 'After three rounds under 70 and only four bogeys, I must be doing something right,' he smiled.

Going into the final day, the top six included four Johnnie Walker Ryder Cup men, plus Chapman – would he break his duck? – and Haeggman, the young Swede with great potential. Everything was set for a thrilling finish but as the weather worsened, so did the scoring although Swede Robert Karlsson collected the third 65 and Andrew Murray a 66. How the contenders must have wished for such scores. In fact, they all stumbled somewhere along the way. No-one seriously challenged Broadhurst who, with

Crowds gather on the 18th

for the finale.

five holes to play, was 15 under par and three ahead of James and Olazabal. Then he began to feel the pressure. He bogeyed the 15th and the 17th. With James having birdied the 17th a few minutes earlier, they were level.

Then James missed the fairway off the 18th tee, couldn't reach the green, laid up in front of the pond and pitched his third through the back. His recovery failed to reach the putting surface and two more to get down meant a double-bogey six for 69 and 277.

Broadhurst could afford to bogey the 18th and still win. He drove long and true but his six-iron approach, like James', missed the green and finished on the bank. 'I said to myself, "If you don't make five you're probably the biggest choker ever",' said Broadhurst. His chip was short but he got down in two more for his victory.

Olazabal (70) needed a last hole birdie to force a play-off but it wasn't to be. Brand Junior had a see-saw 72 to finish joint fourth with Haeggman while poor Chapman had a nightmare 76 to miss out yet again. But Faldo, having cured his ills, roared back with his best-of-the-week 67 for sixth spot.

With the trophy, a first prize of £91,660, and his first title since 1991 in his grasp, Broadhurst could afford to smile. 'This has been a long time coming,' he said.

COURSE: ST MELLION GOLF CLUB, CORNWALL   YARDAGE: 7054   PAR: 72

POS	NAME	CTY	1	2	3	4	TOTAL	PRIZE MONEY
1	Paul BROADHURST	Eng	69	69	67	71	276	£91660
2	Mark JAMES	Eng	68	71	69	69	277	47765
	Jose Maria OLAZABAL	Sp	67	72	68	70	277	47765
4	Joakim HAEGGMAN	Swe	69	69	71	70	279	25400
	Gordon BRAND Jnr	Scot	67	69	71	72	279	25400
6	Nick FALDO	Eng	70	70	74	67	281	19250
7	Roger CHAPMAN	Eng	70	72	65	76	283	14176
	Vijay SINGH	Fij	68	75	70	70	283	14176
	Colin MONTGOMERIE	Scot	70	72	71	70	283	14176
10	Anders GILLNER	Swe	74	68	72	71	285	10186
	Andrew MURRAY	Eng	73	72	74	66	285	10186
	Stephen AMES	T&T	75	67	70	73	285	10186
13	Marc FARRY	Fr	73	74	70	69	286	7778
	Paul McGINLEY	Ire	72	70	73	71	286	7778
	Carl MASON	Eng	74	73	69	70	286	7778
	Retief GOOSEN	SA	76	68	69	73	286	7778
	Paul LAWRIE	Scot	72	77	65	72	286	7778
	Costantino ROCCA	It	70	72	74	70	286	7778
	David A RUSSELL	Eng	70	72	70	74	286	7778
20	Robert KARLSSON	Swe	73	74	75	65	287	6435
	Gary EVANS	Eng	72	69	72	74	287	6435
	Stephen FIELD	Eng	76	71	71	69	287	6435
23	De Wet BASSON	SA	74	71	70	73	288	6105
24	David GILFORD	Eng	69	76	72	72	289	5610
	Darren CLARKE	N.Ire	76	68	74	71	289	5610
	Miguel Angel JIMENEZ	Sp	74	73	69	73	289	5610
	Mark ROE	Eng	73	71	74	71	289	5610
	Martin POXON	Eng	72	72	74	71	289	5610
29	Peter SENIOR	Aus	74	69	77	70	290	4867
	Andrew OLDCORN	Eng	71	70	71	78	290	4867
	Paul CURRY	Eng	72	77	68	73	290	4867
	Jonathan SEWELL	Eng	70	76	70	74	290	4867
33	Adam HUNTER	Scot	77	68	71	75	291	4235
	Jose Manuel CARRILES	Sp	75	72	72	72	291	4235
	Barry LANE	Eng	69	75	75	72	291	4235
	Wayne RILEY	Aus	75	73	72	71	291	4235
	Jesper PARNEVIK	Swe	81	68	70	72	291	4235
	Sven STRUVER	Ger	67	74	78	72	291	4235
39	Paul AFFLECK	Wal	70	76	75	71	292	3740
	Patrick HALL	Eng	74	73	74	71	292	3740
	Sam TORRANCE	Scot	71	75	73	73	292	3740
42	David CURRY	Eng	74	71	73	75	293	3355
	Howard CLARK	Eng	74	75	72	72	293	3355
	Malcolm MACKENZIE	Eng	72	74	73	74	293	3355
	Tony JOHNSTONE	Zim	74	71	78	70	293	3355
46	Anders FORSBRAND	Swe	73	76	72	73	294	2915
	Christy O'CONNOR JNR	Ire	71	74	72	77	294	2915
	Richard BOXALL	Eng	74	75	76	69	294	2915
	Thomas LEVET	Fr	74	73	72	75	294	2915
50	Greg TURNER	NZ	74	73	76	72	295	2365
	Anders SORENSEN	Den	74	73	74	74	295	2365
	Rodger DAVIS	Aus	71	73	75	76	295	2365
	Eoghan O'CONNELL	Ire	72	75	78	70	295	2365
	Jay TOWNSEND	USA	72	76	71	76	295	2365
	Gordon J BRAND	Eng	69	78	72	76	295	2365
56	Peter TERAVAINEN	USA	75	74	72	75	296	1793
	Russell CLAYDON	Eng	71	77	76	72	296	1793
	Magnus SUNESSON	Swe	75	72	72	77	296	1793
	Olle KARLSSON	Swe	73	75	76	72	296	1793
	Ross McFARLANE	Eng	75	71	72	78	296	1793
61	Ove SELLBERG	Swe	74	71	77	75	297	1375
	Martin GATES	Eng	74	74	74	75	297	1375
	Mark MOULAND	Wal	70	77	77	73	297	1375
	Steven RICHARDSON	Eng	75	74	76	72	297	1375
	Ricky WILLISON	Eng	74	73	74	76	297	1375
	Gary ORR	Scot	74	73	77	73	297	1375
67	David FEHERTY	N.Ire	77	71	72	78	298	819
	Steven BOWMAN	USA	76	73	75	74	298	819
	Vicente FERNANDEZ	Arg	73	76	78	71	298	819
	Stephen McALLISTER	Scot	75	70	79	74	298	819
	Mats LANNER	Swe	76	72	75	75	298	819
72	Mike McLEAN	Eng	74	73	79	75	301	813
73	Gary WOLSTENHOLME (Am)	Eng	74	74	76	79	303	–
	Bill MALLEY	USA	74	75	78	75	302	811
74	Peter BAKER	Eng	75	69	84	76	304	809
75	Heinz P THUL	Ger	74	73	88	79	314	807

13 mg TAR 1·1 mg NICOTINE
SMOKING WHEN PREGNANT HARMS YOUR BABY
Health Departments' Chief Medical Officers

HAEGGMAN THE MASTER IN MADRID

Joakim Haeggman held off a strong field to win his first Volvo Tour title

You do not expect the weather to be the dominant factor at a golf tournament in Spain – not in May at any rate. Yet it was for much of the Peugeot Open de Espana at the Real Automovil Club de Espagne outside Madrid. And when eventually discussions about cold fronts, thunderstorms and lightning bolts were finished, then it was time to talk of a young Swede, another young Swede, who made us pay attention to him by the quality of his play which ended in him claiming victory by two strokes.

A new generation is rising in Europe, the one to follow the Faldos, Lyles and Langers. Joakim Haeggman is the latest member of it, the sixth first-time winner on the Volvo Tour so far this year. The 23-year old became the fifth Swede to win on the Volvo Tour behind Mats Lanner, Ove Sellberg, Anders Forsbrand and Per-Ulrik Johansson. And, like it or not, he became the subject of speculation: would he be the first Swede to participate in the Ryder Cup by Johnnie Walker?

One of the best fields to gather for an event on the Volvo Tour thus far in 1993 found themselves struggling with the weather from the start. Of Europe's major championship winners, only Bernhard Langer was missing at RACE. Woosnam made the best start, a 67, one ahead of Nick Faldo, Ronan Rafferty, Gordon Brand Junior, Peter Mitchell and two ahead of Severiano Ballesteros, Mark James, Steven Richardson, Eduardo Romero and Glen Day.

The golf was good over a tricky course

that looked in good condition but at the end of the first day it was not the scores everyone was talking about but the weather. For Heinz Peter Thul, a thunderstorm that broke in the early afternoon came too close for comfort. He was between the 12th and 13th greens when a flash of lightning struck his umbrella and sent him sprawling. A bolt of lightning stopped the clock on the first tee. Play was suspended for three and a half hours. With a 15-minute stoppage in the morning and another in the early evening, it was a disjointed, not to say, damp day. Only 75 players completed their rounds.

The second day began soon after first light and ended long after darkness, one of golf's longest ever days. At the end of it, after the moment when Nick Faldo holed a long putt on the 18th green that was lit by nearby car lights, the tournaments was nearly back on schedule. Only 14 matches involving 42 players had to complete their second round early on the third morning.

Mats Lanner, who had started with a level par 72, took over the lead from Woosnam with an eight-under-par round of 64. He could scarcely believe it. He holed every putt he looked at, six of 18 feet or more. In addition, he sank a couple from six feet and one from 12 feet. He was still rubbing his eyes at the improbability of it all an hour after he had finished. Faldo was moving ominously towards his best form with a 69 and a 36-hole total of 137, level with Woosnam.

But little was going right for Ballesteros. He had begun with a 69, a rare flash of form in an otherwise dark spell. He followed it with a 74 and then took another 69 in the third round. He was weighed down by the weight of the expectations of his countrymen. 'I feel like I have committed a crime, like I have done something bad,' Ballesteros said of the reaction to his continued bad form. His back was sore, which stopped him practising and he had lost confidence. 'On the practice ground Seve's swing looks good,' reported Woosnam after the first round. 'But on the course he is trying to guide the ball. It is not flowing.'

In a week in which the peseta was devalued by eight per cent little was going right for any of the Spaniards. Jose Maria Olazabal was showing glimpses of form but no more. Santiago Luna moved into joint third place after two rounds and Miguel Angel Jimenez was joint third after 54 holes. But names such as these merely reminded us of how the game is changing in Spain. At this time last year there had been six Spanish victories on the Volvo Tour; this year there had been none.

Haeggman took over the lead after 54 holes, his third 69 in a row putting him on nine under par, level with Ernie Els. These two rising stars had a formidable pack breathing down their necks and one wondered whether they could cope with the pressure. Woosnam, Faldo and Olazabal were all close behind.

Haeggman did not turn a hair. He hit a 40-yard bunker shot to ten feet and holed the putt on the first, then holed from five feet for par on the second. On the ninth he holed a putt of 30 feet to give himself a cushion over Faldo who had missed from five feet on the same green. The Swede was looking cool. He faced down an incipient crisis on the par five 14th when his second finished behind a tree. He chose a six iron to keep the ball below the branches of the tree and skilfully landed the ball within inches of

where he had aimed. He watched with satisfaction as the ball rolled to six feet from the flag. When he holed that putt for his fourth birdie of the day he looked as though he was going to win. Els was now two strokes behind; Faldo too.

It was Haeggman's tournament to win and his to lose – and he emphatically did the former. He held his nerve and did not drop a stroke in his last round of 68, four under par. He won by two strokes from Faldo and three from Woosnam, Olazabal and Lanner.

So Forsbrand had been right just after lunch when he had spoken warmly of his countryman. 'He is a solid striker, a good player, certainly good enough to win here,' Forsbrand said.

Haeggman is a new European, a man who speaks several languages, has homes in two countries, travels easily from continent to continent. It was his third victory as a professional (he won twice on the PGA European Challenge Tour) and it is unlikely to be his last.

Right, Joakim Haeggman drives off the ninth tee. Below, rain stopped play on the first day.

Left, Nick Faldo had to settle for second place.

Right, a hard road for Jose Maria Olazabal.

— 84 —

POS	NAME	CTY	1	2	3	4	TOTAL	PRIZE MONEY
	COURSE: REAL AUTOMOVIL CLUB DE ESPANA, MADRID				**YARDAGE: 7105**		**PAR: 72**	
1	Joakim HAEGGMAN	Swe	69	69	69	68	275	£83330
2	Nick FALDO	Eng	68	69	72	68	277	43425
	Ernie ELS	SA	70	68	69	70	277	43425
4	Mats LANNER	Swe	72	64	73	69	278	21233
	José Maria OLAZABAL	Sp	74	69	67	68	278	21233
	Ian WOOSNAM	Wal	67	70	72	69	278	21233
7	Justin HOBDAY	SA	70	70	70	69	279	15000
8	Peter BAKER	Eng	70	69	70	71	280	11216
	Roger CHAPMAN	Eng	70	72	71	67	280	11216
	Heinz P THUL	SA	70	70	69	??	279	11216
11	Carl MASON	Eng	70	70	74	67	281	9190
12	Gordon BRAND Jnr	Scot	68	73	74	67	282	7907
	Mikael KRANTZ	Swe	70	71	69	72	282	7907
	Costantino ROCCA	It	76	68	69	69	282	7907
	Mark JAMES	Eng	69	71	70	72	282	7907
16	Glen DAY	USA	69	71	75	68	283	6900
	Marc FARRY	Fr	72	68	74	69	283	6900
18	Ronan RAFFERTY	N.Ire	68	74	70	72	284	6450
19	José RIVERO	Sp	71	71	74	69	285	5707
	Manuel PINERO	Sp	72	68	73	72	285	5707
	Per-Ulrik JOHANSSON	Swe	74	69	72	70	285	5707
	Paul BROADHURST	Eng	69	75	70	71	285	5707
	Miguel Angel JIMENEZ	Sp	71	72	65	77	285	5707
	Paul McGINLEY	Ire	74	70	72	69	285	5707
	Santiago LUNA	Sp	71	67	75	72	285	5707
26	José COCERES	Arg	71	74	72	69	286	4650
	Anders FORSBRAND	Swe	70	73	72	71	286	4650
	Ian GARBUTT	Eng	70	73	71	72	286	4650
	Darren CLARKE	N.Ire	69	71	70	76	286	4650
	Russell CLAYDON	Eng	72	71	72	71	286	4650
	David GILFORD	Eng	73	70	68	75	286	4650
	Vijay SINGH	Fij	72	70	73	71	286	4650
33	Steven RICHARDSON	Eng	69	74	75	69	287	3950
	Jorge BERENDT	Arg	71	74	69	73	287	3950
	Andrew SHERBORNE	Eng	70	72	72	73	287	3950
	Jim PAYNE	Eng	71	72	71	73	287	3950
37	Rodger DAVIS	Aus	70	70	76	72	288	3350
	Seve BALLESTEROS	Sp	69	74	69	76	288	3350
	Michel BESANCENEY	Fr	74	69	69	76	288	3350
	Mark MOULAND	Wal	72	72	72	72	288	3350
	Mark DAVIS	Eng	71	72	72	73	288	3350
	David CURRY	Eng	70	74	72	72	288	3350
	Gary ORR	Scot	76	67	72	73	288	3350
	Martin GATES	Eng	71	74	72	71	288	3350
45	Richard BOXALL	Eng	72	72	72	73	289	2750
	Peter FOWLER	Aus	71	71	75	72	289	2750
	Miguel Angel MARTIN	Sp	74	70	74	71	289	2750
	Paul MAYO	Wal	75	70	73	71	289	2750
49	Eduardo ROMERO	Arg	69	71	77	73	290	2450
	Magnus SUNESSON	Swe	71	72	73	74	290	2450
51	Stephen AMES	T&T	69	72	77	73	291	2050
	David FEHERTY	N.Ire	72	72	73	74	291	2050
	Jeff HAWKES	SA	72	70	74	75	291	2050
	Steve REY	Swi	71	73	77	70	291	2050
	Giuseppe CALI	It	73	71	72	75	291	2050
	Jay TOWNSEND	USA	72	71	73	75	291	2050
57	Eric GIRAUD	Fr	72	72	77	71	292	1616
	Juan QUIROS	Sp	71	72	77	72	292	1616
	Peter MITCHELL	Eng	68	71	77	76	292	1616
60	Paul CURRY	Eng	73	72	72	76	293	1500
61	Ove SELLBERG	Swe	74	69	78	73	294	1350
	Wayne RILEY	Aus	71	70	74	79	294	1350
	Anders GILLNER	Swe	74	68	76	76	294	1350
	Antoine LEBOUC	Fr	73	70	76	75	294	1350
	Mike CLAYTON	Aus	74	71	72	77	294	1350
66	Silvio GRAPPASONNI	It	74	71	75	75	295	749
	Chris MOODY	Eng	71	74	76	74	295	749
68	Andrew HARE	Eng	73	70	75	79	297	746

TURNER LEADS IN ANNIVERSARY CELEBRATION

It took New Zealander Greg Turner just five weeks to erase the memory of defeat in the Roma Masters in Italy. On his very next trip to that country he won the 50th anniversary Lancia Martini Italian Open at Bernhard Langer's new course at Modena although, in all fairness, it looked for a time as if he would again be involved in a play-off.

At Castelgandolfo he had lost a play-off to Frenchman Jean van de Velde but at Modena a deft pitch from the bank of the lake guarding the final green and a short putt finally shook off the spirited challenge of Argentinian Jose Coceres.

The 29-year-old Coceres suddenly found the form in Modena that had deserted him in early season play when he missed eight of his first nine cuts. The second prize cheque of nearly £50,000 was welcomed not only by him but by his ten brothers and one sister back in Argentina.

It might have been Coceres week but it was Turner's. It might have been Barry Lane's or early leader David Gilford's or Seve Ballesteros' week but it was Turner's. Seve's fans were among the most

The 50th anniversary of the Italian Open saw Greg Turner join an impressive list of winners

disappointed because the Italian Championship is one the Spaniard has never won in his remarkable career. The closest he came was losing a play-off in 1983 to Bernhard Langer.

When Seve fired a course record-equalling 64 on the second day there

were hopes among his multitude of admirers around the world – and particularly those at Modena – that he was back. Naturally Seve was far more cautious about the situation, pointing out wisely and honestly that he had not in fact hit the ball all that well tee-to-green on a course playing far easier than designer Langer would have liked because of the dry weather which gave additional fairway run. Closing rounds of 72 and 75 would back up his concern and he ended the Italian anniversary week 14 shots behind Turner.

The organisers hoped they had produced a master-stroke by inviting not only former USPGA champion Wayne Grady to play but also John Cook, the American who had had the disappointment of finishing runner-up to Nick Faldo and Nick Price in the Open and USPGA Championships a year earlier. American Billy Casper had won the title in 1975, maybe Cook could do the same. In the end Cook trailed the winner of the £73,392 first prize by ten shots while Grady finished 13 behind Turner.

For the New Zealander, whose previous

season had been dogged by wrist trouble, the triumph at Modena with rounds of 65, 70, 68 and 64 justified not only his decision two years earlier to re-build his swing with coach Denis Pugh but also his switch two weeks earlier to a new putting style – the reverse grip he had adopted in Valencia six weeks earlier. On the final day it certainly worked well. He used up only 23 putts and none more testing than the one he holed on the last to win, although not after a certain amount of drama.

He and Coceres were both tied as they played the par five last where there is water to catch the pushed tee shot and also water guarding the green. Turner hooked to avoid the first stretch of water but left himself with a longer than usual 238-yard second shot. Going for the green he finished unplayable on the far bank of the lake. He took a penalty drop but made five.

Coceres, off a perfect tee-shot, needed five to tie and a birdie four to win but he hit his 229-yard second on the head and it skipped across the lake before disap-

pearing into the water. After dropping a second ball, he too hit up to four feet but he missed. His title chance was gone. Adding to Coceres' disappointment was the fact that his last hole bogey was only his second dropped shot of the week but Turner had closed with a record-equalling round to beat him.

So it was Turner's name that went on the silver trophy, becoming the first New Zealander to win a title that in the past has gone to such as Langer, Lyle, Greg Norman, Tony Jacklin, Peter Oosterhuis, Peter and Percy Alliss, Henry Cotton and Aldo Casera, the winner in the 15th Italian Open at San Remo in 1948 and still playing in the Championship 45 years later.

Below, the signs looked good for Jose Coceres.

Below, reflective moment for Steven Richardson and Greg Turner.

| COURSE: MODENA G & CC | | | | | | | YARDAGE: 6733 | | PAR: 72 |

POS	NAME	CTY	1	2	3	4	TOTAL	PRIZE MONEY
1	Greg TURNER	NZ	65	70	68	64	267	£73392
2	José COCERES	Arg	64	70	66	68	268	48898
3	Wayne WESTNER	SA	66	72	69	65	272	22760
	David GILFORD	Eng	65	66	73	68	272	22760
	Barry LANE	Eng	67	69	66	70	272	22760
6	Steven RICHARDSON	Eng	65	69	70	69	273	15418
7	Ronan RAFFERTY	N.Ire	67	71	71	65	274	13215
8	Brian MARCHBANK	Scot	69	67	70	69	275	11013
9	Wayne RILEY	Aus	72	70	66	68	276	9339
	José Maria OLAZABAL	Sp	68	70	69	69	276	9339
11	Jim PAYNE	Eng	67	69	73	68	277	7033
	Derrick COOPER	Eng	71	70	69	67	277	7033
	John COOK	USA	72	69	69	67	277	7033
	Justin HOBDAY	SA	68	71	73	65	277	7033
	De Wet BASSON	SA	70	68	67	72	277	7033
	Danny MIJOVIC	Can	66	72	70	69	277	7033
17	Eduardo ROMERO	Arg	72	64	72	70	278	5594
	Mike HARWOOD	Aus	71	69	66	72	278	5594
	Mike CLAYTON	Aus	68	71	72	67	278	5594
	Mats LANNER	Swe	68	72	72	66	278	5594
21	Fredrik LINDGREN	Swe	71	69	74	65	279	5088
	Eric GIRAUD	Fr	68	71	68	72	279	5088
23	Jeremy ROBINSON	Eng	69	72	69	70	280	4493
	Stephen BENNETT	Eng	64	76	72	68	280	4493
	Richard BOXALL	Eng	69	70	72	69	280	4493
	Stephen McALLISTER	Scot	68	74	71	67	280	4493
	Wayne GRADY	Aus	67	71	71	71	280	4493
	Miguel Angel MARTIN	Sp	67	72	68	73	280	4493
	Peter O'MALLEY	Aus	69	73	70	68	280	4493
30	Pierre FULKE	Swe	66	71	73	71	281	3898
	Seve BALLESTEROS	Sp	70	64	72	75	281	3898
32	Sven STRUVER	Ger	65	72	73	72	282	3480
	Jorge BERENDT	Arg	71	71	72	68	282	3480
	Glen DAY	USA	69	71	73	69	282	3480
	Ulrich ZILG	Ger	67	71	72	72	282	3480
	Peter SENIOR	Aus	68	69	73	72	282	3480
	Stephen AMES	T&T	67	70	71	74	282	3480
38	Haydn SELBY-GREEN	Eng	70	72	71	70	283	2951
	Jon ROBSON	Eng	72	69	72	70	283	2951
	Steven BOWMAN	USA	69	69	77	68	283	2951
	Robert KARLSSON	Swe	72	68	69	74	283	2951
	Charles RAULERSON	USA	70	72	69	72	283	2951
	Michel BESANCENEY	Fr	73	69	73	68	283	2951
44	Costantino ROCCA	It	72	70	73	69	284	2422
	David CURRY	Eng	71	69	73	71	284	2422
	Mikael KRANTZ	Swe	73	68	72	71	284	2422
	Ruben ALVAREZ	Arg	69	73	72	70	284	2422
	Jon EVANS	Eng	67	73	72	72	284	2422
50	David WILLIAMS	Eng	67	74	70	74	285	1938
	Jeff HAWKES	SA	68	71	71	75	285	1938
	André BOSSERT	Swi	72	69	72	72	285	1938
	Keith WATERS	Eng	73	68	75	69	285	1938
	Robin MANN	Eng	67	72	72	74	285	1938
55	Baldovino DASSU	It	68	71	73	74	286	1447
	Silvano LOCATELLI	It	68	72	74	72	286	1447
	Marc FARRY	Fr	71	71	73	71	286	1447
	Gordon J BRAND	Eng	70	68	72	76	286	1447
	Vicente FERNANDEZ	Arg	73	67	74	72	286	1447
	Bernard GALLACHER	Scot	70	70	74	72	286	1447
	Torsten GIEDEON	Ger	68	74	72	72	286	1447
62	Giuseppe CALI	It	70	72	73	72	287	1066
	Andrew HARE	Eng	68	71	72	76	287	1066
	Phillip PRICE	Wal	67	74	74	72	287	1066
	David RAY	Eng	73	69	72	73	287	1066
	Mike McLEAN	Eng	69	73	72	73	287	1066
67	Peter TERAVAINEN	USA	67	72	77	72	288	657
	Frank NOBILO	NZ	64	74	74	76	288	657
	Michele REALE	It	74	67	72	75	288	657
70	Ian GARBUTT	Eng	73	67	76	73	289	652
	David R JONES	Eng	67	74	74	74	289	652
72	Steve REY	Swi	68	73	77	73	291	649

Above, Pierre Fulke faces a piece of ancient history and below, home-cooked food for Costantino Rocca.

LANGER SOARS WITH THE EAGLES

Bernhard Langer dominated the Volvo PGA Championship at Wentworth thanks to his mastery of the par five holes

Par five holes are meat and drink to professional golfers. Two good hits and a couple of putts and they've put one over on the implacable enemy of par and there's always the chance of a single putt for that elusive bird, the eagle.

In the Volvo PGA Championship Bernhard Langer found that three of these *avis raris* had alighted on his scorecards during the four rounds at Wentworth and when he added all the pieces together he was six strokes ahead of his nearest rivals, the proud owner of a second PGA title and £116,660 richer.

Six years previously Langer had put in another stellar performance when he won the Championship with an 18-under par total of 270 to win by four strokes from Severiano Ballesteros. This victory was equally as good, if not better, since the course was playing extremely long after a period of heavy rain and the weather was dominated by blustery winds.

There was unstinting praise for the condition of the course and also for the organisation of the Championship itself, which is firmly established as the flagship event of the Volvo Tour. It is now an integral part of the summer season of great sporting events, a place where the cognoscenti gather and where the game's future is planned. Prime evidence of this occured during the week when it was announced at a press conference attended by the Spanish Secretary for Sport, the Spanish Secretary General of Tourism, the President of the Royal Spanish Golf Federation and members of the Ryder Cup Committee that the 1997 Ryder Cup would be held in Spain. It was a momentous decision and one which fully recognised the part that Spain and Spanish players have played in the growth of European golf.

Still with the Ryder Cup in mind, it was also announced that Delta Air Lines had entered a three-year agreement with the Tour as official airline to the Volvo PGA Championship and nine other Volvo Tour events. This association will extend to 1994 and 1995 and will therefore include the 1995 Ryder Cup at Oak Hill, New York.

Before any jostling began in the Championship there was a little jostling of a political nature. Tim Yeo, Conservative MP for Suffolk South and captain of the Parliamentary Golfing Society was about to play in the Corporate Cup when he was summoned from the course by a telephone call from Number Ten Downing Street. Having left the course as a junior Health Minister, he returned as the new Secretary of State for the Environment and therefore, master of all he surveyed at Wentworth.

There was little re-shuffling at the head of the field after the first round in so far as the favourites, Langer and Nick Faldo had to bow to Gary Evans with a 66, Magnus Sunesson with a 67 and a bunch of players on 68. Langer opened with a 70 and Faldo with a 71. Among that group on 68 was Mark James,

winner of two Volvo Tour titles already this season and it was he who thrust himself to the forefront after two rounds when he repeated his opening score. One stroke behind lay Argentina's Jose Coceres who the week before had finished runner-up in Italy, and Ronan Rafferty. Langer had added a 69 but the shock of the day was the 75 from Faldo which caused him to miss the cut for the first time in Britain since 1985. Joining him on the road home was Ballesteros, whose season of despair continued with rounds of 78-71, double winner this season David Gilford, and Johnnie Walker Ryder Cup points leader, Barry Lane.

The third day found the West course a very different proposition as a strong wind swirled through the avenues of trees, making club selection difficult and sending the scores soaring. Into this maelstrom stepped Langer. He reached the turn in a one-under-par 34 and then on the par five 12th, although blocked out by the trees on the left from his drive, took a three iron, closed the face and hooked the ball round to seven feet. It was the same club which he had used on the 13th at Augusta in the final round en route to his

**Right, Ronan Rafferty in
purple patch.**

**Nick Faldo was out of sorts and on his
way home after two rounds.**

Right, Colin Montgomerie struck out for joint second place.

Below, Frank Nobilo's classic swing took him to joint second place.

Bernhard Langer drives from the 15th tee at Wentworth.

second US Masters title and the result was the same – an eagle. A birdie was pocketed at the dangerous 15th and two woods to the final green and a putt from 15 feet put another eagle against his name and sealed a round of 67.

It was by two shots the best round of the day and Langer rated it among his best, given the conditions. From being three strokes behind James, Langer now moved to three strokes in front as the Englishman took 73 and was joined by Frank Nobilo and defending champion, Tony Johnstone. Johnstone confessed that he was doing his utmost to stop somebody else enjoying the experience of winning the title and his round of 69, which contained an eagle two at the seventh where his six-iron second ran back into the hole, kept him in the hunt. Nobilo's round of 70 contained fives at the 17th and 18th, which he felt were damaging, but he had a run of three consecutive birdies from the 13th. Also within striking distance was Colin Montgomerie, runner-up to Ballesteros two years ago, who lay four strokes behind Langer.

Two things had to happen if Langer's position was to be threatened. First, one of his nearest challengers had to post a low score and second, Langer himself had to suffer a relapse. While all things are possible in golf, the way Langer was playing there was little likelihood of the latter occurring and the weather was not conducive for the former.

As it was, Langer gave no quarter. Birdies at the sixth and 13th plus his second eagle in two days at the 12th, where his one iron second shot finished only 12 inches from the flag, had extended his lead to seven shots. A 'fat' six iron to the short 14th which he later jokingly referred to as 'a bad lie' and three putts at the next were minor aberrations as he regrouped with a long putt for a birdie on the 16th and then chipped close for another on the final hole to complete the round in 68.

Gordon Brand Junior put in a storming finish with a 67 to join Nobilo and Montgomerie in joint second place but poor James had one of those days when

Victory salute from the champion.

nothing went right and was round in 80.

It was the 39th victory of Langer's career worldwide and his first place cheque for £116,660 took him into third place in the all-time money list behind Greg Norman and Tom Kite with £6,561,735. A very considerable player is Bernhard Langer and everyone present at Wentworth for the 1993 Volvo PGA Championship will vouch for that.

Below, last round 67 pulled Gordon Brand Junior into joint second place.

Above, Tony Johnstone put up a stout defence of his title.

Below, international referees gathered at Wentworth.

A week in the life of Bernhard Langer
as he works out in the PGA European
Tour Physio Unit...

...finds there's many a slip 'twixt cup and
lip... and finally gets it all together for
happy family group picture.

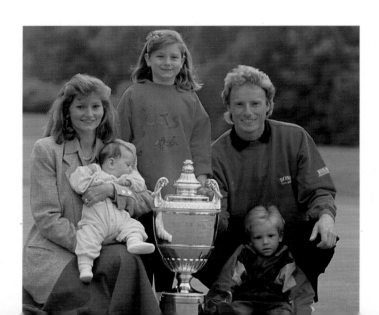

			COURSE: WENTWORTH (WEST COURSE)			YARDAGE: 6957		PAR: 72	
POS	NAME	CTY	1	2	3	4	TOTAL	PRIZE MONEY
1	Bernhard LANGER	Ger	70	69	67	68	274	£116660
2	Frank NOBILO	NZ	72	67	70	71	280	52196
	Colin MONTGOMERIE	Scot	70	69	71	70	280	52196
	Gordon BRAND Jnr	Scot	69	71	73	67	280	52196
5	Mark McNULTY	Zim	72	71	69	69	281	29640
6	Tony JOHNSTONE	Zim	74	66	69	74	283	24500
7	Eduardo ROMERO	Arg	71	71	71	71	284	18036
	Glen DAY	USA	72	67	74	71	284	18036
	Greg TURNER	NZ	73	69	71	71	284	18036
10	José Maria OLAZABAL	Sp	74	70	73	68	285	11865
	Peter FOWLER	Aus	73	71	71	70	285	11865
	José COCERES	Arg	70	67	79	69	285	11865
	Peter MITCHELL	Eng	73	70	69	73	285	11865
	Andrew SHERBORNE	Eng	68	72	73	72	285	11865
	De Wet BASSON	SA	68	75	70	72	285	11865
16	Andrew OLDCORN	Eng	70	68	76	72	286	9257
	Mark ROE	Eng	73	70	72	71	286	9257
	Ronan RAFFERTY	N.Ire	68	69	75	74	286	9257
	Joakim HAEGGMAN	Swe	70	69	75	72	286	9257
20	David FEHERTY	N.Ire	72	71	76	68	287	8085
	Stephen AMES	T&T	69	75	72	71	287	8085
	Mark MOULAND	Wal	72	68	73	74	287	8085
	Carl MASON	Eng	71	71	71	74	287	8085
24	Derrick COOPER	Eng	77	67	72	72	288	7035
	Howard CLARK	Eng	69	73	72	74	288	7035
	Roger CHAPMAN	Eng	74	69	73	72	288	7035
	Gordon J BRAND	Eng	73	67	74	74	288	7035
	Ian WOOSNAM	Wal	72	72	71	73	288	7035
	Gary EVANS	Eng	66	77	77	68	288	7035
30	Ernie ELS	SA	71	71	73	74	289	6002
	Mark JAMES	Eng	68	68	73	80	289	6002
	Jesper PARNEVIK	Swe	70	68	77	74	289	6002
	Andrew MURRAY	Eng	69	69	78	73	289	6002
34	Steen TINNING	Den	69	72	74	75	290	5390
	Peter O'MALLEY	Aus	68	71	76	75	290	5390
	Peter BAKER	Eng	69	72	74	75	290	5390
	Gavin LEVENSON	SA	71	72	74	73	290	5390
38	Sam TORRANCE	Scot	69	75	73	74	291	4970
	Vijay SINGH	Fij	73	70	74	74	291	4970
40	Jean VAN DE VELDE	Fr	71	71	76	74	292	4480
	Ricky WILLISON	Eng	75	69	73	75	292	4480
	Juan QUIROS	Sp	74	70	73	75	292	4480
	Des SMYTH	Ire	70	71	76	75	292	4480
	Wayne WESTNER	SA	69	75	74	74	292	4480
45	Mats LANNER	Swe	71	71	77	74	293	3640
	Magnus SUNESSON	Swe	67	73	77	76	293	3640
	Danny MIJOVIC	Can	68	76	73	76	293	3640
	Jorge BERENDT	Arg	72	70	73	78	293	3640
	Jim PAYNE	Eng	72	70	74	77	293	3640
	José Manuel CARRILES	Sp	71	72	78	72	293	3640
	Retief GOOSEN	SA	73	69	72	79	293	3640
52	Per-Ulrik JOHANSSON	Swe	70	73	76	75	294	2870
	Stephen McALLISTER	Scot	72	72	73	77	294	2870
	Russell CLAYDON	Eng	73	68	78	75	294	2870
	Paul MAYO	Wal	75	69	78	72	294	2870
56	Joe HIGGINS	Eng	73	71	76	75	295	2282
	Giuseppe CALI	It	72	70	77	76	295	2282
	Steven RICHARDSON	Eng	72	72	76	75	295	2282
	Paul McGINLEY	Ire	75	69	74	77	295	2282
	Peter SENIOR	Aus	73	69	76	77	295	2282
61	Thomas LEVET	Fr	70	74	81	71	296	1960
	Jay TOWNSEND	USA	70	72	76	78	296	1960
	Wayne RILEY	Aus	70	71	77	78	296	1960
64	Mark DAVIS	Eng	71	72	75	79	297	1820
65	Sandy LYLE	Scot	72	72	76	79	299	1750
66	David JONES	N.Ire	73	71	84	80	308	1050

More Nonstops To The U.S.A. Than Any Other Airline In The World.

Every day, Delta Air Lines makes it easier for people all over Europe to do business in the U.S.A.

By offering more nonstops from Europe to the U.S.A. than any other airline in the world. As well as convenient service to over 250 destinations across America.

So no matter where your business takes you, chances are so can we.

▲ DELTA AIR LINES

The Official Airline Of The PGA European Tour

THE FABULOUS BAKER BOY

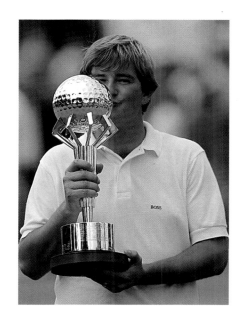

*A superlative
performance by
Peter Baker saw
him set all kinds
of records at
Woburn*

There was no disguising what was at stake for Peter Baker on the eve of the final round of the Dunhill British Masters. The leader by one with 18 long, long holes stretching out in front of him the next afternoon, this was unquestionably going to be the most important round of golf in his life.

As he retired that evening to his Woburn hotel, the implications of those four hours to come whirred in his head. Five years ago, too young to be nervous, he had beaten Nick Faldo in a play-off to win the Benson and Hedges International Open. He had eagled the final hole to tie Faldo and then eagled it again to defeat him in extra time. 'He's the one we've been waiting for,' Faldo had said generously afterwards. Predicting future greatness was always the most precarious of professions.

While Faldo went on to rule the world, Baker went into recession. He finished 104th in the Volvo Order of Merit in 1989 and 108th the following year. Baker continued to accumulate scar tissue over the next two years as well, so much so that the position he was in at Woburn was one to which he was wholly unaccustomed.

So that, then, is a brief outline as to what Baker had to contend with that evening. The fact a jazz band played until the early hours in his hotel would have been the final straw for many. Baker

slept soundly through the easy New Orleans noise. No getting up in the middle of the night for him, sick with nerves. Others the next day would have shot themselves in the foot. Baker went out and shot a new course record.

Woburn proved quite a sanctuary that

week for those who had fallen on hard times. Tony Jacklin, who had hitherto not made a cut since returning to play a limited Tour schedule the previous year, opened with a 67 to be just one behind the leaders, Jean van de Velde and David Feherty. What a wonderful sight this was to see Jacko back at something close to his pomp.

What a sight too, to be able to witness it in glorious sunshine. For you know the Dunhill British Masters, that's the tournament where the heavens save up all their rain and dump it on Woburn in the first week in June. Not this year. The skies were cloudless from start to finish. Jacklin made the cut by one. And hang gliders glistened overhead as Baker started his final round, the one that would tell us so much about him.

All through his distinguished amateur days, Baker had stood out because of his watertight nerve; this would be an enormous test to see whether that inner strength was still there.

One behind was the talented young Swede, Joakim Haeggman, and then came a bunch that included former winners like Sandy Lyle and Mark James, and Bernhard Langer was there on the periphery as well.

Baker parred the first three holes and just three shots separated the first 13 players. He had led since he eagled the tenth in the second round on his way to

Bunkers frame the third
green at Woburn Golf and
Country Club.

Peter Baker drives from the
17th tee in the final round of the
Dunhill British Masters.

equalling the course record with a 64. But the three stroke advantage he enjoyed after round two had of course dwindled the next day, and when his birdie putt stopped breathless on the edge of the third hole in round four, was he gasping for air too?

Not likely. What followed over the next eleven holes was as perfect as golf ever gets. For Baker had reached the zone, that blessed state that even the best players achieve but half a dozen times in a career. Now everything he did only put more distance between himself and his pursuers. Pity Carl Mason, chasing his first ever Tour victory. What a valiant effort he

made, picking up three shots in his first 11 holes. Normally that would have been good enough to take him to the front. But not on this day. Such was Baker's performance that Mason found himself pedalling backwards.

The lad from Wolverhampton, another product of the peerless Shropshire youth system that spawned Lyle and Ian Woosnam, played those ten holes in nine under par. The final holes therefore were lined not with potential disaster but glory, and the game's cheekiest grin was much in evidence, as he conducted what amounted to a lap of honour. A final birdie at the last gave him a 63, and he

Birdie from Jose Maria Olazabal on the 12th.

lowered Faldo's record winning margin of 21-under by a shot into the bargain. Mason finished second to claim his biggest-ever cheque, but seven strokes separated him from the winner.

The fabulous Baker boy was back and Faldo's prophecy resounded around the arena of the 18th, as he basked in the warm and thoroughly-earned applause.

**Weight training for
Joakim Haeggman.**

**Baker family's celebration
on the final hole.**

COURSE: WOBURN DUKE'S COURSE							YARDAGE: 6940	PAR: 72
POS	NAME	CTY	1	2	3	4	TOTAL	PRIZE MONEY
1	Peter BAKER	Eng	67	64	72	63	266	£100000
2	Carl MASON	Eng	68	67	69	69	273	66660
3	Tony JOHNSTONE	Zim	70	70	68	66	274	37560
4	Roger CHAPMAN	Eng	70	69	69	67	275	27700
	Ronan RAFFERTY	N.Ire	68	66	70	71	275	27700
6	Joakim HAEGGMAN	Swe	68	67	69	72	276	18000
	Jim PAYNE	Eng	68	70	68	70	276	18000
	David FEHERTY	N.Ire	66	68	72	70	276	18000
9	Glen DAY	USA	68	73	71	65	277	13440
10	Peter MITCHELL	Eng	71	69	70	68	278	10428
	Sandy LYLE	Scot	70	65	70	73	278	10428
	Jesper PARNEVIK	Swe	69	66	71	72	278	10428
	Mark JAMES	Eng	70	65	71	72	278	10428
	Colin MONTGOMERIE	Scot	70	69	71	68	278	10428
15	Sam TORRANCE	Scot	69	67	73	70	279	8280
	Richard BOXALL	Eng	67	69	71	72	279	8280
	Derrick COOPER	Eng	68	70	68	73	279	8280
	Bernhard LANGER	Ger	70	67	71	71	279	8280
19	Mark DAVIS	Eng	68	73	72	67	280	7320
	Mark McNULTY	Zim	70	72	67	71	280	7320
21	Rodger DAVIS	Aus	71	70	71	69	281	6660
	Peter FOWLER	Aus	73	69	67	72	281	6660
	Ernie ELS	SA	68	71	70	72	281	6660
	Eduardo ROMERO	Arg	71	71	71	68	281	6660
	Mark MOULAND	Wal	67	74	68	72	281	6660
26	Barry LANE	Eng	69	72	72	69	282	5580
	Paul CURRY	Eng	73	67	71	71	282	5580
	Mark ROE	Eng	68	71	70	73	282	5580
	Ian PALMER	SA	67	71	70	74	282	5580
	Gordon BRAND Jnr	Scot	69	71	72	70	282	5580
	Costantino ROCCA	It	70	68	73	71	282	5580
	Frank NOBILO	NZ	68	75	70	69	282	5580
33	Martin GATES	Eng	70	70	72	71	283	4500
	Darren CLARKE	N.Ire	72	69	70	72	283	4500
	Paul LAWRIE	Scot	73	67	75	68	283	4500
	Andrew OLDCORN	Eng	72	71	70	70	283	4500
	Paul BROADHURST	Eng	71	70	72	70	283	4500
	Gavin LEVENSON	SA	70	70	76	67	283	4500
	Nick FALDO	Eng	68	73	72	70	283	4500
	José RIVERO	Sp	67	74	72	70	283	4500
41	Christy O'CONNOR Jnr	Ire	70	69	71	74	284	3780
	Jonathan SEWELL	Eng	70	68	74	72	284	3780
	Malcolm MACKENZIE	Eng	72	69	72	71	284	3780
	Jean VAN DE VELDE	Fr	66	71	75	72	284	3780
45	José Maria OLAZABAL	Sp	72	71	66	76	285	3240
	David GILFORD	Eng	71	72	70	72	285	3240
	Mike HARWOOD	Aus	72	69	69	75	285	3240
	Silvio GRAPPASONNI	It	70	70	73	72	285	3240
	Jay TOWNSEND	USA	71	67	72	75	285	3240
50	Eamonn DARCY	Ire	72	68	71	75	286	2760
	Greg TURNER	NZ	72	69	72	73	286	2760
	Howard CLARK	Eng	73	69	74	70	286	2760
53	Jorge BERENDT	Arg	73	69	75	70	287	2460
	Gordon J BRAND	Eng	70	72	72	73	287	2460
55	Andrew MURRAY	Eng	72	70	76	70	288	2100
	José Manuel CARRILES	Sp	71	69	73	75	288	2100
	Phillip PRICE	Wal	73	69	71	75	288	2100
	José Maria CANIZARES	Sp	68	71	77	72	288	2100
59	Alberto BINAGHI	It	68	70	74	77	289	1800
	Juan QUIROS	Sp	73	70	73	73	289	1800
	Andrew SHERBORNE	Eng	72	67	76	74	289	1800
62	Manuel PINERO	Sp	70	72	74	74	290	1620
	Robert KARLSSON	Swe	69	73	75	73	290	1620
	Justin HOBDAY	SA	75	68	75	72	290	1620
65	Rick HARTMANN	USA	71	70	73	77	291	1048
	Giuseppe CALI	It	74	68	72	77	291	1048
	Magnus SUNESSON	Swe	70	70	73	78	291	1048
	Tony JACKLIN	Eng	67	76	73	75	291	1048
69	Mats LANNER	Swe	70	70	78	74	292	894
70	Patrick HALL	Eng	71	71	72	79	293	892
71	Steven RICHARDSON	Eng	71	72	76	78	297	890

The Royal Bank of Scotland is delighted to be associated with the PGA European Tour.

The Royal Bank of Scotland is the official bank to the PGA European Tour.

The Royal Bank of Scotland

WHERE PEOPLE MATTER

The Royal Bank of Scotland plc. Registered Office: 36 St. Andrew Square, Edinburgh EH2 2YB. Registered in Scotland No. 90312.

TORRANCE'S TRIPLE TRIUMPH

Sam Torrance won his third Volvo Tour title of the year after a four man play-off

Sam Torrance began his 1993 tournament campaign with the declaration that it was imperative he maintained his place among Europe's elite by qualifying for a seventh successive Ryder Cup appearance.

There were many who thought it was a tall order for a player entering his 40th year, even one as talented as the hugely popular Scot, particularly as he had finished 62nd on the Volvo Order of Merit the previous season. Yet amazingly, 'slamming' Sam was almost able to celebrate his third appearance at The Belfry by the middle of June with his third victory in the space of eleven weeks.

First it was the Kronenbourg Open in Italy, then it was the Heineken Open Catalonia which fell to his superior stroke-play and consistent putting. Then at Hamburg's Gut Kaden club he prised the Honda Open from Ryder Cup rivals Ian Woosnam and Paul Broadhurst, and Sweden's Johan Rystrom.

When Torrance wielded his broom-handle putter with deadly precision to birdie the first play-off hole from 35 feet he felt he would be returning to the Midlands course where his emotional 1985 victory over Andy North had ended 28 years of American tenure of the coveted trophy.

That putt, for the only birdie of the final day at the 450-yards 18th hole, gave Torrance his 18th victory in 22 years in Europe, took him to the head of the Volvo Order of Merit and gave him over 248,000 points in the Ryder Cup

by Johnnie Walker qualifying process.

While Torrance was proving just how competitive he still is, although suffering from a sore wrist, a heavy cold and an attack of hay fever, Woosnam was making positive strides to regain his best form, and Rystrom, who came so agonisingly close to gaining a maiden victory, showed how deep is the reservoir of Scandinavian golf talent. Then there was US Masters champion Bernhard Langer, who had been given a hero's welcome by the German fans.

Langer was the inaugural Honda champion, but after a bright start to his title defence the incessant rain during Saturday's third round put a dampener on his progress, and instead of an eighth European victory in his own country he had to settle for fifth place alongside Joakim Haeggman, one shot behind the play-off quartet.

Only Broadhurst, the Benson and Hedges International Open champion at St Mellion, was unhappy with his performance, describing his golf as 'plodding' rather than inspired. Yet he came closest to avoiding the need for extra time when he struck a perfect drive and three iron some eight feet behind the flag at the 72nd hole. His putt for outright victory brushed the lip, then when Broadhurst got a second chance he put his approach into a bunker, and his putter was not given a chance to redeem itself.

The principle contenders were all among the 55 par-beaters who found Gut Kaden in benign mood on the opening day, South African Ernie Els taking the lead with a 66 which featured nine birdies. At the halfway mark it was Anders Gillner, the Swede who had been runner-up to Jim Payne in the Turespana Iberia Open de Baleares, who was out in front at ten under par by virtue of a record equalling 65 in which he came home in 30 after commencing at the tenth. Rystrom and Ireland's John McHenry who had just begun to putt in the Langer style by clasping his putter handle against his left wrist, had 66 to be one behind with Torrance

and Langer on 137. Els, who had fallen back with a 73, was alongside Woosnam and Broadhurst two shots further back.

The stage was set for an enthralling weekend but the weather was anything but when Saturday dawned wet and unseasonably chilly. For Torrance and Woosnam it was no handicap. Both returned 68s and only the experienced Mats Lanner could match them. Torrance went into the lead at eleven under when he claimed the second of only two birdies at the 18th with a putt of 30 feet. Rystrom, despite four-putting from 20 feet at the eighth in his 71, and Woosnam were just behind, while Masters hero Langer was within striking distance on 209.

Rystrom was out in front after the fourth hole of the final round after Torrance had three-putted both the third and fourth, and when the tall Swede turned for home in 34 against the 37 of Torrance with Woosnam in second place and Langer four shots back, there seemed every likelihood he could hang on. Just why Rystrom was doing so well after failing to survive the halfway axe in his six previous tournament was a mystery to everyone but himself and his sports psychologist.

Johan's explanation was that because his confidence had plunged to such a low level he had resolved just to hit golf shots and see what happened. His mental adviser had told him he had been committing the cardinal sin of worrying about what was going to happen to his ball before he struck it. Rystrom found a happy medium between execution and expectation for almost the entire week, arriving on the final tee one shot ahead of four golfers who between them had achieved more than 60 European victories. But all week the huge tree and cunningly sited bunker that guarded the 18th hole left-hand dog-leg had bothered Rystrom, whose natural shot goes in the opposite direction.

His drive found heavy rough and he could not reach the green with his recovery. When he failed to get up and down from 60 yards short a play-off was inevitable. Broadhurst's 68 gave him a second chance, then Woosnam, and

finally Torrance followed suit. Only Langer, to the chagrin of the large German gallery, could not make his par four, his approach finding sand and his putt screwing wide.

'It just did not happen last year,' said Torrance after coaxing home a putt that rolled unerringly across the sloping green, climbed the tier, and fell precisely into the cup. 'But here I got the right putt in at the right time and I know now that Ryder Cup place is mine.'

Four men with a play-off
mission.

Ian Woosnam showed a resurgence
of form.

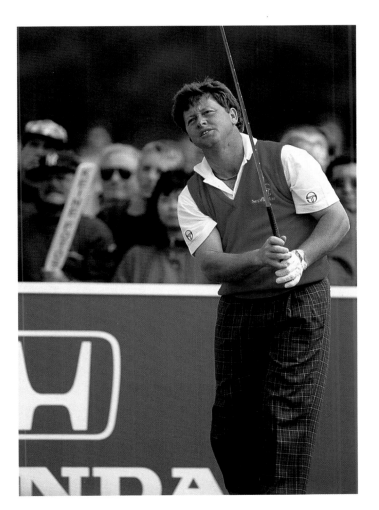

			COURSE: GUT KADEN, HAMBURG				YARDAGE: 6822		PAR: 72

POS	NAME	CTY	1	2	3	4	TOTAL	PRIZE MONEY
1	Sam TORRANCE	Scot	68	69	68	73	278	£83330
2	Paul BROADHURST	Eng	71	68	71	68	278	37283
	Johan RYSTROM	Swe	69	66	71	72	278	37283
	Ian WOOSNAM	Wal	67	72	68	71	278	37283
5	Joakim HAEGGMAN	Swe	71	71	71	66	279	19350
	Bernhard LANGER	Ger	69	68	72	70	279	19350
7	Jamie SPENCE	Eng	70	66	73	71	280	12883
	Mats LANNER	Swe	71	72	68	69	280	12883
	Ian PALMER	SA	67	72	72	69	280	12883
10	Ernie ELS	SA	66	73	70	72	281	9595
	Miguel Angel JIMENEZ	Sp	69	69	74	69	281	9595
12	Jim PAYNE	Eng	74	65	73	70	282	7907
	Mike McLEAN	Eng	72	71	70	69	282	7907
	Chris WILLIAMS	Eng	71	72	69	70	282	7907
	Ronan RAFFERTY	N.Ire	71	67	72	72	282	7907
16	Gordon BRAND Jnr	Scot	70	70	73	70	283	6490
	Wayne WESTNER	SA	73	70	73	67	283	6490
	Silvio GRAPPASONNI	It	71	69	71	72	283	6490
	Thomas LEVET	Fr	68	69	74	72	283	6490
	Domingo HOSPITAL	Sp	70	73	70	70	283	6490
21	Jeremy ROBINSON	Eng	70	68	74	72	284	5550
	Olle KARLSSON	Swe	78	65	70	71	284	5550
	Andrew HARE	Eng	70	67	77	70	284	5550
	Anders GILLNER	Swe	70	64	76	74	284	5550
	Mikael KRANTZ	Swe	74	67	73	70	284	5550
26	Ross DRUMMOND	Scot	75	67	69	74	285	4516
	Paul McGINLEY	Ire	71	67	73	74	285	4516
	Sandy LYLE	Scot	68	72	70	75	285	4516
	David FEHERTY	N.Ire	69	74	72	70	285	4516
	Gary EVANS	Eng	69	68	76	72	285	4516
	Steen TINNING	Den	71	71	75	68	285	4516
	Russell CLAYDON	Eng	70	72	69	74	285	4516
	Craig CASSELLS	Eng	69	71	74	71	285	4516
	John McHENRY	Ire	69	66	79	71	285	4516
35	Rodger DAVIS	Aus	69	73	73	71	286	3500
	Andrew OLDCORN	Eng	73	68	73	72	286	3500
	Brian MARCHBANK	Scot	70	71	75	70	286	3500
	Darren CLARKE	N.Ire	72	71	69	74	286	3500
	Stephen BENNETT	Eng	71	69	71	75	286	3500
	Keith WATERS	Eng	68	71	78	69	286	3500
	Paul EALES	Eng	70	73	73	70	286	3500
	Paul MAYO	Wal	70	73	73	70	286	3500
	Roger CHAPMAN	Eng	68	68	82	68	286	3500
44	Gary ORR	Scot	68	72	77	70	287	2850
	Ove SELLBERG	Swe	68	74	78	67	287	2850
	Jon ROBSON	Eng	73	70	72	72	287	2850
	Stuart LITTLE	Eng	71	72	73	71	287	2850
48	Mark DAVIS	Eng	69	72	75	72	288	2300
	Wayne RILEY	Aus	72	66	75	75	288	2300
	Alberto BINAGHI	It	72	70	73	73	288	2300
	José RIVERO	Sp	69	71	73	75	288	2300
	Miguel Angel MARTIN	Sp	73	69	73	73	288	2300
	José Manuel CARRILES	Sp	72	70	72	74	288	2300
	Gabriel HJERTSTEDT	Swe	68	68	76	76	288	2300
55	Paul AFFLECK	Wal	67	73	76	73	289	1750
	Andrew SHERBORNE	Eng	75	68	75	71	289	1750
	Martin GATES	Eng	73	68	74	74	289	1750
	Eoghan O'CONNELL	Ire	75	66	74	74	289	1750
59	Carl MASON	Eng	69	68	76	77	290	1525
	Lucien TINKLER	Aus	70	73	73	74	290	1525
61	Mark McNULTY	Zim	72	71	77	71	291	1450
62	Tom PERNICE	USA	72	70	76	74	292	1375
	Ralf BERHORST	Ger	76	66	74	76	292	1375
64	Mats HALLBERG	Swe	73	67	80	74	294	1275
	Dennis EDLUND	Swe	74	69	77	74	294	1275
66	Sven STROVER	Ger	71	72	77	75	295	750
67	Mike HARWOOD	Aus	71	71	77	77	296	748
68	David RAY	Eng	74	69	75	79	297	746

PALMER TAKES CHARGE

Ian Palmer captured his second Volvo Tour title with a final round that was reminiscent of his illustrious namesake

It is hard to remember when the world of golf last witnessed a Palmer charge like it. Who would have thought Palmer would break out of the pack with a nine-under-par 63 to set up a memorable victory? And do it in US Open week of all weeks.

The Palmer in question, however, was not Arnold it was Ian. And although the round came on US Open Sunday, it came not at Baltusrol, New Jersey, but on the other side of the world at La Moye, Old Jersey, the Channel Isles.

Ian Palmer was little more than a toddler when his famous namesake was bludgeoning his way to tournament glory, but the curly-haired South African took a leaf out of the Arnold Palmer Book of Last Day Charges to win the Jersey European Airways Open.

The 35-year old from Johannesburg had looked to be meandering his way to just another top-25 finish when he bogeyed the first hole on Sunday to fall five shots behind the tournament leader Sam Torrance. With the Scot displaying some of the best form of his career – and fresh from a Honda Open triumph the week before – there seemed little chance of Palmer springing any springbok surprise. He had been having a miserable time with the putter for weeks, and in Jersey was experimenting again with an old Zebra putter. Secondly, he was without his regular caddie and his bag was

being carried by John Bland's brother. Finally (and maybe this should have been a warning) he had a ricked neck. 'Before going out I though if I could shoot 70 I would finish in the top 25,' said Palmer. 'I wasn't very happy when I dropped a shot at the first hole. But then I just relaxed and played my normal game.'

Make that an abnormal game. Four holes later Palmer's Zebra putter was earning its stripes, rolling in a putt from 30 feet for an unlikely birdie at the 449-yard fifth. From the ridiculous things went to the sublime, as Palmer played the stretch from the fifth to the 17th in ten under par. He set up a glorious eagle three with a three iron to three feet at the par-five sixth, then wedged to eight feet at the next for a birdie to turn in 33. There were more birdies at the tenth and 11th, then a quartet of birdies from the 14th topped off with a putt of 25 feet at the 419-yard 17th to get to 20 under. Back in 30 for a 63, a stroke shy of the course record, but enough for Palmer to secure his second Volvo Tour triumph by two shots and a handy £50,000 prize.

Unceremoniously bundled into runner-up spot was Torrance, searching for his fourth win of the season. The day before the Ryder Cup man had shot a 63 of his own. He had been so hot that playing partner Mark Roe quipped: 'I was afraid to get his card out of the bag in case it ignited'. Torrance agreed: 'This is as good as I have played in my career. My irons are as good as they have ever been, my driving is not bad either. I'm playing as well as at any time.'

Roe's unlikely successor wielding Torrance's red hot pencil on Sunday was the former PGA Cup player Ged Furey, playing in his first ever Volvo Tour event.

Right, Brian Barnes was joint first round leader.

Right, Brian Barnes was joint first round leader.

Furey had received an 11th hour invitation from the millionaire owner of Jersey European Airways and chairman of Blackburn Rovers, Jack Walker (who also happens to be a member at Furey's club Pleasington, just outside Blackburn). He found himself out in the final pairing after shooting 69, 66, 68. Before Palmer went berserk, Furey even got to within a stroke of Torrance's lead after birdieing two of the first four holes during the fourth round. His closing 73, however, pushed the 33-year old down the field but was still enough to earn £4,273 – double his previous best earnings as a pro. 'My aim was just to make the cut.' said Furey, 'and not to let Jack Walker down for giving me a special invitation. I wanted to prove I was good enough to take someone's place.'

While Furey was proving himself worthy of a place, Torrance was having his place as odds-on winner taken by Palmer. The first the Scot knew of what the South African had done was when he glanced at a scoreboard beside the 16th fairway. 'I couldn't believe it,' said Torrance who was 17 under at the time, 'Palmer had finished at 20 under! I thought at best he would finish at 18 under – but not 20 under.'

With holes disappearing the Ryder Cup man went in search of the three birdies he needed to force a play-off. At the 482-yard 16th his third shot, a wedge from 100 yards, crashed against the flagstick, hit the hole, and flipped out. 'It was in, guaranteed. It was in,' said Torrance on what would have been an extraordinary eagle. 'It just hit the stick and came out. It was no more than a foot away.' The resulting birdie was Torrance's last of the tournament and he finished two behind the champion.

Palmer's first win on the Volvo Tour had come a year earlier at the Johnnie Walker Asian classic. That victory had been notable as it marked the South African's return to Europe after a gap of eight years. He had kept away because of sanctions against South African sportsmen which existed in Spain and

Right, Greg Turner and Mark James in close scrutiny.

Sweden at the time – important stops on the Volvo Tour.

If victory in Thailand signalled Palmer's return in some style, victory in Jersey suggests the quiet South African is here to stay. 'I have learned a lot since winning in Thailand,' he said. 'I have played my own game this year, I've started getting better, getting to know the courses and getting used to the travelling again. Winning the first tournament put a lot of pressure on me. Everyone said it was just a flash in the pan – I wanted to prove it wasn't.'

Above, crowds gather round the 18th
at La Moye.

Below, former champion Sam Torrance
had to be content with second place.

	COURSE: LA MOYE, JERSEY					YARDAGE: 6826		PAR: 72	
POS	NAME	CTY	1	2	3	4	TOTAL	PRIZE MONEY
1	Ian PALMER	SA	68	67	70	63	268	£50000
2	Sam TORRANCE	Scot	70	68	63	69	270	33330
3	Mark JAMES	Eng	68	65	71	67	271	18780
4	Greg TURNER	NZ	66	69	69	68	272	12733
	Martin GATES	Eng	72	67	67	66	272	12733
	Jim PAYNE	Eng	70	66	70	66	272	12733
7	Mark ROE	Eng	68	70	66	69	273	9000
8	Carl MASON	Eng	71	67	66	71	275	6427
	Gordon BRAND Jnr	Scot	67	67	73	68	275	6427
	Peter BAKER	Eng	70	64	69	72	275	6427
	Ross DRUMMOND	Scot	65	69	72	69	275	6427
12	Derrick COOPER	Eng	70	70	67	69	276	4273
	Howard CLARK	Eng	68	68	72	68	276	4273
	Jamie SPENCE	Eng	67	73	72	64	276	4273
	Robert LEE	Eng	70	70	70	66	276	4273
	Brian MARCHBANK	Scot	66	69	72	69	276	4273
	Wayne STEPHENS	Eng	71	70	69	66	276	4273
	André BOSSERT	Swi	70	69	67	70	276	4273
	Ruben ALVAREZ	Arg	65	70	69	72	276	4273
	Ged FUREY	Eng	69	66	68	73	276	4273
21	Torsten GIEDEON	Ger	67	74	65	71	277	3330
	Pierre FULKE	Swe	72	69	68	68	277	3330
	Eoghan O'CONNELL	Ire	72	69	70	66	277	3330
	Mark MOULAND	Wal	68	74	67	68	277	3330
	Richard BOXALL	Eng	70	71	66	70	277	3330
26	Andrew HARE	Eng	73	67	66	72	278	2568
	Chris MOODY	Eng	73	68	69	68	278	2568
	Paul CURRY	Eng	71	67	72	68	278	2568
	Malcolm MACKENZIE	Eng	70	68	71	69	278	2568
	Stephen BENNETT	Eng	67	68	74	69	278	2568
	Clinton WHITELAW	SA	75	66	70	67	278	2568
	Brian BARNES	Scot	65	70	70	73	278	2568
	Russell CLAYDON	Eng	69	69	70	70	278	2568
	Mike McLEAN	Eng	69	70	70	69	278	2568
	John McHENRY	Ire	68	69	71	70	278	2568
	Wayne WESTNER	SA	68	69	72	69	278	2568
	Andrew SHERBORNE	Eng	72	70	68	68	278	2568
	Des SMYTH	Ire	70	69	68	71	278	2568
39	Tom PERNICE	USA	72	66	69	72	279	1980
	Craig CASSELLS	Eng	68	66	72	73	279	1980
	Martin POXON	Eng	69	68	71	71	279	1980
	Ole ESKILDSEN	Den	73	68	68	70	279	1980
	Thomas LEVET	Fr	68	69	70	72	279	1980
44	Philip WALTON	Ire	72	68	69	71	280	1710
	Peter MITCHELL	Eng	73	68	71	68	280	1710
	Mike CLAYTON	Aus	68	68	69	75	280	1710
	Steven RICHARDSON	Eng	68	71	72	69	280	1710
48	Paul BROADHURST	Eng	75	67	71	68	281	1500
	Mikael KRANTZ	Swe	71	70	72	68	281	1500
	David CURRY	Eng	71	68	73	69	281	1500
51	Paul WAY	Eng	70	70	72	70	282	1320
	Robin MANN	Eng	70	68	74	70	282	1320
	Paul LAWRIE	Scot	71	69	69	73	282	1320
54	Jonathan SEWELL	Eng	70	72	70	71	283	1140
	José Maria CANIZARES	Sp	68	70	73	72	283	1140
	Stuart SMITH	Eng	71	71	71	70	283	1140
57	Philip TALBOT	Eng	70	69	73	72	284	970
	Adam HUNTER	Scot	69	69	72	74	284	970
	Bill MALLEY	USA	70	69	75	70	284	970
60	David WILLIAMS	Eng	73	66	74	72	285	900
61	Tony CHARNLEY	Eng	70	71	71	74	286	840
	David RAY	Eng	71	71	72	72	286	840
	Jon ROBSON	Eng	70	71	76	69	286	840
64	Ross McFARLANE	Eng	70	71	73	73	287	765
	Ian GARBUTT	Eng	72	70	68	77	287	765
66	Tommy HORTON	Eng	71	71	72	74	288	450
67	Gabriel HJERTSTEDT	Swe	71	68	74	76	289	448

ROCCA FLUENT IN FRENCH DOUBLE

Costantino Rocca took his second Volvo Tour title of the season on French soil

Once upon a time there lived in Bergamo in northern Italy a young man who dreamed of becoming a professional golfer. But in his country, where golf was still a game for the rich, there seemed no way into the game for a son of a humble family, so he continued to bend his back in the polystyrene factory where he was forced to make his living.

He had fallen in love with the game at the age of seven, when he used to caddie for the lucky few at the club near his home. He had the aptitude, he had the determination, but still there was no way in, and he was well into his twenties already, and still working in the factory.

Then, out of the blue, came the moment that was to change his life. He landed a job as a caddie master, and he won, then lost, a coveted place on the Volvo Tour three times before he arrived to stay. The man's name was Costantino Rocca, and on Sunday, June 27, 1993, another dream came true when he won the Peugeot Open de France. He smiles a lot, does Signor Rocca, and his face after he had completed his triumph threatened to split into two.

Rocca, who tied with Paul McGinley on 273, 11 under par, went on to beat the young Irishman at the first hole of a sudden-death play-off and win £83,330, which almost goes without saying was the biggest pay-day of his life, doubling the cheque he had picked up in his first Volvo Tour victory in Lyon in April.

Rocca did not collect his prize without more than the odd alarum, however. With McGinley in the clubhouse after a closing 68, Rocca extended his lead to three strokes after birdieing the 15th from

35 feet. It seemed that all he had to do was stay upright and the spoils would be his. Then came calamity as he pushed his tee shot through the green and on to a bank at the 176-yard 16th. He had a horrible downhill lie and no green to play with; he took three to get down, and the lead was back to two.

His final hiccup came on the 18th, a monstrously testing hole with water a constant menace, when the guidance system that had put him in such a powerful position suddenly went wildly out of kilter. He drove into the rough, and might have been better advised to lay up. Instead, he took the bold route with a four iron and

succeeded only in putting his ball into the briny. He dropped out under penalty then sank to his knees in frustration when his putt from 40 feet for victory stopped one roll from the cup. A double-bogey six and a round of 70 left him facing extra time against McGinley, the 26-year-old former Walker Cup player.

The play-off hole on the 15th, another horror with a long carry over water to an island green that it shares with the 18th, and that one hole carried enough tension to fill a whole day.

McGinley pulled his drive into thick rough and could only hack out, and with Rocca in prime position he had to hope for a disaster from his opponent. He nearly got it, too, when Rocca hit a 150-yard seven-iron through the green and not more than ten feet from the water. In the end it mattered little because McGinley, caught between an eight and nine-iron 138 yards from the flag, hit the nine, but did not have enough club, and planted his ball into the water. Rocca chipped to six feet and missed the putt, but by then he had the tournament won. It was an error-strewn finish by both men, but the quality of the golf over those crucial, final 15 minutes was an irrelevance in the drama of it all.

The play-off was a fitting climax to a tournament that had thrown up many a sub-text along the way. On the first day, for example, David Williams, who lost his card at the end of 1992 and failed to get it back at the PGA European Tour Qualifying School, shot an eight-birdie 64. Williams only knew he had got into the tournament the Monday before it started, and he had to forgo his daughter

Lucy's fourth birthday party to play. He eventually finished in a tie for 25th, led by a shot by Gary Orr, a big Scot, who was in turn a stroke in front of a group of eight players.

Peter Mitchell was one of the octet, but he would have been singing a duet with Williams had he not arrived 20 seconds late on the first tee and found himself on the wrong end of a two-stroke penalty. Mitchell, as chirpily philosophical as ever, blamed nobody but himself.

The next day Jean van de Velde, carrying the hopes of his compatriots, equalled Williams' 64, but incurred the displeasure of David Garland, the Tournament Director, for his slow play. Van de Velde had two breaches of the time allowance and would have had a third – and a fine – had he taken a second longer over a putt. Still, he proved his point by taking the lead on 11 under par.

Van de Velde slipped to a 73 in the third round, but was still only one shot behind Rocca, who had opened with two 66s and followed it with a 71, and Johan Rystrom. Mark Roe, meanwhile, was proving he was more than just the joker in the Tour pack by producing a 67 to put himself in contention.

Van de Velde was still in the hunt when he pitched in from 60 yards at the fifth on the final day, but he moved out of contention with a plug-ugly finish in which he dropped three shots in the last three holes.

Out in front, Rocca continued to play composed golf, and when he birdied the 14th and 15th he looked a clear winner. Although he did not know it then, the drama was yet to come. It was time for the Italian's resolve to be tested, and he probably hated every minute of that climactic extra hole.

One thing was certain, though – however unpleasant, however tortuous, it beat the living daylights out of slaving away in a polystyrene factory.

Right, the island green on the 18th became the play-off battleground.

Below, double image of Jean van de Velde.

Above, Costantino Rocca agonises as putt to win stays out.

COURSE: LE GOLF NATIONAL, PARIS						YARDAGE: 6965	PAR: 71	
POS	NAME	CTY	1	2	3	4	TOTAL	PRIZE MONEY
1	Costantino ROCCA	It	66	66	71	70	273	£83330
2	Paul McGINLEY	Ire	69	67	69	68	273	55550
3	Mark JAMES	Eng	69	69	68	68	274	31300
4	Mark ROE	Eng	67	71	67	70	275	23100
	Anders FORSBRAND	Swe	68	71	69	67	275	23100
6	Jean VAN DE VELDE	Fr	67	64	73	72	276	13230
	Johan RYSTROM	Swe	66	70	67	73	276	13230
	Tony JOHNSTONE	Zim	67	71	71	67	276	13230
	Jay TOWNSEND	USA	71	71	68	66	276	13230
	David FEHERTY	N.Ire	67	70	70	69	276	13230
11	Ronan RAFFERTY	N.Ire	69	69	69	70	277	8367
	Gary ORR	Scot	65	67	72	73	277	8367
	Santiago LUNA	Sp	70	68	67	72	277	8367
	Malcolm MACKENZIE	Eng	70	70	69	68	277	8367
15	Vicente FERNANDEZ	Arg	72	70	69	67	278	6521
	Ross DRUMMOND	Scot	71	66	72	69	278	6521
	José Maria OLAZABAL	Sp	71	66	72	69	278	6521
	Mike HARWOOD	Aus	67	71	72	68	278	6521
	Peter O'MALLEY	Aus	66	69	70	73	278	6521
	Ernie ELS	SA	69	68	71	70	278	6521
	Retief GOOSEN	SA	68	71	71	68	278	6521
22	Barry LANE	Eng	70	67	74	68	279	5550
	Howard CLARK	Eng	68	67	72	72	279	5550
	Adam HUNTER	Scot	69	72	68	70	279	5550
25	Martin POXON	Eng	72	70	72	66	280	5025
	David WILLIAMS	Eng	64	73	72	71	280	5025
	Peter MITCHELL	Eng	66	71	73	70	280	5025
	Frank NOBILO	NZ	69	69	71	71	280	5025
29	Manuel PINERO	Sp	71	67	72	71	281	4300
	Robert LEE	Eng	69	70	71	71	281	4300
	Paul WAY	Eng	66	67	75	73	281	4300
	Sam TORRANCE	Scot	68	68	72	73	281	4300
	Paul MAYO	Wal	69	71	74	67	281	4300
	Stephen McALLISTER	Scot	68	70	72	71	281	4300
35	Mikael KRANTZ	Swe	69	73	71	69	282	3650
	Chris MOODY	Eng	71	70	68	73	282	3650
	Steven RICHARDSON	Eng	72	68	71	71	282	3650
	Mark McNULTY	Zim	71	70	70	71	282	3650
	Emmanuel DUSSART	Fr	71	69	66	76	282	3650
	Eoghan O'CONNELL	Ire	70	70	74	68	282	3650
41	Thomas LEVET	Fr	71	66	71	75	283	3050
	Alberto BINAGHI	It	72	70	70	71	283	3050
	Paul AFFLECK	Wal	66	70	71	76	283	3050
	Giuseppe CALI	It	71	69	72	71	283	3050
	Greg TURNER	NZ	73	68	75	67	283	3050
	Philip WALTON	Ire	73	67	71	72	283	3050
47	Mark DAVIS	Eng	71	71	70	72	284	2600
	Jeremy ROBINSON	Eng	71	71	71	71	284	2600
	Michel BESANCENEY	Fr	68	72	67	77	284	2600
50	Roy MACKENZIE	Chil	69	72	70	74	285	2200
	Jean Ignace MOUHICA	Fr	70	71	75	69	285	2200
	Haydn SELBY-GREEN	Eng	69	71	75	70	285	2200
	Gordon BRAND Jnr	Scot	66	72	70	77	285	2200
	Andrew HARE	Eng	68	72	74	71	285	2200
55	Gary EVANS	Eng	70	70	69	77	286	1675
	André BOSSERT	Swi	74	68	70	74	286	1675
	John McHENRY	Ire	70	70	74	72	286	1675
	Mark MOULAND	Wal	66	73	75	72	286	1675
	Patrick HALL	Eng	72	70	71	73	286	1675
	Mike McLEAN	Eng	70	70	76	70	286	1675
61	Marc PENDARIES	Fr	69	71	74	73	287	1375
	Phillip PRICE	Wal	70	70	75	72	287	1375
	Andrew MURRAY	Eng	68	72	74	73	287	1375
	Jeff HAWKES	SA	70	67	79	71	287	1375
65	David A RUSSELL	Eng	71	71	71	75	288	916
	Paul CURRY	Eng	71	71	73	73	288	916
	Jamie SPENCE	Eng	68	74	73	73	288	916
68	Dominique NOUAILHAC	Fr	70	70	75	74	289	745
	Alfonso PINERO	Sp	70	71	75	73	289	745
70	Anders GILLNER	Swe	73	68	74	75	290	739
	Ross McFARLANE	Eng	68	74	77	71	290	739
	Philip TATAURANGI (AM)	NZ	70	72	80	69	291	739

Left, home hero van de Velde was left holding the baby.

Left, Gary Orr in tiger country.

FALDO RELAXES FOR IRISH HAT-TRICK

Nick Faldo smiles a lot when he goes to Ireland. The splendid fishing there could be a factor. Then again, it might have something to do with a dominance of the Carrolls Irish Open which he captured for a record third successive year when the event moved to the new, Jack Nicklaus-designed course at Mount Juliet, Co Kilkenny.

By way of explaining his first tournament victory since the Johnnie Walker Classic in Singapore five months previously, the world number one suggested: 'There is something about the country – nobody dies of ulcers here. It helps me to relax.'

Faldo did little for the digestive system of Jose Maria Olazabal, however, as these Ryder Cup colleagues became implacable rivals in a breathtaking climax to the tournament. Finishing on 12-under-par 276, two matches ahead of the Spaniard, Faldo shot a course record final round of 65 in an effort reminiscent of his first US Masters triumph at Augusta National in 1989. And, as happened on that occasion, it sent him into a play-off for the title. Instead of the hapless Scott Hoch his opponent this time was the 1990 Carrolls Irish Open champion Olazabal, who came from two strokes adrift to draw level with birdies on the 16th and 17th.

The par four 18th at Mount Juliet presented a fearsome, climactic challenge. Measuring 476 yards off the back tee,

Nick Faldo recorded his third successive Carrolls Irish Open victory and decided it was something about the country

it was perceived to be so difficult that Tournament Director Andy McFee decided to reduce it by 27 yards before the event got under way. Even that concession, however, failed to avert some horrendous casualties, including a ten by the gifted South African David Frost in the opening round.

Apart from its length, there was an intimidating lake bordering the left side of the fairway and an intrusive tree at driving distance down the right. Given these factors, then, Faldo and Olazabal hit

splendid tee shots on the play-off hole.

Then came the critical second shots. The defending champion was first into action, hitting a two iron arrow-straight for the target. Its trajectory, however, was lower than intended and the ball overshot the green to finish in heavy rough off the back fringe. The attendance of 27,000 packed along the 17th fairway and around the finishing hole sensed a door opening invitingly for the Spaniard.

But Olazabal stumbled on the threshold. His three iron was pulled into the large bunker guarding the left side of the green and from there he recovered to six feet below the hole. Faldo, meanwhile, did well to get a sand wedge recovery to stop 12 feet past the flag.

The illustrious amateur, Joe Carr, was close by the green in his capacity as President of the host club. Turning to Mount Juliet captain Tom Duggan, he remarked: 'You know this fellow holes these ones.' Faldo stood over the putt and in the finest tradition of great players in death-or-glory situations, he seemed to will the ball into the hole. The head never moved, the stroke was perfect and the target was found.

Olazabal then eyed his putt which, moments earlier, he must have felt would be for the title. Now it was for survival. When he had parred the 18th to force a play-off, the Spaniard had holed from four feet below the hole but from a different

angle. This time, there was a slight break to the right. In the event, the pace of the putt was such that it is doubtful if it took any break: it hit the right edge of the hole and ran past.

Faldo emulated the achievement of Ian Woosnam, winner of the Monte Carlo Open in 1990, 1991 and 1992 by winning the same title in three successive years. And it become the Englishman's seventh win in ten play-offs on the PGA European Tour.

'It's a wonderful feeling to have played well and done something I'd never done before,' said Faldo afterwards. 'My game had been a bit off for the last few months but things began to come together during a session with David (Leadbetter) this morning.' In fact the champion had changed to a driver he had never used before, a metal wood with a Founder head and a Mizuno shaft which combined to produce a club three swing-weights lighter than his old persimmon MacGregor. 'The shaft was the key,' he added. 'I could tell immediately that my timing was better.'

In moving to Mount Juliet, Carrolls were pursuing a policy upon which they had embarked in 1991 when the tournament was moved from Portmarnock to Killarney. In view of his three Open triumphs, it is therefore ironic that the change from links to parkland terrain culminated in a hat-trick of victories for Faldo in Ireland.

'This is a very impressive course,' he said of Mount Juliet which was officially opened only two years previously. 'It has set a standard in finish that others can follow. The greens are the best I have played on this season with the exception of Dubai. Its arrival as a European venue is great for the game. Our players are certain to benefit from experience of playing an excellently-conditioned, American-style course which incidentally, we were led to believe was an impossibility because of our climate.'

Splendid scoring standards were set from the start, with Scotland's Brian

**Below, Jose Maria Olazabal flew the
Spanish flag for the runner-up spot.**

**Below, Nick Faldo put a stop to
anyone else taking the title.**

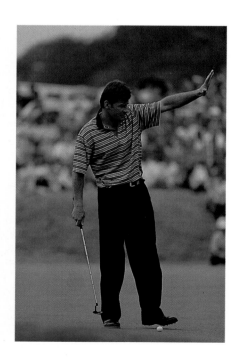

Above, Olazabal takes a close look at the rushes.

Marchbank leading the first round with a six-under-par 66, three strokes ahead of Olazabal and six ahead of Faldo. Marchbank putted conventionally on the way to the top of the leaderboard but as an exponent also of the so-called Bernhard Langer method, he protested: 'My father Ian was putting that way 30 years ago.'

When the cut was made on 147, three over par, Olazabal had taken over the lead on 136, one stroke ahead of Irish challenger John McHenry, Swede Per-Ulrik Johansson and Bernhard Langer who, incidentally, was still afflicted by a neck injury which he had first sustained in the run up to the US Open. But with a second round of 67, Faldo had moved menacingly into a share of sixth place.

The third round saw no significant movement at the top. McHenry had become joint leader with Olazabal; Johansson was third and Faldo was four strokes off the lead in the somewhat unlikely company of Frost. Given his wretched ten at the 18th on the opening day when he was twice in the water and incurred a two-stroke penalty for an incorrect drop, Frost's revival was quite stunning. It seemed unthinkable that he would be partnering Faldo in the final round.

On Sunday morning somebody had suggested to Faldo that he would need to shoot 67 to win. 'I replied that 65 was the figure – that would be my target,' the champion had said. The putter soon began to deliver a rich harvest. With nine putts over the opening seven holes, he carded five birdies and two pars to claim the lead on ten under par. It was impeccable play. Further birdies followed on the 12th, where he sank a putt of 40 feet, and on the long 17th, which he reached in two.

He had set a target which Olazabal would later equal through a holed bunker shot on the 16th and a majestic pitch and putt from six feet on the next. But for the Spaniard, it proved to be fruitless battle against a master at the peak of his form.

Nick Faldo smiles a lot when he goes to Ireland, and fishing in the River Nore can be both relaxing and fruitful. On the night after the first round he caught eight trout which he returned to the river. Would he be pursuing a fourth successive Carrolls Irish Open title at Mount Juliet next year? 'What a question!' came the ambiguous reply. And he smiled.

Left, majestic Mount Juliet.

Triple champion and caddie traverse

the emerald fairway.

COURSE: MOUNT JULIET G.C.				YARDAGE: 7143			PAR: 72	
POS	NAME	CTY	1	2	3	4	TOTAL	PRIZE MONEY
1	Nick FALDO	Eng	72	67	72	65	276	£96630
2	José Maria OLAZABAL	Sp	69	67	71	69	276	64380
3	David FROST	SA	74	69	68	68	279	36310
4	Steven RICHARDSON	Eng	71	68	72	69	280	29000
5	Costantino ROCCA	It	71	70	71	69	281	24590
6	Olle KARLSSON	Swe	71	67	72	72	282	18850
	Retief GOOSEN	SA	69	72	75	66	282	18850
8	Per-Ulrik JOHANSSON	Swe	69	68	72	74	283	13030
	Wayne WESTNER	SA	73	69	73	68	283	13030
	Joakim HAEGGMAN	Swe	71	68	72	72	283	13030
11	Ian WOOSNAM	Wal	71	72	72	69	284	10670
12	Steven BOWMAN	USA	70	71	71	73	285	9657
	Paul McGINLEY	Ire	75	71	69	70	285	9657
14	John McHENRY	Ire	67	70	70	79	286	8352
	Bernhard LANGER	Ger	68	69	76	73	286	8352
	De Wet BASSON	SA	70	73	72	71	286	8352
	Wayne RILEY	Aus	69	74	73	70	286	8352
18	Rodger DAVIS	Aus	71	73	71	72	287	7002
	Adam HUNTER	Scot	72	70	74	71	287	7002
	Santiago LUNA	Sp	68	71	76	72	287	7002
	Tony JOHNSTONE	Zim	72	70	74	71	287	7002
	Mark JAMES	Eng	72	70	72	73	287	7002
23	Brian MARCHBANK	Scot	66	76	72	74	288	5884
	Peter O'MALLEY	Aus	75	72	73	68	288	5884
	Frank NOBILO	NZ	73	70	73	72	288	5884
	Colin MONTGOMERIE	Scot	74	71	70	73	288	5884
	Seve BALLESTEROS	Sp	73	73	70	72	288	5884
	Ross McFARLANE	Eng	72	72	71	73	288	5884
	Des SMYTH	Ire	73	70	70	75	288	5884
30	Russell CLAYDON	Eng	75	71	71	72	289	4947
	Antoine LEBOUC	Fr	68	74	76	71	289	4947
	Ronan RAFFERTY	N.Ire	76	71	67	75	289	4947
	Carl MASON	Eng	72	74	73	70	289	4947
34	Darren CLARKE	N.Ire	70	75	72	73	290	4310
	Philip WALTON	Ire	67	75	74	74	290	4310
	Paul MAYO	Wal	72	71	75	72	290	4310
	Andrew OLDCORN	Eng	71	73	73	73	290	4310
	Peter BAKER	Eng	73	73	71	73	290	4310
	Anders FORSBRAND	Swe	71	69	78	72	290	4310
40	Mark DAVIS	Eng	78	69	70	74	291	3717
	Vijay SINGH	Fij	68	79	73	71	291	3717
	Jean VAN DE VELDE	Fr	73	74	71	73	291	3717
	David FEHERTY	N.Ire	72	72	76	71	291	3717
44	Robin MANN	Eng	72	74	75	71	292	3200
	Stephen AMES	T&T	72	75	74	71	292	3200
	Eduardo ROMERO	Arg	73	71	76	72	292	3200
	Marc FARRY	Fr	72	66	76	78	292	3200
	Stuart LITTLE	Eng	74	72	71	75	292	3200
49	Paul EALES	Eng	73	71	76	73	293	2720
	Jon ROBSON	Eng	72	73	71	77	293	2720
	Stephen FIELD	Eng	74	72	76	71	293	2720
	Paul BROADHURST	Eng	72	71	72	78	293	2720
53	Robert LEE	Eng	71	73	75	75	294	2420
	Jay TOWNSEND	USA	73	73	73	75	294	2420
55	Jorge BERENDT	Arg	77	70	72	76	295	2126
	Patrick HALL	Eng	71	75	74	75	295	2126
	Glen DAY	USA	71	73	73	78	295	2126
	Miguel Angel MARTIN	Sp	76	70	70	79	295	2126
59	Hugh BAIOCCHI	SA	75	70	72	79	296	1811
	Clinton WHITELAW	SA	73	73	78	72	296	1811
	David J RUSSELL	Eng	72	75	78	71	296	1811
	Peter FOWLER	Aus	79	68	77	72	296	1811
63	Chris MOODY	Eng	72	75	76	74	297	1571
	Craig CASSELLS	Eng	72	75	74	76	297	1571
	Domingo HOSPITAL	Sp	73	71	73	80	297	1571
66	Keith WATERS	Eng	76	70	74	78	298	869
	André BOSSERT	Swi	70	72	77	79	298	869
68	Andrew COLTART	Scot	73	74	77	75	299	864
	David R JONES	Eng	74	72	77	76	299	864
	Jim PAYNE	Eng	71	75	73	80	299	864

HORTON HAS THE MOST MILEAGE

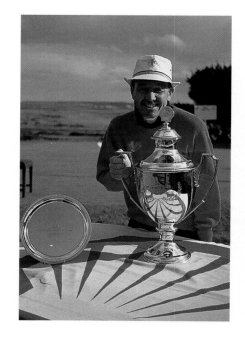

***Tommy Horton
outlasted his
opponents to win the
inaugural Shell
Scottish Seniors Open
at Royal Aberdeen***

Now and then at the Shell Scottish Seniors Open, nothing seemed different. George Will was still the great iron player, punching a four iron through the wind to the 18th green on the second day. Neil Coles was magical as ever with wedges, holing a bunker shot at the 17th in round three. Harry Bannerman, himself an Aberdonian, looked as good as he had in the 1971 Ryder Cup.

But we were looking at the future as well as the past. National championships for senior professionals are the shape of things to come.

Royal Aberdeen, though, is inextricably tied to earlier times. There are no new versions of this place. It is the way golf courses used to be – out and back along the linksland, all humps and hollows with scarcely a lie that isn't uphill, downhill or sidehill, each well-bunkered fairway encased in knee-high rough and gorse, ending in a true, quick, rolling green. An unusual wind blew across these holes, everything ensuring that the champion would be truly skilled in all facets of the game.

The 127 entries from 15 countries were reduced in a pre-qualifying round to 80. One of those had learned his golf on a links, was professional at a links, and had recent tournament experience on a links. This was Tommy Horton, of Royal Jersey, who had hurt his neck in the Jersey European Airways Open at La Moye and was taking mild painkillers. He led the field on the first day with a 69.

Brian Huggett, already winner of two events on the PGA European Seniors Tour was a stroke behind, as were Ireland's Michael Murphy and Hugh Inggs, a

South African who was second in a USPGA event in the United States in 1969. Brian Carter, winner at La Bresse, Neil Coles, no special lover of links, Bob Thatcher, American owner of three courses near Philadelphia, and his countryman Rafe Botts were all on 71, with 23 others better than 75.

Next day, in a little less wind,

Huggett's one mistake was to overclub at the 14th. A 68 put him two strokes ahead of Horton, with Coles one behind. Thatcher had his second 71 and was tied with Murphy. David Butler needed a four at the last for a 67 but the day's one bad tee shot cost him a six, placing him level with Joe Carr, owner of Bedrock Golf Club in Massachusetts and commonly dubbed Fred Flintstone. Bobby Verwey, the 1991 Senior British Open Champion, was also on 143.

In the final round Huggett immediately lost his advantage, having to hack out of the left-hand rough at the first, then pitching down the dune behind the green for a six. Horton chipped stiff at the second for a birdie four going ahead.

Further misfortunes saw Huggett slump to two over par for the tournament after five holes, and Coles, who had a run of four holes in which he dropped five strokes, went to four over. Steady play by Horton to the 14th, where he scored his fifth birdie of the round and went four under par for the Championship, put him out of reach. Tommy could afford to drop shots at the 16th and the 17th. There he was bunkered and missed a short putt whilst Coles holed his bunker shot for a two and Huggett, in rough behind the green, took five.

Horton finished it off by holing from six feet for his par on the final green. Coles and Huggett, five behind, were joint second. Verwey was fourth, Thatcher was the best American, Michael Murphy the leading Irishman and George Will the top Scot. No doubt they were hoping that Royal Lytham would be easier than Royal Aberdeen.

Tommy Horton pointed the way to victory.

The perennial Neil Coles finished joint second.

The 16th green at Royal Aberdeen.

POS	NAME	CTY	1	2	3	TOTAL	PRIZE MONEY
1	Tommy HORTON	Eng	69	71	68	208	£10000
2	Neil COLES	Eng	71	70	72	213	7300
	Brian HUGGETT	Wal	70	68	75	213	7300
4	Bobby VERWEY	SA	72	71	72	215	5500
5	David BUTLER	Eng	74	69	75	218	4400
6	Bob THATCHER	USA	71	71	79	221	3202
	David SNELL	Eng	73	71	77	221	3262
	Michael MURPHY	Ire	70	72	79	221	3262
	Hugh INGGS	SA	70	76	75	221	3262
10	John FOURIE	SA	74	74	74	222	2400
	Joe CARR	USA	74	69	79	222	2400
	Terry SQUIRES	Eng	74	71	77	222	2400
13	George WILL	Scot	73	77	73	223	1833
	Jose Maria ROCA	Sp	74	72	77	223	1833
	Matt MCCRORIE	Scot	72	73	78	223	1833
16	Denis HUTCHINSON	SA	77	74	79	224	1350
	Jim MCALISTER	Scot	76	72	77	224	1350
	Ramon SOTA	Sp	74	74	76	224	1350
	Peterb BUTLER	Eng	74	75	75	224	1350
	Hugh BOYLE	Ire	75	76	73	224	1350
	Rafe BOTTS	USA	71	74	79	224	1350
22	Peter GILL	Eng	73	77	75	225	950
	Frederick BOOBYER	Eng	75	72	78	225	950
	Jim O'HERN	USA	72	77	76	225	950
25	Brian WAITES	Eng	76	74	76	226	850
26	Jack WILKSHIRE	Eng	75	74	78	227	800
	Fred MARTI	USA	73	77	77	227	800
	Austin SKERRITT	Ire	72	78	77	227	800
29	David TALBOT	Eng	76	76	76	228	730
	Bryan CARTER	Eng	71	74	83	228	730
	John DONOGHUE	Eng	76	75	77	228	730
	Hugh JACKSON	N Ire	76	76	76	228	730
33	Roger FIDLER	Eng	76	71	82	229	640
	Howell FRASER	USA	79	75	75	229	640
	Bernard HUNT	Eng	78	73	78	229	640
	Hedley MUSCROFT	Eng	73	78	78	229	640
38	Stuart MURHAY	Scot	74	76	80	230	580
	Clifford HARTLAND (AM)	Eng	73	76	81	230	—
39	Tony COVENEY	Ire	77	77	77	231	526
	Russ WHITEHEAD	Eng	74	78	79	231	526
	Frank RENNIE	Scot	78	74	81	231	520
	Lionel PLATTS	Eng	80	75	70	231	526
	Malcolm COLE	Eng	76	80	75	231	526
44	Bryon HUTCHINSON	Eng	75	77	80	232	490
	James HAY (AM)	Scot	78	76	78	232	—

COURSE: ROYAL ABERDEEN **YARDAGE: 6739** **PAR: 72**

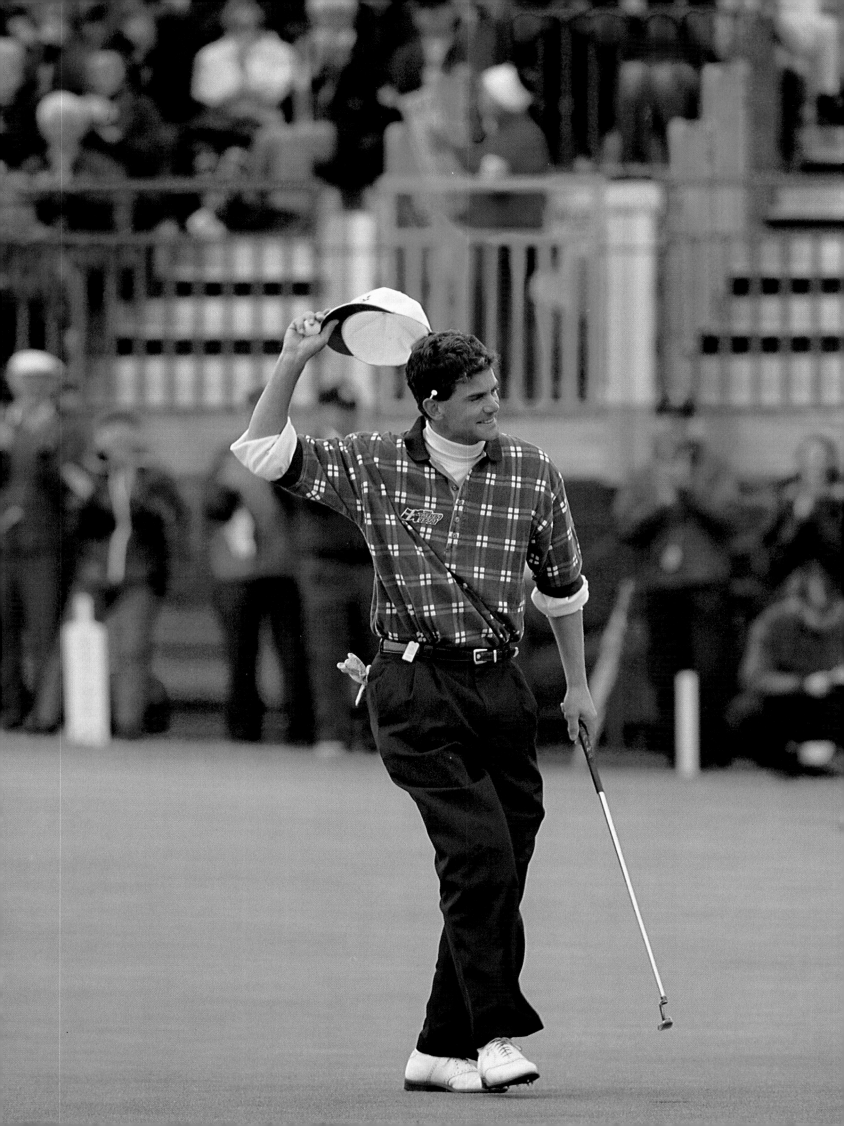

PARNEVIK IS UNSTOPPABLE

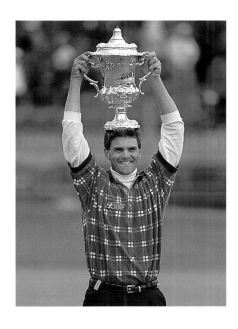

*'I*t wasn't how I'd dreamed of winning my first Volvo Tour event,' said Sweden's Jesper Parnevik after wrapping up the Bell's Scottish Open and, in truth, it would have taken a fair flight of fancy to come up with a scenario which included leading from start to finish and winning by five shots from Payne Stewart

What the 28-year old from Stockholm had had in mind was more along the lines of having to sink a long putt on the last green. As it was, he shot a first-round 64 – six under par – which gave him a three-shot lead over the Londoner, Robert Lee, whose 67 put him closer to Parnevik than anyone else was to get in the course of the week.

This early skewering of the field and Parnevik's subsequent domination of it were the major features of a remarkable week. To begin with, the King's course, a pretty playground where professionals could disport themselves before the Open, suddenly got nasty.

The wind was heavy and gusting, the greens firm, the rough luxuriant. Paul Curry, who had set the record with his 60 the previous year, took 20 more to get round this time and, in spite of a second-round 70, failed to qualify. One of the difficulties was trying to stop the ball on the greens with the wind behind, which it was, for the most part, on the inward nine. Seasoned Parnevik observers reckoned that his steep attack on the ball with the irons – he takes divots that would grace many a hearth – gave him a vital

Jesper Parnevik recorded his maiden Volvo Tour victory when he led from start to finish at Gleneagles

edge in this department.

Whatever the explanation, he came home in 29. In the best traditions of a showbiz family – his father, Bo, is a professional entertainer – Parnevik, who likes to imitate the swings of other golfers, did his Greg Norman bit at the last hole with a high-flying nine-iron second which brought him his sixth successive birdie.

Apart from Lee, Parnevik's closest challengers were the South African, De Wet Basson, 68, and a flock of 69s. Handily placed on 71 was Stewart, while Sam Torrance and the two late entries, Sandy Lyle and Ian Woosnam, were all round in 73. The story of golf being riddled with first-round leaders who are never heard of thereafter, the Swede, seven years on the Tour, faced a few questions in the second and answered most of them with a 66, this time finishing 3, 3, 3, 3, 4 from the 14th against the par of 4, 4, 3, 4, 5.

He finished in the heavy rain which was to have such an effect on the day's play that the leaderboard was not resolved until getting on for 11pm. Players were called in from the flooded course around two o'clock and play did not get underway again until 5pm.

Before that, Torrance had slipped in with a 65 and for most of a long day the Scot sat tied with Lee on 138 – eight behind Parnevik, one ahead of Brian Marchbank and Carl Mason and two ahead of Lyle and Stewart. Marchbank, Mason and Lyle were round in 67, Stewart in 69.

Meanwhile, out in the gathering gloom, Gary Evans of Worthing, in his second full professional season, was soldiering on. With play officially ended and 11 players due to complete their rounds early next morning, he elected to play on, having eagled the 14th to move to four under par – six off the lead. A

Payne Stewart rejoices after holed chip.

Gary Orr salutes home supporters.

cruel double-bogey at the 17th was to dispel the euphoria, but a birdie at the last saw him file in seven shots behind Parnevik.

The cut fell at 147 and brought the departure of the holder, Peter O'Malley, whose electrifying finish last year (eagle-birdie-birdie-birdie-eagle) stunned, among others, Colin Montgomerie, Nick Faldo and Bernhard Langer. It also saw the departure of David J Russell and Howard Clark, who packed up and went home thinking they were out, only to discover that they were on the mark. They got into their cars and hurtled back.

The main development in the third round was Payne Stewart's confirmation that he had a heart condition which might or might not necessitate the fitting of a pacemaker in the fullness of time. As far as Parnevik was concerned, it was business as usual, his par 70 leaving his seven-shot lead intact, though Stewart was now in hottest pursuit after a 67, with Lyle and Torrance on 209, one ahead of Evans and Marchbank.

To further mutilate a well-worn phrase: 'All Parnevik had to do now...' or as the player himself put it: 'I was so close. All I could do was lose it. It was as if I'd already won, but I still had to play the round.'

What he did, in fact, was birdie the first two holes of the final round. When he answered Stewart's birdie at the sixth by way of a chip and a putt, he was nine ahead. Such was his grip on the tournament that after he'd faltered with three bogeys in a row from the eighth, he still held the seven-shot lead he started with.

That was the nearest thing to an opening Parnevik was to allow and when Stewart failed to step in, his last realistic chance was gone. The 1991 US Open champion took five at the par three eighth where the Swede's brief slide began and that was no way to set about reducing such a lead.

In the event, Parnevik was able to indulge in a sketchy bogey-par finish for 71 and a nine-under-par total of 271 which left him five clear of Stewart, who signed off with a 69. Two shots further

Stewart applauds the winner home.

adrift were Scotland's Gary Orr, a Tour rookie who closed as Parnevik had opened, with a 64, and the Spaniard, Jose Rivero, who followed a first-round 77 with rounds of 66, 68, and 67.

Torrance shared fifth place with Paul Way, whose final 66 gained him one of the Bell's Scottish Open's traditional 'perks' – a place in the Open, along with Orr, Christy O'Connor Junior, Evans and, of course, the winner.

For Parnevik, victory brought a trophy, £100,000 and new-found status. For those who witnessed his performance it revealed another dimension to a man previously best known for his plunge into a duck pond at stormy St Mellion two years ago when he reckoned it couldn't be any wetter in than out.

Stewart aimed for a crock of gold but settled for second place.

Right, Miguel Angel Martin was the best shot of the week.

Perthshire hills form backdrop to the 16th tee.

POS	NAME	CTY	1	2	3	4	TOTAL	PRIZE MONEY
	COURSE: GLENEAGLES HOTEL, KING'S COURSE				**YARDAGE: 6739**			**PAR: 70**
1	Jesper PARNEVIK	Swe	64	66	70	71	271	£100000
2	Payne STEWART	USA	71	69	67	69	276	66660
3	Gary ORR	Scot	70	72	72	64	278	33780
	José RIVERO	Sp	77	66	68	67	278	33780
5	Paul WAY	Eng	69	74	70	66	279	23200
	Sam TORRANCE	Scot	73	65	71	70	279	23200
7	Christy O'CONNOR JNR	Ire	71	70	70	70	281	18000
8	Roger CHAPMAN	Eng	69	71	73	69	282	12352
	Mark ROE	Eng	73	72	68	69	282	12352
	Gary EVANS	Eng	69	68	73	72	282	12352
	Robert LEE	Eng	71	73	71	71	282	12352
	Sandy LYLE	Scot	73	67	69	73	282	12352
13	Peter SENIOR	Aus	71	76	71	65	283	9213
	Santiago LUNA	Sp	71	70	72	70	283	9213
	Steven RICHARDSON	Eng	73	71	70	69	283	9213
16	Sven STRUVER	Ger	72	75	69	68	284	7788
	Alastair WEBSTER	Scot	73	69	74	68	284	7788
	Peter BAKER	Eng	69	74	68	73	284	7788
	Richard BOXALL	Eng	73	68	72	71	284	7788
	Steven BOWMAN	USA	73	69	71	71	284	7788
21	Peter FOWLER	Aus	71	73	72	69	285	6840
	Haydn SELBY-GREEN	Eng	78	68	71	68	285	6840
	Paul BROADHURST	Eng	76	70	69	70	285	6840
24	Ian WOOSNAM	Wal	73	69	75	69	286	6030
	Donnie HAMMOND	USA	73	71	71	71	286	6030
	Brian MARCHBANK	Scot	73	67	70	76	286	6030
	Darren CLARKE	N Ire	69	73	70	74	286	6030
	Eoghan O'CONNELL	Ire	77	65	71	73	286	6030
	Brian BARNES	Scot	70	76	68	72	286	6030
30	Rodger DAVIS	Aus	73	73	70	71	287	4820
	Eduardo ROMERO	Arg	72	70	74	71	287	4820
	Miguel Angel JIMENEZ	Sp	71	72	74	70	287	4820
	Fredrik LINDGREN	Swe	77	70	71	69	287	4820
	Barry LANE	Eng	75	69	70	73	287	4820
	Duffy WALDORF	USA	72	75	68	72	287	4820
	Howard CLARKE	Eng	76	71	70	70	287	4820
	Craig CASSELLS	Eng	73	74	69	71	287	4820
	Gordon J BRAND	Eng	73	73	70	71	287	4820
39	Jean VAN DE VELDE	Fr	72	71	73	72	288	3840
	Miguel Angel MARTIN	Sp	73	73	72	70	288	3840
	Carl MASON	Eng	72	67	74	75	288	3840
	Joakim HAEGGMAN	Swe	73	73	68	74	288	3840
	Andrew OLDCORN	Eng	74	71	72	71	288	3840
	Mats LANNER	Swe	72	73	71	72	288	3840
	Hugh BAIOCCHI	SA	70	76	70	72	288	3840
46	Ian PALMER	SA	72	73	73	71	289	3180
	Devin STABLES	Scot	73	74	70	72	289	3180
	Olle KARLSSON	Swe	76	71	68	74	289	3180
	David FEHERTY	N Ire	73	72	72	72	289	3180
50	Keith WATERS	Eng	71	74	72	73	290	2460
	Colin MONTGOMERIE	Scot	70	71	76	73	290	2460
	Seve BALLESTEROS	Sp	74	73	73	70	290	2460
	Glen DAY	USA	74	73	72	71	290	2460
	Magnus SUNESSON	Swe	69	76	73	72	290	2460
	Derrick COOPER	Eng	72	71	68	79	290	2460
	Ricky WILLISON	Eng	76	70	72	72	290	2460
	Wayne WESTNER	SA	73	72	72	73	290	2460
58	Paul EALES	Eng	78	68	72	73	291	1920
59	Anders SORENSEN	Den	70	75	72	75	292	1770
	Robin MANN	Eng	70	73	73	76	292	1770
	Johan RYSTROM	Swe	72	72	72	76	292	1770
	Colin GILLIES	Scot	71	73	73	75	292	1770
63	Malcolm MACKENZIE	Eng	70	74	75	74	293	1295
	Glenn RALPH	Eng	73	71	74	75	293	1295
	Stephen FIELD	Eng	76	71	69	77	293	1295
	David J RUSSELL	Eng	75	72	69	77	293	1295
	Gary NICKLAUS	USA	69	76	77	71	293	1295
68	De Wet BASSON	SA	68	77	73	76	294	893
	Steen TINNING	Den	76	71	73	74	294	893
	Kenny WALKER	Scot	75	72	75	72	294	893
	Jorge BERENDT	Arg	73	74	77	70	294	893
72	Justin HOBDAY	SA	75	71	73	76	295	888

NORMAN DEVOURS SANDWICH

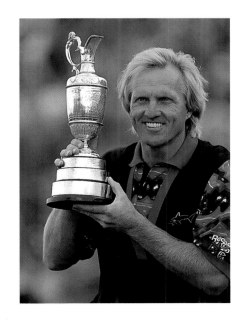

Records tumbled at Royal St George's as Greg Norman produced an outstanding final round to win his second Open title

In the realms of golf's what might have beens Greg Norman stood as the supreme exception to the old sporting cliché that nobody remembers who finished second. Most players can only take the anguish of one major championship trophy being dashed from their grasp before disappearing into the background; Norman had imprinted himself on everyone's memory on four occasions.

The flaxen-haired idol of the marketing men appeared destined to remain ranked alongside such players as George Archer, Orvilly Moody, Lou Graham and Bill Rogers as one-shot major winners. The 1986 Open champion had been robbed by outrageous pieces of good fortune from other players in the 1986 US PGA Championship and in the 1987 US Masters while in the 1986 Masters and the 1989 Open Championship had fallen victim to his own miscalculation.

The fact that Norman had been involved in so many denouments of this nature was in itself a tribute to his ability but his inability to finish off the job still haunted him. Were the problems therefore, technical or mental? One follows the other for if a golfer is not totally confident in his method then the doubts begin to gnaw at the psyche, particularly under the stress of a final round.

Norman recognised his and placed himself in the hands of Butch Harmon, son of Claude the 1948 US Masters champion. Harmon gave Norman a shorter, tighter backswing and emphasised the synchronisation of his body through the ball. At Royal St George's in the 122nd Open Championship the results were there for all to see as Norman took the game to heights which hitherto had been unapproached.

Following a prolonged dry spell, most of the early opinion among the players was focused on the difficulty of controlling the ball on crumpled fairways the texture of concrete. Given a piece of wind, said some players, then quite a few holes were going to be unplayable. This, they continued, was going to be the toughest Open course for many a year and Bill Rogers' winning score in 1981 of 276, four under par, would remain a distant target.

They had however, reckoned without St Swithin for on that particular saint's day, on the evening before the Championship started, the heavens opened and gave St George's an extensive soaking. The dragon that was St George's had its teeth thoroughly blunted and the fairways and greens became soft havens for a well-struck shot.

Put the best players in the world out in conditions like that with just a light breeze blowing and a flock of birdies will be scattered across the scoreboards. Such was the case on the first day when nearly a third of the field broke 70, including most of the significant names. Peter Senior, Mark Calcavecchia, Fuzzy Zoeller and Norman led the way with 66s while behind them lay Bernhard Langer on 67, Nick Price and Fred Couples on 68 with defending champion Nick Faldo on 69. Even Severiano Ballesteros stirred from his slumbering season with a 68 which contained flashes of his old magic.

If the cream was rising to the top after the first round it positively bubbled over

the rim on the second day. First Langer came in with a 66 to set the pace at 133, Couples matched Langer's round as did Corey Pavin to lie one stroke off the pace and Norman added a 68 to join them. All this was going on while Faldo was just starting his round and the world's most relentless golfer decided to redress the balance. Four birdies on the first nine put him out in 31 and he notched up another birdie at the difficult 13th to move to five under par for the round and six under for the Championship. Then came the crisis.

A pulled tee shot on the 14th finished in deep rough, the recovery still found the rough and the third shot finished 50 yards short in the light rough. Suddenly the crisis was over for the pitch shot ran sweetly into the hole for an unexpected birdie bonus and Faldo was off and running

again. Solid pars were obtained on the next three holes and then Faldo staged his grand finale on the 18th by hitting the most perfect second shot to that most elusive green – a two iron which was Hoganesque in its execution and set up a birdie putt from 15 feet which was willed into the hole by the collective power of the watching thousands for a 63.

Bernhard Langer just misses a birdie on the tenth in the final round.

Greg Norman points the way.

Left, Nick Faldo was in charge after two rounds.

Trouble at the sixth as Gary Evans,

inset, takes three to get out of

a bunker.

Thus Faldo became the sixth man to shoot the lowest round in the Open (Payne Stewart became the seventh in the final round) and he also broke Christy O'Connor Junior's course record of 64, set in the 1985 Open. More importantly, it gave Faldo the lead at eight under par and demonstrated that the defender was not going to relinquish his title easily.

The cut fell at 143 and among those who departed were Jack Nicklaus, Tom Watson, Davis Love III, Colin Montgomerie, Jose Maria Olazabal and perhaps saddest of all, Sandy Lyle, the man who brought glory to Britain over the same links in 1985. Among the 77 players who remained was British Amateur champion, Iain Pyman, who after rounds of 68 and 72 went on to add a 70 and a 71 to win not only the amateur medal but to record the lowest aggregate by an amateur in the history of the Championship.

The third round saw the big guns somewhat muffled, largely due to some tricky pin positions which made it difficult to attack the flag. Faldo posted a 70 to stay in the lead but was joined by Pavin with a 68. Langer also had a 70 to lie one behind along with Norman who had a 69. Price and Senior were three off the pace and a stroke behind them were Couples, Ernie Els and Wayne Grady whose 64 was the lowest of the day.

So the stage was set for a rousing finish with the only question being who would provide it? It was Norman who was fastest out of the blocks with three birdies in the first six holes while Faldo picked up two birdies in the same run but dropped a stroke at the fourth. Langer had also slipped two shots behind the Australian by the turn and Pavin was well out of it. Norman turned in 31 and appeared to be in total control of himself and his game. Faldo nearly holed his tee shot to the short 11th to get one back but then Norman birdied the 12th in response. Langer went on to birdie the 12th and 13th so that when he and Norman arrived on the 14th tee the

**Corey Pavin finished
top American.**

**Langer grimaces as drive on the 14th
goes out of bounds.**

margin was still two in favour of the latter.

Then Langer made a fatal error. All week he had taken an iron from the tee for safety but knowing he had to try for a birdie or a possible eagle he took a driver. The ball finished in the rough belonging to the adjacent Prince's course and that meant three off the tee for Langer and finally, a destructive seven on his card.

Norman obtained his customary birdie so now he only had Faldo behind him to worry about. Faldo, 'the most tenacious golfer on the planet' according to Norman, hung on with a birdie at the 14th but that was to be his last thrust.

Ahead of him Norman was in majestic mode, striding after his tee shots in the manner of a man who knows that this time

nothing will stop him. There was a slight hiccup on the 17th when a putt from 18 inches stayed out but two magnificent shots onto the final green put the finishing touch to one of the great last rounds of the Championship – a 64 in which every shot went where its perpetrator meant it to go and most of the putts followed suit.

Faldo's tenacity enabled him to take second place, ahead of Langer. Both were round in 67 which in normal circumstances would have seen off most challenges.

Right, the scoreboard tells

the story.

Left, huge crowds enjoy the view from the Maiden.

Above, Fred Couples drives on the 17th.

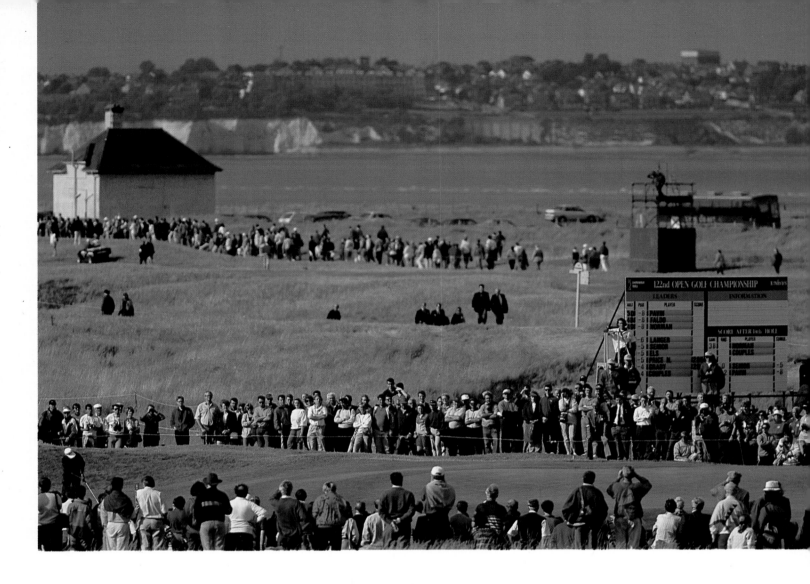

Placid waters provide tranquil background on the final day.

Faldo strikes for home in second round 63.

For the statistically minded, Norman's final round was the lowest ever by a winner, his aggregate of 267 was a new record and he was the first winner to break 70 in all four rounds. All this was incidental to a man who had put the past into perspective. 'I'm not out there to prove anybody wrong,' said Norman after his pulsating final round, 'I'm out there to prove myself right.' So he did and at the same time put to rest another old sporting cliché – the one that says they never come back.

Above, champions past and present:

Gene Sarazen congratulates Norman.

Below, Mr and Mrs Norman are

reunited with an old friend.

COURSE: ROYAL ST GEORGE'S			**YARDAGE: 6860**				**PAR: 70**	
POS	NAME	CTY	1	2	3	4	TOTAL	PRIZE MONEY
1	Greg NORMAN	Aus	66	68	69	64	267	£100000
2	Nick FALDO	Eng	69	63	70	67	269	80000
3	Bernhard LANGER	Ger	67	66	70	67	270	67000
4	Corey PAVIN	USA	68	66	68	70	272	50500
	Peter SENIOR	Aus	66	69	70	67	272	50500
6	Nick PRICE	Zim	68	70	67	69	274	33166
	Paul LAWRIE	Scot	72	68	69	65	274	33166
	Ernie ELS	SA	68	69	69	68	274	33166
9	Fred COUPLES	USA	68	66	72	69	275	25500
	Scott SIMPSON	USA	68	70	71	66	275	25500
	Wayne GRADY	Aus	74	68	64	69	275	25500
12	Payne STEWART	USA	71	72	70	63	276	21500
13	Barry LANE	Eng	70	68	71	68	277	20500
14	Fuzzy ZOELLER	USA	66	70	71	71	278	15214
	Tom KITE	USA	72	70	68	68	278	15214
	José RIVERO	Sp	68	73	67	70	278	15214
	Gil MORGAN	USA	70	68	70	70	278	15214
	John DALY	USA	71	66	70	71	278	15214
	Mark CALCAVECCHIA	USA	66	73	71	68	278	15214
	Mark McNULTY	Zim	67	71	71	69	278	15214
21	Peter BAKER	Eng	70	67	74	68	279	10000
	Jesper PARNEVIK	Swe	68	74	68	69	279	10000
	Howard CLARK	Eng	67	72	70	70	279	10000
24	Mark ROE	Eng	70	71	73	66	280	8400
	Rodger DAVIS	Aus	68	71	71	70	280	8400
	David FROST	SA	69	73	70	68	280	8400
27	Larry MIZE	USA	67	69	74	71	281	7225
	Des SMYTH	Ire	67	74	70	70	281	7225
	Iain PYMAN (AM)	Eng	68	72	70	71	281	–
	Yoshinori MIZUMAKI	Jap	69	69	73	70	281	7225
	Seve BALLESTEROS	Sp	68	73	69	71	281	7225
	Malcolm MACKENZIE	Eng	72	71	71	67	281	7225
	Mark JAMES	Eng	70	70	70	71	281	7225
33	Jean VAN DE VELDE	Fr	75	67	73	67	282	6180
	Raymond FLOYD	USA	70	72	67	73	282	6180
	Paul BROADHURST	Eng	71	69	74	68	282	6180
	Howard TWITTY	USA	71	71	67	73	282	6180
	Wayne WESTNER	SA	67	73	72	70	282	6180
38	Duffy WALDORF	USA	68	71	73	71	283	5327
	Rocco MEDIATE	USA	71	71	72	69	283	5327
	Christy O'CONNOR Jnr	Ire	72	68	69	74	283	5327
	Darren CLARKE	N.Ire	69	71	69	74	283	5327
	Carl MASON	Eng	69	73	72	69	283	5327
	Paul MOLONEY	Aus	70	71	71	71	283	5327
	Andrew MAGEE	USA	71	72	71	69	283	5327
	Greg TURNER	NZ	67	76	70	70	283	5327
	Anders SORENSEN	Den	69	70	72	72	283	5327
47	John HUSTON	USA	68	73	76	67	284	4850
	Lee JANZEN	USA	69	71	73	71	284	4850
	Steve ELKINGTON	Aus	72	71	71	70	284	4850
50	Manuel PINERO	Sp	70	72	71	72	285	4356
	Ian WOOSNAM	Wal	72	71	72	70	285	4356
	Sam TORRANCE	Scot	72	70	72	71	285	4356
	Miguel Angel JIMENEZ	Sp	69	74	72	70	285	4356
	Stephen AMES	T&T	67	75	73	70	285	4356
	Jonathan SEWELL	Eng	70	72	69	74	285	4356
	Frank NOBILO	NZ	69	70	74	72	285	4356
	Ian GARBUTT	Eng	68	75	73	69	285	4356
58	Vijay SINGH	Fij	69	72	72	73	286	4025
	Craig PARRY	Aus	72	69	71	74	286	4025
	Paul AZINGER	USA	69	73	74	70	286	4025
	Tom LEHMAN	USA	69	71	73	73	286	4025
62	Jamie SPENCE	Eng	69	72	72	74	287	3850
	Ross DRUMMOND	Scot	73	67	76	71	287	3850
	Olle KARLSSON	Swe	70	71	73	73	287	3850
65	Tom PERNICE	USA	73	70	70	75	288	3675
	James COOK	Eng	71	71	74	72	288	3675
	William GUY	Scot	70	73	73	72	288	3675
	Magnus SUNESSON	Swe	70	73	73	72	288	3675
69	Mike MILLER	Scot	73	68	76	72	289	3516
	Ian BAKER-FINCH	Aus	73	69	67	80	289	3516
	Tom PURTZER	USA	70	70	74	75	289	3516

CHARLES IS KING
OF ROYAL LYTHAM AGAIN

Before the Senior British Open, attention at Royal Lytham & St Annes focused on Bob Charles. The most successful senior golfer in history, he had senior winnings of $4,253,380, headed the 1993 United States senior money list with $610,841 and had become Open Champion on the course 30 years previously.

In the six Senior British Opens, he had won once, been second three times, and never finished worse than sixth. This record was unsurpassed. Also, nobody was as match-fit. Gary Player, winner in 1988 and 1990, declared: 'Bob is hitting the ball further and playing better than he did when he won the Open.'

Charles' said deteriorating eyesight affected his putting, but his most serious problems were jet lag and the change from 90 degree temperatures in America to wind, rain and 50s cool in Lancashire. Without Neil Coles, who was unwell, his likely challengers were Tommy Horton, the new Shell Scottish Senior Open champion who was used to links courses and who also had recent top-level experience, and Player. But Player said he was playing poorly.

On the first day, Arnold Palmer deservedly drew the biggest crowds, but did so because he's still the most exciting player in the game, not because his Army expected him to win. The surprise leader was Bob Zimmerman, nowadays a golf equipment salesman. He hit only one bad shot in a two-under-par 69.

Liam Higgins, the new Irish Senior champion, lay second on 70, a stroke ahead of American amateurs Dick Horne and Michael Sanger. Charles, Player

Thirty years after winning the Open Championship, Bob Charles made a successful return to Royal Lytham & St Annes

and Horton were among those on 73.

Next day Higgins, who had once set long-distance driving records, made prodigious hits and took a three stroke lead after a 71, with Chicago amateur Joel Hirsch, who had already played seven big tournaments in 1993, on 144, a stroke ahead of Brian Huggett and Horton. Charles was five behind, in a group that included the cigar-chewing 1992 US Senior champion Larry Laoretti.

Higgins stretched his lead to six in the third round, but at the tenth his second shot landed near a sprinkler head. He should have asked for a free drop and, if that had been refused, ought to have chipped the ball. Instead he decided to putt, and took three to get down. This worried him so much that he dropped six shots in the remaining eight holes and Charles, who played a brilliant back nine in conditions that were too much for almost everyone else, took 71 to tie with Higgins on 217, a stroke ahead of Horton and Hirsch.

In the final round, Charles tried to play for safety, knowing that a loose shot would probably mean a bogey, but Higgins tried to blast his way round and dropped back. Meanwhile, Tony Grubb, reverting to the slow swing with which he had won the 1964 PGA Match-Play Championship, eagled the sixth and caught Charles and Hirsch.

In a frenetic climax, the amateur faded and Charles seemed well on the way to victory until, as heavy squalls swept over the course, his ball plugged in a bunker at the short 12th, and his six left Horton two ahead. That lead became three when Player bogeyed the 14th. Horton, penalised at the 15th earlier when he slipped and moved his ball whilst removing a leaf, was plugged unplayable in the rough off his second shot this time, and also took six.

Needing a par four at the last, Horton drove into the rough, bunkered his second, and from an awkward lie came out strong, missing the putt. Charles hit a four iron to seven feet and holed for a birdie and a one-stroke victory.

Above, familiar finishing flourish from Arnold Palmer.

Above, Tommy Horton strikes for home on the 72nd.

	COURSE: ROYAL LYTHAM & ST ANNES					YARDAGE: 6673		PAR: 71
POS	NAME	CTY	1	2	3	4	TOTAL	PRIZE MONEY
1	Bob CHARLES	NZ	73	73	71	74	291	£36550
2	Gary PLAYER	SA	73	74	72	73	292	18905
	Tommy HORTON	Eng	73	72	73	74	292	18905
4	Anthony GRUBB	Eng	77	73	71	72	293	11000
	Joel S HIRSCH (AM)	USA	78	71	74	77	295	—
5	Liam HIGGINS	Ire	70	71	76	79	296	8515
	Brian HUGGETT	Wal	72	73	75	76	296	8515
7	Arthur PROCTOR	USA	73	76	73	75	297	6600
8	John FOURIE	SA	72	77	75	74	298	5500
9	Norman DREW	N Ire	73	73	73	80	299	4292
	David SNELL	Eng	74	78	69	78	299	4292
	Christy O'CONNOR	Ire	72	77	72	78	299	4292
	José Maria ROCCA	Sp	75	72	75	77	299	4292
13	Arnold PALMER	USA	73	76	75	76	300	3455
	Brian WAITES	Eng	77	75	73	76	300	3455
15	Bob ZIMMERMAN	USA	69	77	75	80	301	3230
	Charles GREEN (AM)	Scot	72	78	75	76	301	—
16	Larry LAORETTI	USA	75	71	78	78	302	3035
	Simon HOBDAY	SA	74	77	75	76	302	3035
18	Frederick BOOBYER	Eng	74	73	72	84	303	2785
	Ralph TERRY	USA	75	79	71	78	303	2785
	James STAHL (AM)	Eng	74	75	76	78	303	—
20	Roger FIDLER	Eng	77	74	75	78	304	2605
	David TALBOT	Eng	77	77	74	76	304	2605
22	Michel DAMIANO	Fr	75	79	75	76	305	2440
	Frank RENNIE	Scot	77	78	75	77	305	2440
	Hedley MUSCROFT	Eng	72	78	74	83	305	2440
25	Michael MURPHY	Ire	77	77	76	76	306	2115
	Vincent TSHABALALA	SA	77	75	72	82	306	2115
	Bobby VERWEY	SA	74	80	76	76	306	2115
	Hugh INGGS	SA	72	77	72	85	306	2115
	Joe CARR	USA	73	77	78	78	306	2115
	Bernard HUNT	Eng	77	73	78	78	306	2115
	Austin SKERRITT	Ire	73	77	74	82	306	2115
	Gordon MURRAY (AM)	Scot	74	75	82	75	306	—
32	Billy DUNK	Aus	74	72	84	77	307	1855
33	Deray SIMON	USA	82	72	81	73	308	1782
	Ross WHITEHEAD	Eng	73	77	77	81	308	1782
	Michael SANGER (AM)	USA	71	78	81	78	308	—
35	Akio TOYODA	Jap	78	74	77	80	309	1715
	Brian Neville DICK (AM)	SA	76	77	76	80	309	—
36	Robert BROWNE	Ire	81	73	78	80	310	1580
	Howell FRASER	USA	77	75	79	79	310	1580
	James DOLAN III	USA	74	75	80	81	310	1580
	Jimmy KINSELLA	Ire	78	78	79	77	310	1580
	Derek STRACHAN	Scot	75	78	74	83	310	1580
	Roy SMETHURST (AM)	Eng	76	77	75	82	310	—
	Jonathan MARKS (AM)	Eng	77	73	78	82	310	—
41	Brian ALLEN	Eng	77	78	77	79	311	1377
	John FREW	Scot	79	75	76	81	311	1377
	Rafe BOTTS	USA	75	77	83	76	311	1377
	Terry SQUIRES	Eng	73	82	75	81	311	1377
45	Robert RAWLINS	USA	79	75	77	81	312	1190
	Jean GARAIALDE	Fr	75	78	79	80	312	1190
	Lionel PLATTS	Eng	76	79	74	83	312	1190
	Chick EVANS	USA	76	78	80	78	312	1190
	Charles MEHOR	USA	77	78	83	74	312	1190
50	Peter BUTLER	Eng	77	73	79	84	313	1030
	Vance MOXOM	USA	75	80	78	80	313	1030
	Jim O'HERN	USA	78	82	80	78	313	1030
53	Thomas DEMENT	USA	74	76	82	82	314	950
54	James ALRED	USA	73	75	79	88	315	890
	Hugh BOYLE	Ire	76	79	77	83	315	890
56	John DONOGHUE	Eng	77	76	76	87	316	793
	Peter BLAZE	Eng	73	74	79	90	316	793
	Denis SCANLAN	Eng	74	80	82	80	315	793
	Dick HORNE (AM)	USA	71	80	84	81	316	—
59	Rick JETTER	USA	74	78	81	84	317	780
60	Kenneth MAGNUSSON	Swe	76	75	89	78	318	550

MONTGOMERIE ENDS
THE FAMINE

***After nearly two years
without a victory
Colin Montgomerie
finally triumphed in
Holland***

Colin Montgomerie arrived in Holland for the Heineken Dutch Open in an unusually serene state of mind, induced by a recent conversion to fatalism. If it's meant to happen, it will happen, mused the Scot as he attempted to end a tournament famine lasting precisely 103 weeks.

In the event, it did happen. After countless close calls, including five second place finishes since his victory in the 1991 Scandinavian Masters, Montgomerie's faith in the doctrine of predestiny was vindicated with a one stroke win in dismal, squally conditions at Noordwijkse.

Montgomerie came from four shots back to overtake third round leader Jose Coceres of Argentina and capture his third Volvo Tour title with a closing 69 and seven under par total of 281.

The previous week at Sandwich, Montgomerie had dashed from Royal St George's having missed the cut in the Open by a single stroke. He decided to take a week off to seek a remedy for problems which subsequently transpired to be figments of his brittle imagination.

In terms of technique, there was little cause for alarm. He just needed to cast out the demons of self-doubt which had been gnawing at his mind during those long months without success. The best way to do that, he decided, was to 'play my way out of the rut I was in'.

Hastily reconsidering his plans to spend a week with his coaches and advisers, Montgomerie confronted the issue head-on and won in a style which confirmed him as one of the best rough weather golfers in Europe, if not in the world.

Memories of the 1992 US Open at Pebble Beach were revived as Montgomerie tackled the gusts with gusto, and his closing 69 was beaten by only one man, Frenchman Jean van de Velde, who fired a marvellously controlled 68 to share second place with Coceres. 'There's no doubt it was all psycho-

logical. It's true that this game is played on a six-inch golf course,' smiled the sturdy Ryder Cup player, indicating the distance between his ears.

'I had been reading books about the mind, and reached the conclusion that fate has a lot to do with things. I wasn't supposed to play this event but I was glad I did. Tom Kite was fated to win at Pebble Beach, not me. Maybe I was fated to win this one.'

Montgomerie had decided that he needed to be more patient, less anxious to win again. Instead of being paralysed by uncertainty, his more relaxed mental approach paid off handsomely with a cheque for £108,330. 'I'm being more patient with myself. I'm not desperate any more. I now know that if I play good golf I'll win sometimes,' he said.

On that wet and windy final afternoon, Montgomerie played exceptional golf, an apt description also of the score delivered by David A Russell on a bright first day. The 35-year old from Kent chipped in twice and holed a bunker shot in compiling an adventurous 65 to lead by two strokes from Ronan Rafferty and De Wet Basson. Russell, who only retained his card thanks to a medical exemption following major surgery on his left thumb the previous year, was to take ten strokes more in the second round to drift out of contention.

Rafferty picked up the gauntlet and eased smoothly into the halfway lead on

137 with a second round of 70 for a seven-under-par total and a two-stroke advantage over Coceres, Carl Mason, Ross Drummond and Anders Sorensen. Montgomerie, who opened with rounds of 68 and 73, was tucked away in share of ninth place as American John Daly bade a premature farewell to Holland. The former US PGA champion, visiting the Heineken-sponsored event for the first time, found some exotic locations among the Noordwijk dunes no other golfers could reach as he missed the cut by six shots with rounds of 77 and 76.

Reigning US Open champion Lee Janzen and Bernhard Langer, the 1993 US Masters winner, fared only marginally better. After matching starts of 68, Janzen figured in a nine-way tie for 19th place while Langer, drained by his Open exertions, dropped to 41st.

Coceres, after a third round 69, led going into the last day on 208, with Rafferty (72) on 209 and Ian Woosnam

and Steen Tinning a further stroke behind, one ahead of Montgomerie. But as the conditions deteriorated, Montgomerie's iron-will refused to bend or break. He two-putted the last as the lightning crackled overhead, bringing a downpour which resulted in a 35-minute suspension.

When play resumed, Woosnam and Coceres – who had both held the lead in the closing stages – made critical, and ultimately fatal, errors. Just as Van de Velde had done in posting his superb 68, both men bogeyed the 16th, leaving Montgomerie time to prepare his victory speech and reflect that fate, having kicked him in the teeth a few times, had been a generous benefactor this time.

Above, defending champion Bernhard Langer failed to make an impact.

Below, John Daly at full stretch.

Below, Steen Tinning takes a sideways
look at the course.

Above, Colin Montgomerie was on top
of the world in Holland

Above, US Open champion Lee Janzen

shoulders arms.

Eduardo Romero finds that trees are sometimes 90 per cent wood.

Happy hour for Montgomerie as victory looms.

COURSE: NORDWIJKSE			YARDAGE: 6839					PAR: 72
POS	NAME	CTY	1	2	3	4	TOTAL	PRIZE MONEY
1	Colin MONTGOMERIE	Scot	68	73	71	69	281	£108330
2	Jean VAN DE VELDE	Fr	73	70	71	68	282	56450
	José COCERES	Arg	69	70	69	74	282	56450
4	Ian WOOSNAM	Wal	71	70	69	73	283	32500
5	Ronan RAFFERTY	N.Ire	67	70	72	75	284	27530
6	Steen TINNING	Den	71	70	69	75	285	21125
	Mark ROE	Eng	70	71	74	70	285	21125
8	Paul EALES	Eng	68	74	74	70	286	16250
9	Jesper PARNEVIK	Swe	71	71	70	75	287	12662
	Jorge BERENDT	Arg	68	73	73	73	287	12662
	Eamonn DARCY	Ire	70	74	69	74	287	12662
	Olle KARLSSON	Swe	76	71	69	71	287	12662
13	Tony JOHNSTONE	Zim	75	69	73	71	288	10460
14	Paul McGINLEY	Ire	74	73	70	72	289	9162
	Anders SORENSEN	Den	70	69	73	77	289	9162
	Marc FARRY	Fr	71	74	72	72	289	9162
	Vijay SINGH	Fij	72	70	73	74	289	9162
	Sam TORRANCE	Scot	72	69	72	76	289	9162
19	Peter O'MALLEY	Aus	74	72	69	75	290	7222
	Per-Ulrik JOHANSSON	Swe	70	75	69	76	290	7222
	Lee JANZEN	USA	68	72	74	76	290	7222
	Silvio GRAPPASONNI	It	70	76	72	72	290	7222
	Frank NOBILO	NZ	73	74	70	73	290	7222
	David A RUSSELL	Eng	65	75	72	78	290	7222
	Anders FORSBRAND	Swe	71	73	71	75	290	7222
	Philip WALTON	Ire	72	72	74	72	290	7222
	Wayne WESTNER	SA	74	73	71	72	290	7222
28	Ross DRUMMOND	Scot	69	70	76	76	291	5850
	Miguel Angel JIMENEZ	Sp	68	74	71	78	291	5850
	Gavin LEVENSON	SA	72	75	69	75	291	5850
	Eduardo ROMERO	Arg	70	76	72	73	291	5850
	Mark MOULAND	Wal	73	72	70	76	291	5850
33	Peter BAKER	Eng	68	76	76	72	292	4875
	Gary EVANS	Eng	69	71	75	77	292	4875
	Carl MASON	Eng	71	68	74	79	292	4875
	Gary ORR	Scot	73	70	76	73	292	4875
	Roderick WATKINS	Scot	74	73	74	71	292	4875
	Gordon BRAND Jnr	Scot	70	72	76	74	292	4875
	José Maria OLAZABAL	Sp	71	76	70	75	292	4875
	Juan QUIROS	Sp	70	75	75	72	292	4875
41	Richard BOXALL	Eng	74	73	71	75	293	3965
	Bernhard LANGER	Ger	68	74	74	77	293	3965
	Wayne RILEY	Aus	71	74	73	75	293	3965
	Andrew MURRAY	Eng	71	73	74	75	293	3965
	De Wet BASSON	SA	67	80	72	74	293	3965
	Des SMYTH	Ire	71	71	70	81	293	3965
47	Sven STROVER	Ger	72	74	72	76	294	3055
	Retief GOOSEN	SA	69	76	76	73	294	3055
	Brian BARNES	Scot	74	73	71	76	294	3055
	Barry LANE	Eng	71	74	76	73	294	3055
	Thomas LEVET	Fr	68	79	74	73	294	3055
	David CURRY	Eng	71	75	75	73	294	3055
	John McHENRY	Ire	70	77	75	72	294	3055
	Christy O'CONNOR Jnr	Ire	73	74	72	75	294	3055
55	David J RUSSELL	Eng	72	73	73	77	295	2223
	Alberto BINAGHI	It	74	73	75	73	295	2223
	Russell CLAYDON	Eng	72	74	76	73	295	2223
	Roger WINCHESTER	Eng	70	77	69	79	295	2223
	John WOOF	Eng	70	74	73	78	295	2223
60	Paul MOLONEY	Aus	74	73	73	76	296	1917
	Stephen AMES	T&T	71	73	77	75	296	1917
62	Brian GEE	Hol	73	74	74	76	297	1573
	Jamie SPENCE	Eng	73	73	79	72	297	1573
	Robert LEE	Eng	74	72	75	76	297	1573
	Joost STEENKAMER	Hol	74	72	75	76	297	1573
	Greg TURNER	NZ	68	77	75	77	297	1573
67	Peter FOWLER	Aus	68	75	76	79	298	971
	Steve BOWMAN	USA	73	74	78	73	298	971
	Paul WAY	Eng	73	73	78	74	298	971
70	Bill MALLEY	USA	71	76	74	79	300	967
71	Manuel PINERO	Sp	69	77	77	78	301	961
	André BOSSERT	Swi	73	74	76	78	301	961
	Derrick COOPER	Eng	70	76	77	78	301	961
	Johan RYSTROM	Swe	73	74	73	81	301	961
	Fredrik LINDGREN	Swe	71	76	78	76	301	961

Ideal for a drive in the country

There's never been a better time to head straight for the open – with only your Sony for company.

While others might wait with baited breath over the results of the British Open, the results are plain to see in the XR-U441 RDS (EON).

That's short for their latest tuner cassette (which can control a 10 disc CD autochanger, conveniently stashed away in the boot).

The RDS bit constantly tunes the radio to the best signal, wherever you happen to be in the country.

The EON part means the latest traffic news will, if you wish, interrupt whatever BBC station you are listening to, local or national, or even your CD or cassette. Making sure you never end up stuck in the rough.

The rest of the machine's no Sunday driver, either. The amp offers 4 x 20 watts of output power, and of course, you get all those luxurious finishing touches like Dolby B and automatic music search.

All in all, a machine that's well above par – so drive one soon.

SONY

Why compromise?

IT'S MASTER BAKER AGAIN

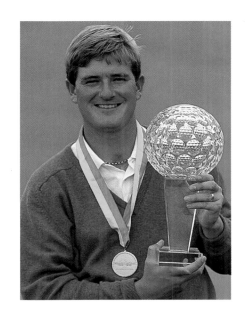

Peter Baker captured his second Masters title of the season when he triumphed in Gothenburg

Long before Peter Baker foundered in the rainswept, treacherous conditions of Forsgardens during the final round of the Scandinavian Masters, righted himself and then sailed home to victory, he had gained a well-deserved reputation for weathering storms in the face of the fiercest opposition.

First, he had beaten Nick Faldo with two eagles in the 1988 Benson and Hedges International Open, then, this year, he had stormed to a landslide victory in the Dunhill British Masters at Woburn, finishing six strokes ahead of the field. At Forsgardens, however, Baker almost met his match. Even as he reached, in his mind's eye, for the trophy and the £108,000 first prize, he found himself confronted by Anders Forsbrand, a man with his heart set on becoming the first Swede to win the Scandinavian Masters and, worst of all, by his own fear; the shadow of those long, lonely seasons in the wilderness still loomed large in Baker's world.

But all that had yet to come. The week began with Baker taking the lead in the opening round – a position he was to hold throughout the event – with a four-under-par 67. Forsbrand soon joined him, while David Feherty and Colin Montgomerie were among those on 68. Much of the limelight focussed on Nick Faldo, the defending champion, who was a stroke further behind. Having spent the weekend trout fishing in the north of Sweden, and Monday evening watching his children enjoy the rides in Gothenburg's famous theme park, Faldo

looked relaxed and invincible, capable of almost anything.

Nevertheless, the vagaries of Forsgardens' and Gothenburg's weather system proved too much even for the world number one in the second round. As grey sheets of rain sluiced the fairways and slowed the greens until they became as mysterious as corn circles, Faldo slipped to a level par 72 for a total of 141. It had left him three strokes adrift of

Baker and Forsbrand, who had matched each other stride for stride for the second day running. Stephen Ames of Trinidad and Tobago also moved into contention with a 68, ahead of Feherty, Robert Karlsson, Montgomerie, Jamie Spence, Paul Way and Frank Nobilo.

Ronan Rafferty was among the unfortunates on the Friday night plane home. Forgetting that under local rules players were supposed to move advertising signs positioned around the greens and not their golf balls, he took a wrong drop at the ninth hole, which cost him a two stroke penalty and turned a five into a triple bogey. His first round 71 was followed by an 81, and he missed the cut by five strokes.

In professional golf, the third round is often the most crucial, a time for strategic manoeuvring and power-play. The Scandinavian Masters was no different. Though the rain fell relentlessly, hampering the progress of all except the 20,000 strong gallery, who squelched joyfully along through a vast sea of mud, Baker refused to settle for pars. He rammed in birdie putts from 15 and 40 feet at the opening holes, had just birdied the eighth when play was suspended, and went on to birdie the tenth from six feet for an eventual 68. When the battle lines were drawn at the close of play, Baker was on ten under par, three strokes ahead of Forsbrand and one ahead of Ames. Montgomerie, Steven Richardson, Way, Feherty and Karlsson shared fourth place.

And so to the final round. Once more, the day dawned bleak and cold, and once more the huge crowds, their spirits undampened, swarmed across the golf course, creating an atmosphere rarely found outside a major championship. At first it seemed that Baker had gained the upper hand and might prove unstoppable. He was quickly into his stride, swinging sweetly and with confidence and, despite being caught at the 12th by Forsbrand, calmly rolled in an eight foot putt for a birdie to the Swede's bogey at the 16th, and was leading by two strokes when he teed up at the last.

However, one of the things that makes golf the greatest game ever played is its unpredictability. Just as Baker seemed to be preparing to take a slow waltz down the 18th and into the winner's circle, destiny chose to intervene. First, he drove into a fairway bunker on the left, then he played into the rough on the right. His third shot ran into the thick rough fringing the green, his fourth was duffed two feet and he took two to get down for a double bogey. It was like something out of a nightmare, one where the victim tries vainly to escape on leaden feet.

When his putt finally dropped for a 72, Baker was led away in a daze for the play-off with Forsbrand. Down the 18th they went again. Both men drove well but Forsbrand hit his second into a bunker. He left his recovery eight feet short and closed his eyes in despair as his putt wobbled past the hole. Then Baker, who had left his two-iron approach just short of the green, did much the same thing as his six-footer rimmed the hole and stayed out.

They returned to the 18th tee once again. By now Baker had recovered his composure. Later, he was to say that he had counselled himself not to be too hard on himself after the disaster on the 72nd. Now he hit a perfect drive as Forsbrand, his nerves raw, blocked his own tee shot into a bunker. The Swede had no choice but to lay up and when his third shot came to a halt 30 feet short of the pin, he put his hands over his eyes in a weary gesture of defeat.

The gracious gallery acknowledged Baker's victory putt rapturously and with affection. The Scandinavian Masters title proved beyond doubt that Baker could hold his own in any company and, more importantly, it proved he was back – with a vengeance.

Above, largest divot of the year prize went to Ernie Els.

Below, Nick Faldo's hopes were dampened.

Above, Peter Baker en route to final
hole double bogey.

Below left and right, hopes of a home
victory were denied Anders Forsbrand.

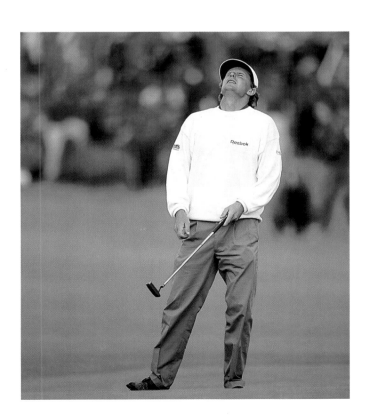

Above, sign of what was at stake in the play-off. Right, second Masters title of the season for Baker.

The new champion is congratulated by Faldo as large crowds look on, below.

COURSE: FORSGÅRDENS GC			YARDAGE: 6893				PAR: 72	
POS	NAME	CTY	1	2	3	4	TOTAL	PRIZE MONEY
1	Peter BAKER	Eng	67	71	68	72	278	£108330
2	Anders FORSBRAND	Swe	67	71	71	69	278	72210
3	Nick FALDO	Eng	69	72	71	68	280	40690
4	David FEHERTY	N.Ire	68	73	70	71	282	30015
	Rodger DAVIS	Aus	72	71	70	69	282	30015
6	Stephen AMES	T&T	71	68	71	73	283	22750
7	Robert KARLSSON	Swe	72	69	70	73	284	17875
	Colin MONTGOMERIE	Scot	68	72	71	73	284	17875
9	Frank NOBILO	NZ	69	72	73	71	285	12222
	Costantino ROCCA	It	72	73	70	70	285	12222
	Steven RICHARDSON	Eng	70	71	70	74	285	12222
	Paul WAY	Eng	71	69	71	74	285	12222
	Brian MARCHBANK	Scot	71	71	70	73	285	12222
14	Sven STRÜVER	Ger	71	73	71	71	286	9550
	Vijay SINGH	Fij	73	66	74	73	286	9550
	Gordon BRAND Jnr	Scot	71	70	74	71	286	9550
17	Darren CLARKE	N.Ire	71	74	72	70	287	8255
	Per-Ulrik JOHANSSON	Swe	72	70	72	73	287	8255
	De Wet BASSON	SA	70	73	72	72	287	8255
	José Maria OLAZABAL	Sp	73	74	71	69	287	8255
21	Mats LANNER	Swe	76	71	72	69	288	7020
	Gary ORR	Scot	72	73	70	73	288	7020
	Jamie SPENCE	Eng	68	73	71	76	288	7020
	Henrik NYSTROM (AM)	Swe	72	71	73	72	288	—
	Des SMYTH	Ire	74	73	71	70	288	7020
	John McHENRY	Ire	70	73	73	72	288	7020
	Nicklas FASTH	Swe	73	72	68	75	288	7020
	David RAY	Eng	72	70	74	72	288	7020
	Leif WESTERBERG (AM)	Swe	71	72	72	73	288	—
28	Ernie ELS	SA	71	74	73	71	289	5947
	Jesper PARNEVIK	Swe	75	69	68	77	289	5947
	Paul AFFLECK	Wal	68	73	72	76	289	5947
	Jim PAYNE	Eng	72	72	72	73	289	5947
32	Juan QUIROS	Sp	73	74	74	69	290	5200
	Ian PALMER	SA	77	70	74	69	290	5200
	Paul BROADHURST	Eng	74	69	75	72	290	5200
	Philip TALBOT	Eng	75	71	73	71	290	5200
	Robin MANN	Eng	70	70	74	76	290	5200
37	David R JONES	Eng	70	73	76	72	291	4355
	Peter MITCHELL	Eng	77	70	72	72	291	4355
	Howard CLARK	Eng	74	71	72	74	291	4355
	Johan RYSTROM	Swe	73	74	69	75	291	4355
	Peter O'MALLEY	Aus	73	69	74	75	291	4355
	Mark McNULTY	Zim	69	74	75	73	291	4355
	Jay TOWNSEND	USA	74	69	74	74	291	4355
	Silvio GRAPPASONNI	It	72	71	76	72	291	4355
45	Sam TORRANCE	Scot	68	72	74	78	292	3445
	Olle NORDBERG	Swe	68	76	74	74	292	3445
	Gary EVANS	Eng	72	75	74	71	292	3445
	Anders GILLNER	Swe	74	71	74	73	292	3445
	Steve BOWMAN	USA	71	73	74	74	292	3445
	Ross McFARLANE	Eng	73	74	74	71	292	3445
51	André BOSSERT	Swi	72	73	75	73	293	2795
	Mark ROE	Eng	70	74	75	74	293	2795
	Ove SELLBERG	Swe	73	73	73	74	293	2795
	Philip WALTON	Ire	71	74	73	75	293	2795
55	Stuart LITTLE	Eng	73	71	75	75	294	2135
	Greg TURNER	NZ	70	70	76	78	294	2135
	Rick HARTMANN	USA	73	73	75	73	294	2135
	José RIVERO	Sp	75	72	70	77	294	2135
	Alberto BINAGHI	It	73	71	75	75	294	2135
	Mark MOULAND	Wal	71	73	71	79	294	2135
	Jon ROBSON	Eng	74	72	73	75	294	2135
62	Mike McLEAN	Eng	73	73	75	74	295	1787
	José Manuel CARRILES	Sp	72	75	72	76	295	1787
64	Tony JOHNSTONE	Zim	71	74	75	76	296	1690
65	Christoffer HANELL (AM)	Swe	71	74	75	77	297	—
	Haydn SELBY-GREEN	Eng	75	70	77	75	297	1625
66	Retief GOOSEN	SA	73	74	77	74	298	972
	Mikael LUNDBERG (AM)	Swe	72	72	73	81	298	—
	Jeremy ROBINSON	Eng	72	74	75	77	298	972
	Miguel Angel JIMENEZ	Sp	72	74	75	77	298	972

FOWLER'S FINISHING FLOURISH

A final round of 63 gave Peter Fowler his first victory in Europe after ten years of trying

Peter Fowler hasn't got the prettiest swing in the world but inelegance doesn't always betoken a lack of skill – Lee Trevino, Ray Floyd, take one step forward.

Fowler couldn't be sure when he set forth on his final round of the BMW International Open what would be needed to take the £83,330 first prize, but he felt it would take eight birdies to come from behind and lift the swag. He overestimated the task a tad, but he exactly achieved his aim, and even threw in an eagle for good measure as he produced an extraordinary burst of scoring around the turn to finish on 267, 21 under par. It brought the Australian victory by three strokes from the favourite, Ian Woosnam.

Fowler is a quiet, unassuming sort of a bloke but he was entitled to celebrate, though, as he brought the Nord-Echenried course to its knees with a final round of 63 to claim his first win in Europe after ten years of trying. They were dancing in the streets of Bagshot, the Surrey village that turns into a kind of rural Earls Court when the Volvo Tour's contingent of Antipodeans descend on it every summer.

The tall, slim Sydneyite has had a house in Bagshot since 1987, and loves it there. But he loved a couple of hundred acres of Bavaria even more as he set a blistering pace that was beyond challenge on the final lap.

Although two under par for the day, Fowler, who had started three strokes behind Woosnam, the leader, was playing for little more than a top ten place when he reached the par five ninth. The hole had been out of reach in two shots all week, but the tee had been moved forward to give players a chance to hit the green with their second shot.

Fowler not only hit the green with his metal three wood, he hit the pin as well, and the ball ricocheted away to no more than a couple of feet. He tapped in for an eagle, and thus inspired he went on to birdie the next four holes, holing a long putt at the tenth, and put himself out of reach of a thoroughbred pursuing pack. He even picked up a further shot on the 72nd hole of the tournament, but by then another birdie was at once an irrelevance and a piece of pure self-indulgence.

At 21 under, he was by now out of reach of a resurgent Woosnam, who dropped only three shots all week and followed a first-round 65 with a pair of 68s and a closing 69. The Welshman was in commanding form all week from tee to green, but perfectionist that he is, pronounced himself 'disgusted' with his putting, especially from short distance.

At the start of the tournament he seemed happy enough with the week's favoured putter, a middle-aged model made by Harold Swash, the ultimate expert in the game within a game. Woosnam fished the club, with which he had won the 1987 Scottish Open, out of his garage the previous week when preparing to move house to Jersey, and thought he would give it a run.

By the end of the third round, the angst had returned; at the short 17th he even resorted to putting with left hand below right and, wouldn't you know it, he sank the putt for a birdie. Needless to say, he putted cack-handed in the last round as well, missed three short putts and still left the final green in despair.

Another couple of Europe's big names were suffering from the greens blues before the tournament started. Mark James said he had been in trouble for four tournaments, so had asked Swash to don his putting coach's hat and pass on a few tips. The next day he shot an eight-birdie 64 to share the lead, and eventually finished tied for 12th place, nine shots behind Fowler. For one man, at least, the problem had been licked.

For Sandy Lyle, meanwhile, there was no such consolation. He had got into such a state over his putting that he was spotted using a Sam Torrance-style long-handled job in the pro-am. He even sank a putt of 40 foot for an eagle with it. He did not use it in the tournament proper, but shot 73 and 72 to miss the cut by four strokes. Long after play was over he was still on the putting green, looking for the answer to his torment.

Level with James at the top of the leaderboard on the first day was David Ray, the tall Bristolian, who defied a strength-sapping dose of food poisoning to record an eagle, seven birdies and only one bogey. He blamed his illness, which struck him in his hotel room the day he arrived in Germany after a visit to a restaurant near his home the night before, on the cream on his dessert. There followed 36 hours of unalloyed misery, and he changed his mind about going home on the first morning of the tournament only after getting up at 6am and feeling he might be able to get round.

Ray, 40th at the PGA European Tour Qualifying School the previous autumn, could not bend to line up his putts without feeling dizzy, but it seemed to make little

Above, Peter Fowler strikes for home.

Below, Gary Orr finished joint third.

Left, delicate touch from Fowler.

difference. He started the week in 120th place in the Volvo Order of Merit, but held on heroically to finish on 276, 12 under par, to collect more than £7,700. He will remember his week in southern Germany with mixed feelings.

Golf of the highest quality was produced by a fistful of players on the final day. Anders Forsbrand had a 65, Bernhard Langer a 66, Peter Mitchell a 67 and Gary Orr, the promising young Scottish professional, a 69, and the quartet finished equal third, four shots behind the winner. Another time they might have won. On this day, they were reduced to matchwood by the irresistible force of Hurricane Peter.

High five for the winner from Joakim Haeggman.

POS	NAME	CTY	1	2	3	4	TOTAL	PRIZE MONEY
1	Peter FOWLER	Aus	67	69	68	63	267	£83330
2	Ian WOOSNAM	Wal	65	68	68	69	270	55550
3	Peter MITCHELL	Eng	69	66	69	67	271	23750
	Bernhard LANGER	Ger	66	69	70	66	271	23750
	Gary ORR	Scot	67	69	66	69	271	23750
	Anders FORSBRAND	Swe	71	67	68	65	271	23750
7	Joakim HAEGGMAN	Swe	68	66	69	69	272	15000
8	Mark McNULTY	Zim	66	70	69	68	273	12500
9	De Wet BASSON	SA	66	68	70	70	274	11150
10	Juan QUIROS	Sp	67	70	69	69	275	9595
	Jesper PARNEVIK	Swe	68	72	67	68	275	9595
12	Miguel Angel JIMENEZ	Sp	70	69	71	66	276	7736
	Silvio GRAPPASONNI	It	68	69	73	66	276	7736
	Mark JAMES	Eng	64	72	68	72	276	7736
	David A RUSSELL	Eng	66	72	69	69	276	7736
	David RAY	Eng	64	72	69	71	276	7736
17	Anders GILLNER	Swe	69	69	70	69	277	6600
	Nolan HENKE	USA	69	70	70	68	277	6600
19	Paul LAWRIE	Scot	66	70	72	70	278	5783
	Alexander CEJKA	Ger	71	69	70	68	278	5783
	Marc FARRY	Fr	68	71	70	69	278	5783
	Mark ROE	Eng	71	70	69	68	278	5783
	Ross McFARLANE	Eng	68	70	70	70	278	5783
	Ronan RAFFERTY	N.Ire	68	71	71	68	278	5783
25	Jeremy ROBINSON	Eng	65	72	70	72	279	4655
	Mike MILLER	Scot	68	70	72	69	279	4655
	Emlyn AUBREY	USA	70	69	69	71	279	4655
	Stuart LITTLE	Eng	67	70	71	71	279	4655
	Magnus SUNESSON	Swe	68	73	70	68	279	4655
	Andrew COLTART	Scot	67	70	72	70	279	4655
	Thomas GOGELE	Ger	67	68	71	73	279	4655
	Brian MARCHBANK	Scot	66	69	73	71	279	4655
	Paul BROADHURST	Eng	68	72	69	70	279	4655
34	Mike McLEAN	Eng	73	68	68	71	280	3900
	Chris WILLIAMS	Eng	68	73	71	68	280	3900
	Lucien TINKLER	Aus	66	72	71	71	280	3900
37	Robert LEE	Eng	70	68	70	73	281	3650
	David FEHERTY	N.Ire	69	69	73	70	281	3650
39	Mike CLAYTON	Aus	69	72	69	72	282	3150
	Jon EVANS	Eng	69	72	69	72	282	3150
	José Manuel CARRILES	Sp	68	71	69	74	282	3150
	Jay TOWNSEND	USA	68	70	74	70	282	3150
	Pierre FULKE	Swe	69	71	70	72	282	3150
	Yago BEAMONTE	Sp	69	68	76	69	282	3150
	Paul MAYO	Wal	72	69	72	69	282	3150
	Scott WATSON	Eng	71	68	73	70	282	3150
47	Tom PURTZER	USA	70	70	71	72	283	2550
	Russell CLAYDON	Eng	69	72	72	70	283	2550
	Sven STRUVER	Ger	72	68	73	70	283	2550
	David GILFORD	Eng	68	70	69	76	283	2550
51	John McHENRY	Ire	66	74	73	71	284	2100
	Peter BAKER	Eng	70	71	68	75	284	2100
	Paul AFFLECK	Wal	71	70	73	70	284	2100
	André BOSSERT	Swi	67	73	70	74	284	2100
	Peter O'MALLEY	Aus	71	70	73	70	284	2100
56	Ole ESKILDSEN	Den	70	70	71	74	285	1750
	Heinz P THUL	Ger	71	70	74	70	285	1750
58	Jonathan SEWELL	Eng	71	68	71	76	286	1525
	Antoine LEBOUC	Fr	73	68	72	73	286	1525
	Gordon J BRAND	Eng	70	71	72	73	286	1525
	Torsten GIEDEON	Ger	72	69	73	72	286	1525
62	Danny MIJOVIC	Can	69	67	74	77	287	1400
63	David WILLIAMS	Eng	70	71	73	74	288	1325
	Rainer MUND	Ger	70	69	73	76	288	1325
65	Oliver ECKSTEIN	Ger	67	74	74	74	289	1250
66	Malcolm MACKENZIE	Eng	71	69	79	74	293	750

COURSE: MUNCHEN NORD-EICHENRIED   YARDAGE: 6910   PAR: 72

VINTAGE STUFF FROM RAFFERTY

Ronan Rafferty found that 1993 was a very good year in Austria

Connoisseur Ronan Rafferty knows a fine wine when he tastes one. In Vienna he reckoned he knew a quality golf course when he saw one. Anyone who had stayed away from the Colony Club course. vintage 1989, Rafferty's favourite year, didn't know what he was missing, was the Irishman's view. Quality, never mind the width of his victory, prevailed in the end, too, with a dramatic first win for Rafferty in 17 months, as he overcame Dane Anders Sorensen in a sudden-death play-off.

Before he could bring home the bacon, though, Rafferty had to overcome a great Danish slice of luck. On the final day, Sorensen homed a three iron approach right into the cup on the tenth for a eagle two. It gave him a two-shot cushion over the field. Rafferty, standing on the 11th tee, having just scrambled par, watched the shot all the way. The 1989 European number one, at last finding some kind of form as he made a last-ditch bid to return to The Belfry, thought it was curtains. It left him four shots behind Sorensen, with eight holes to go. In the end, however, it was Rafferty who brought down the curtain on a first Volvo Tour win for Denmark with a burst of magnificent golf for the second successive day over the tough closing holes.

'I thought he had wrapped it up there and then when he holed that shot,' Rafferty admitted later. Nevertheless Rafferty did not give up. Far from it. Seeing this remarkable shot by Sorensen spurred him to play an amazing spell of holes. He single-putted for par on the 11th, hit a wedge to within inches of the

hole on the 12th, holed from 12 feet on the 16th and three feet on the 17th, both for birdies. As if this was not enough, he then hit a big drive and a five iron over the lake and to the back of the green on the 18th. Two putts gave him his fourth birdie in seven holes and tied him with the Dane.

The opening day belonged to Jamie Spence whose round of 64 was both a new course record and a reminder that he was edging back to form after a debilitating bout of shingles in midsummer. Spence was relieved to be back at the top of the leaderboard. His eight-under-par score brought back memories of the day he burst on the scene when he

recorded the same total in the 1990 Open at St Andrews. He was, however, flattering to deceive and soon Rafferty, who had begun with a 65, took over the lead.

After two rounds Rafferty shared the lead with Eoghan O'Connell. But if anyone thought it was going to develop into a sort of Irish match-play championship the opening nine holes of a hot August Saturday afternoon soon made them think again.

O'Connell, whose new long-tom Polekat putter replaced the weapon broken at the Open, smelt victory when the Kat started to purr on Thursday and Friday. But his Polekat suddenly spat back at him on Saturday, a day when temperatures reached the mid-80s. He took a couple of three putts and generally endured an indifferent afternoon on the greens.

Rafferty's problems began on the fourth hole. A hooked drive avoided the fairway and the adjoining fifth fairway, too, and finished in a bush. Although Rafferty showed the strength of his short game by dropping only one stroke, he started going backwards. By the 14th he had slipped out of the reckoning — until, that is, he produced his trademark finish of four birdies in five holes. After that, he was back in the running.

Charles Raulerson, who was playing with Sven Struver, the German whose 63 on Friday broke Spence's day-old course record, calmed his nerves enough to think perhaps he was in the right place at the right time after all. After 54 holes he was one stroke ahead. The 29-year-old Jacksonville man was loathe to go to

Austria, wanting to play on the PGA European Challenge Tour instead to protect his tenth place which would give him a qualifying spot for the Volvo Tour. However, a last day 76 returned him to the same frame of mind.

Australian Jamie Taylor threatened early on the fourth day but it was Per-Ulrik Johansson who made the strongest challenge. Despite four birdies in five holes after the turn the Swede finished one stroke light of Rafferty, who for the second day running drifted out of contention and then back again with a whirl of birdies. Sorenson, who had trundled in a putt from 60 feet for an eagle on the 18th the day before, now holed from six feet to join Rafferty on 14 under par.

The pair had featured in a play-off before. There had been a cavalry-charge in the 1990 Atlantic Open when both gave best to Steve McAllister in a six-man sudden-death in Portugal.

The magnificent clubhouse at the Colony Club Gutenhof.

Ronan Rafferty was in sparkling form.

This time it was head-to-head, but it took a measurement to decide the losing putt in Vienna. Rafferty missed the green and chipped up. Sorensen approached from 40 feet. Both looked equidistant, but Tournament Director David Probyn adjudged Sorensen to be marginally further away.

Sorensen missed from around four feet, Rafferty made it for par, for £41,660, and for a new favourite vintage.

HOHE BRÜCK ■

AUSTRIAN OPEN

COURSE: COLONY CLUB GUTENOF, HIMBERG						YARDAGE: 6936	PAR: 72
POS	NAME	CTY	1	2	3	4	TOTAL	PRIZE MONEY
1	Ronan RAFFERTY	N.Ire	65	69	72	68	274	£41660
2	Anders SORENSEN	Den	70	67	68	69	274	27770
3	Per-Ulrik JOHANSSON	Swe	70	67	70	68	275	15650
4	Sven STRUVER	Ger	72	63	72	69	276	11550
	Jamie TAYLOR	Aus	66	71	68	71	276	11550
6	Paul MAYO	Wal	68	70	67	73	278	8125
	Greg TURNER	NZ	68	67	71	72	278	8125
8	Steve BOWMAN	USA	72	68	68	72	280	5362
	Charles RAULERSON	USA	68	67	69	76	280	5362
	David R JONES	Eng	72	68	70	70	280	5362
	Brian BARNES	Scot	72	68	69	71	280	5362
12	Mike CLAYTON	Aus	67	73	70	71	281	3950
	Jay TOWNSEND	USA	69	71	70	71	281	3950
	David RAY	Eng	67	75	68	71	281	3950
	André BOSSERT	Swi	77	67	66	71	281	3950
16	Gordon BRAND Jnr	Scot	72	69	69	72	282	3009
	Gabriel HJERTSTEDT	Swe	70	73	70	69	282	3009
	Domingo HOSPITAL	Sp	66	73	70	73	282	3009
	Mike MILLER	Scot	71	67	68	76	282	3009
	Darren CLARKE	N.Ire	73	66	70	73	282	3009
	Paul BROADHURST	Eng	67	73	70	72	282	3009
	Eoghan O'CONNELL	Ire	67	67	74	74	282	3009
	Philip TALBOT	Eng	71	70	72	69	282	3009
	Malcolm MACKENZIE	Eng	68	68	70	76	282	3009
	Paul CURRY	Eng	65	71	72	74	282	3009
26	Jon ROBSON	Eng	70	69	72	72	283	2475
	Peter MITCHELL	Eng	67	69	73	74	283	2475
	Chris WILLIAMS	Eng	71	70	68	74	283	2475
29	Jeff HAWKES	SA	71	72	69	72	284	2180
	Fredrik LINDGREN	Swe	75	68	70	71	284	2180
	David GILFORD	Eng	71	67	73	73	284	2180
	David WILLIAMS	Eng	69	72	71	72	284	2180
	Brian NELSON	USA	68	70	74	72	284	2180
34	John BLAND	SA	68	70	72	75	285	1900
	Robert LEE	Eng	75	69	72	69	285	1900
	José Manuel CARRILES	Sp	74	67	71	73	285	1900
	Stephen BENNETT	Eng	75	69	71	70	285	1900
	Mike McLEAN	Eng	71	71	71	72	285	1900
39	Glenn RALPH	Eng	72	69	71	74	286	1625
	Keith WATERS	Eng	72	72	68	74	286	1625
	Jim PAYNE	Eng	71	69	71	75	286	1625
	Ian GARBUTT	Eng	71	72	68	75	286	1625
	Bill MALLEY	USA	69	72	72	73	286	1625
	Martin POXON	Eng	69	73	75	69	286	1625
45	Andrew COLTART	Scot	70	72	72	73	287	1425
	David A RUSSELL	Eng	72	70	69	76	287	1425
47	Johan RYSTROM	Swe	74	70	72	72	288	1250
	Richard BOXALL	Eng	68	68	79	73	288	1250
	Andrew HARE	Eng	71	71	72	74	288	1250
	Alberto BINAGHI	It	73	68	74	73	288	1250
	Jamie SPENCE	Eng	64	76	73	75	288	1250
52	Scott WATSON	Eng	73	69	72	75	289	1000
	Sam TORRANCE	Scot	68	73	75	73	289	1000
	Paul EALES	Eng	70	74	74	71	289	1000
	Emlyn AUBREY	USA	69	73	73	74	289	1000
	Tony CHARNLEY	Eng	69	74	74	72	289	1000
57	Craig McCLELLAN	USA	73	71	75	71	290	825
	Ruben ALVAREZ	Arg	70	72	73	75	290	825
59	Giuseppe CALI	It	72	70	74	75	291	750
	Maximilian BALTL	Aut	71	72	79	69	291	750
	Karl ABLEIDINGER	Aut	69	70	77	75	291	750
62	Michel BESANCENEY	Fr	72	68	75	77	292	687
	Heinz P THUL	Ger	71	73	73	75	292	687
	Markus BRIER (AM)	Aut	71	69	75	77	292	—
64	Rudi SAILER (AM)	Aut	71	72	78	75	296	—
	Steven THOMPSON	Eng	74	68	78	75	295	650
65	Yago BEAMONTE	Sp	71	73	77	78	299	625
66	Gordon J BRAND	Eng	71	73	76	80	300	400

Per-Ulrik Johansson

seeks a ruling.

DOWN IN THE FOREST
WOOSNAM STIRRED

By late summer, the border-line candidates for Ryder Cup honours begin to get edgy as decision time approaches and they know they are running out of a chance. Indeed it is a curious irony that the act of winning becomes not just the prime objective but simply a means to an end.

In Ian Woosnam's case, there were other considerations too and all of them related to Europe's Ryder Cup by Johnnie Walker prospects and therefore of wider general concern than his own frustrations at not scoring a victory all season nor showing the kind of form that had made him a stalwart of so many previous teams.

It was unthinkable that Bernard Gallacher would take the field of play without the former US Masters champion but unless the diminutive Welshman could edge his way into an automatic place among the top nine qualifiers, he would have to be picked personally by Gallacher who might reasonably have expected a player of such calibre to earn his spot, and to permit a wider freedom of choice. Indeed with Seve Ballesteros and José Maria Olazabal outside the top nine, it seemed that Gallacher's selection had already been made for him; or rather that he had no other course but to take these three obvious candidates.

Moreover it is not always personal form on the fairways that can decide the prospects of a team place because Sam Torrance arrived at the Forest of Arden for the Murphy's English Open in the comforting knowledge that after three victories he

After months of frustration on the greens, Ian Woosnam found the secret at the Forest of Arden

needed only a reasonably proficient finish to be absolutely sure of his place.

All that changed however when he collided with a flower pot in his hotel room as he went sleep walking. The burly Scot has been prone to such nocturnal perambulations since childhood and this particular episode might have been funny but for the implications it held for an in-form Torrance and the team he was expected to serve. He was forced to withdraw from the tournament with chest injuries and obliged to spend the following weeks out of play waiting anxiously to discover whether he would be fit

enough to play in the match.

Woosnam however was something of a puzzle. He had been striking the ball well for several weeks but simply could not find the kind of putting touch he needed to inspire a winning performance. It had been a year of other distractions anyway as he moved family and home from Oswestry, where he had been born and bred, to a new residence in Jersey. His sense of impatience was only heightened by the shoal of hints and tips he received from well-wishers all eager to see him back on form and Woosnam admitted to one newspaper that he felt like taking two months away from the game but realised his Ryder Cup responsibilities took precedence. Indeed, even though he was tired, he promised Bernard Gallacher he would compete in the Volvo German Open, the last qualifying event, if he did not perform well at the formidable Forest of Arden venue.

There was to be no such need. Suddenly the old confidence returned to Woosnam's stride as he rediscovered the elusive putting touch. It happened quite by chance when in an idle moment he practised his putting on the bedroom carpet and decided to adopt the Gary Player stance in which the right knee is pointed inwards. Woosnam called it a 'kink' in the right knee.

The effect was to lock his lower body and transfer the weight to his left side. In fact Nick Faldo adopts a similar stance and Woosnam explained that even though it felt awkward he would persist

Above, Ian Woosnam chips to the final green.

Right, the Forest of Arden says it with flowers

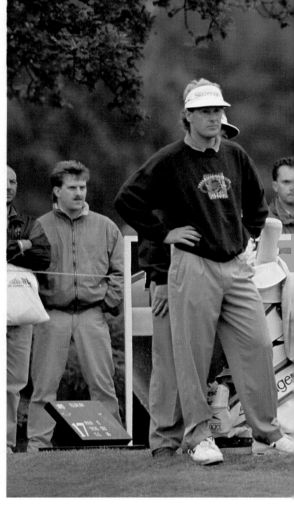

with the method particularly after his second round 67 left him one stroke off the halfway lead shared Tony Johnstone and Jose Maria Canizares who were tied on seven under par 137.

In a sense the Forest of Arden venue, which was hosting its first Volvo Tour event, provided the perfect test for Woosnam because it demanded a succession of challenging, bold and long strokes to well-protected and undulating greens. In truth it required the kind of fearless golf for which he is famed and with his confidence restored, he was more than a match for it.

Meanwhile his fellow Midlander Peter Baker was suddenly confronted with a personal crisis as he realised his own Ryder Cup debut might not be the foregone conclusion it had seemed if he continued to offer the kind of golf that

gave him a 74 on the opening day and reduced him to candidacy for the halfway cut. Accordingly, he clicked back into the kind of form that had earlier made him Dunhill British Masters and Scandinavian Masters champion and put together a seven-under-par 65. In fact he had also shown that he possessed the fighting spirit that is fundamental to successful Ryder Cup golf.

By the third round, there was even better news from the Forest of Arden because Costantino Rocca, already a double Tour winner and the first Italian to become a realistic Ryder Cup candidate, was also running into splendid form with a superlative 64 which gave him the course record and pushed him one stroke ahead of Woosnam whose 65 tied him on 203 with Canizares.

Joakim Haeggman, hoping to become

the first Swedish professional to earn a Ryder Cup place, thought his prospects were fading somewhat as he trailed five strokes behind the leaders going into the final round while in contrast, Sandy Lyle, in 23rd position, was still maintaining his own case for a team place even though the argument was academic and not based on evidence of form. At the beginning of the season, Lyle had seemed an obvious candidate but week-by-week he had slipped down the list and the Volvo Masters champion had not helped his case by refusing to play in more tournaments to boost both points and form.

So it was that Woosnam and Rocca faced each other on the final day in what would be a test of each other's nerve and skill while also presenting an ideal foretaste of the man-to-man pressures involved in Ryder Cup conflict.

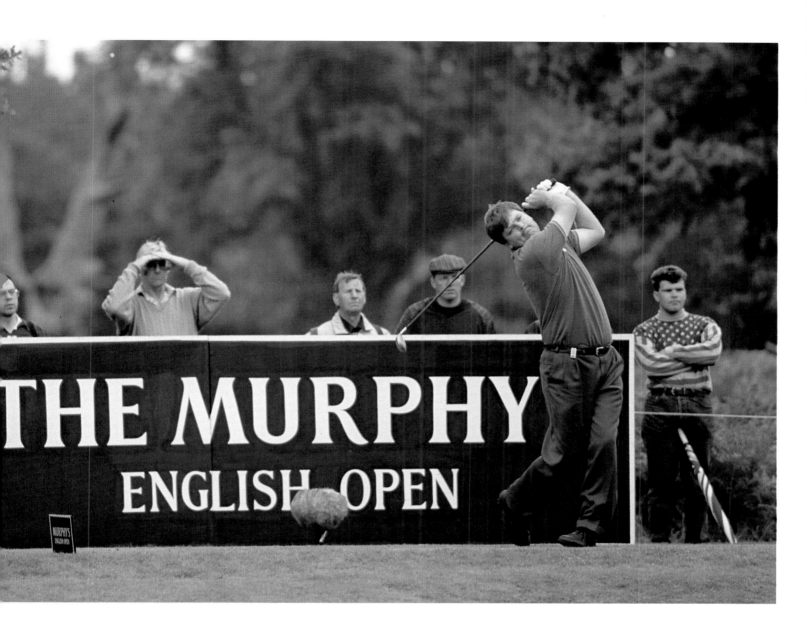

But the truth of it was that Woosnam was simply too close to victory after 13 frustrating months to let this one slip from his grasp and he took command with the impatience of a man who already knew the outcome. He not only erased Rocca's overnight lead but countered every thrust from the genial Italian and after nine holes required only 32 strokes to move clear of his rival.

There was just one anxious moment when the venerable Canizares, who sank the putt which tied the 1989 Ryder Cup match but had subsequently disappeared among the supporting ranks of the Volvo Tour, holed a full five iron of 186 yards for an eagle two on the 13th to move within a stroke. But he was unable make the final push to draw level which meant that Rocca and Woosnam could concentrate solely on each other until the finish

Below, it's no 'fern' for Joakim Haeggman

Above, Mark Roe stands aside as Steven Richardson drives

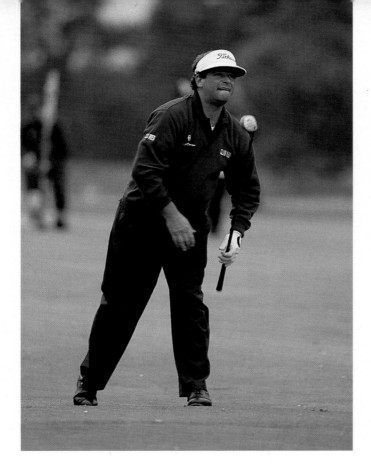

Costantino Rocca leant into second place.

with the Welsh professional scoring a 66 for a 19-under 269 total to take the £100,000 top prize by a two-stroke margin from his potential team-mate.

All in all it had been a satisfying venture. Woosnam was safe because his win had hoisted him to fourth place in the Johnnie Walker Ryder Cup points table. So skipper Gallacher had a wider selection for his eventual team. Rocca was happy too because his second place finish – or rather the £66,660 it offered – confirmed his place while Peter Baker clung on to ninth and the last automatic spot. Even the courtly Canizares for whom Ryder Cup glory had become just a fond and warm memory proved there was still life in the old dog with his third place finish. And what also emerged was that the Volvo Tour had found a new high quality venue in the Forest of Arden.

It ranked equally among more established golf courses on the Tour and indeed some tournament stars placed the Forest of Arden in the same category as its neighbour – The Belfry – just down the road. And – whisper it – there was even talk it held greater potential. Thus, almost everybody came away with a smile.

COURSE: THE FOREST OF ARDEN HOTEL G&C CLUB							YARDAGE: 7079	PAR: 72
POS	NAME	CTY	1	2	3	4	TOTAL	PRIZE MONEY
1	Ian WOOSNAM	Wal	71	67	65	66	269	£100000
2	Costantino ROCCA	It	70	68	64	69	271	66660
3	Jose Maria CANIZARES	Sp	66	71	66	69	272	37560
4	Ronan RAFFERTY	N.Ire	73	68	69	68	278	27700
	Darren CLARKE	N.Ire	68	72	68	70	278	27700
6	Per-Ulrik JOHANSSON	Swe	68	73	69	69	279	16860
	Peter MITCHELL	Eng	70	72	69	68	279	16860
	Mark ROE	Eng	69	73	67	70	279	16860
	Brian MARCHBANK	Scot	70	69	74	66	279	16860
10	Retief GOOSEN	SA	74	67	70	69	280	11106
	Howard CLARK	Eng	71	69	68	72	280	11106
	Joakim HAEGGMAN	Swe	70	69	68	73	280	11106
13	Paul CURRY	Eng	69	70	71	71	281	8322
	Paul BROADHURST	Eng	69	73	69	70	281	8322
	Sandy LYLE	Scot	72	70	69	70	281	8322
	André BOSSERT	Swi	72	72	68	69	281	8322
	Tony JOHNSTONE	Zim	66	71	73	71	281	8322
	José RIVERO	Sp	69	69	70	73	281	8322
	Jeff HAWKES	SA	70	68	69	74	281	8322
	Steven RICHARDSON	Eng	67	72	70	72	281	8322
21	Peter BAKER	Eng	74	65	77	66	282	6930
	Domingo HOSPITAL	Sp	75	68	71	68	282	6930
23	David GILFORD	Eng	70	70	71	72	283	6480
	Gordon BRAND Jnr	Scot	71	69	71	72	283	6480
	Vicente FERNANDEZ	Arg	69	71	71	72	283	6480
26	Gary EVANS	Eng	72	70	69	73	284	5580
	Mark JAMES	Eng	69	73	71	71	284	5580
	Gary ORR	Scot	70	71	72	71	284	5580
	David FEHERTY	N.Ire	69	74	68	73	284	5580
	Jon ROBSON	Eng	69	72	70	73	284	5580
	Mike CLAYTON	Aus	73	70	69	72	284	5580
	Jesper PARNEVIK	Swe	72	69	71	72	284	5580
33	Frank NOBILO	NZ	69	72	70	74	285	4560
	Peter FOWLER	Aus	68	71	73	73	285	4560
	Wayne WESTNER	SA	71	70	73	71	285	4560
	Giuseppe CALI	It	69	72	74	70	285	4560
	Robert ALLENBY	Aus	72	70	68	75	285	4560
	Eduardo ROMERO	Arg	71	73	71	70	285	4560
	Pierre FULKE	Swe	72	70	71	72	285	4560
40	Fredrik LINDGREN	Swe	71	71	75	69	286	3660
	Craig CASSELLS	Eng	70	73	75	68	286	3660
	Christy O'CONNOR Jnr	Ire	70	72	71	73	286	3660
	Paul WAY	Eng	68	75	70	73	286	3660
	Barry LANE	Eng	69	75	71	71	286	3660
	José Manuel CARRILES	Sp	68	72	74	72	286	3660
	Paul AFFLECK	Wal	71	73	70	72	286	3660
	De Wet BASSON	SA	70	71	76	69	286	3660
48	Paul LAWRIE	Scot	70	74	68	75	287	3000
	Greg TURNER	NZ	71	70	71	75	287	3000
	Thomas LEVET	Fr	71	73	73	70	287	3000
51	Gordon J BRAND	Eng	73	71	73	71	288	2580
	Stuart LITTLE	Eng	74	70	70	74	288	2580
	Steen TINNING	Den	69	74	74	71	288	2580
	Phillip PRICE	Wal	73	70	71	74	288	2580
55	Stephen McALLISTER	Scot	73	70	68	78	289	2100
	Ricky WILLISON	Eng	71	72	75	71	289	2100
	Roger WINCHESTER	Eng	68	76	74	71	289	2100
	Michel BESANCENEY	Fr	71	72	70	76	289	2100
59	Olle KARLSSON	Swe	69	73	70	78	290	1770
	Ove SELLBERG	Swe	77	67	78	68	290	1770
	Jorge BERENDT	Arg	71	73	72	74	290	1770
	Martin GATES	Eng	72	72	74	72	290	1770
63	Steve BOWMAN	USA	71	71	75	77	294	1590
	Manuel PINERO	Sp	73	70	77	74	294	1590
65	Ian GARBUTT	Eng	67	76	77	76	296	1500

Declan misunderstood the shout of 'fore', but like the Murphy's he wasn't bitter.

KING LANGER
THE FIFTH

***Bernhard Langer
dominated the
Volvo German Open
and recorded his fifth
victory in the event's
history***

No professional golfer can expect worse in his life than to face, and then miss, the putt that would have retained the Ryder Cup. Such a fate befell in 1991 Bernhard Langer at Kiawah Island as a crowd of many thousands glued its eyes on him and an audience of millions held its breath on television.

Yet within a week Langer faced a putt of much the same length to tie the Mercedes German Masters at Stuttgart, holed it and then won the play-off. Therein lay the inner strength of a man who, to golf in Germany, is what Severiano Ballesteros has been to the game in Spain.

To win is one thing; to win when it is expected of you is quite another. Yet as one looks down Langer's outstanding record, the two pinnacles of which have been his Masters victories of 1985 and 1993, one sees again and again his flair for rising to the occasion when he has his native soil beneath his feet.

His Volvo German Open victory at the Hubbelrath Club in Dusseldorf was his fifth and that equalled the record of the late Percy Alliss between the two world wars, four of the victories in a row from 1926. Langer's have spanned 12 years beginning in 1981 but he has also, in his time, won the German Masters in 1989 and 1991 and the Honda Open, which was also played in Germany, in 1992.

Langer knows he is expected to play well but it is his own belief 'that I expect to play well' that has given his game another dimension when his fellow countrymen flock after him and despite all the demands that are put on his time off the golf course. He is very much public property for the week of the tournament with no escape from media, promoters, sponsors or anyone else.

It is all, Langer accepts, part of the deal and, apart from one unsuspected wobble at the end of the second and beginning of the third rounds of this latest German conquest, he was the commanding figure throughout. Rounds of 65, 68, 70, 66 made him 19 under par and the winner by five strokes from Peter Baker and Robert Allenby, an emerging young Australian. It was Langer's third victory of the year, the others by equally emphatic margins: four strokes in the Masters at Augusta, six in the Volvo PGA Championship at Wentworth.

Only fleetingly during the third round was Langer ever other than at the top of the leaderboard; tied with Johan Rystrom at the end of the first day, one ahead of Baker at the end of the second, two clear of Baker and David Feherty at the end of the third and away on his own when, as it were, the bell sounded for the last lap.

For all that Langer did have an uneasy time. He had said after his first round of 65 that he would be happy 'if I could always putt like that' as he sank putts of anything up to 30 feet, which was for an eagle three at the eighth.

After 13 holes in the second round, which had included a second eagle at the eighth and five other birdies, he was 14 under par and six strokes clear of the field. Quite unaccountably his engine then began to splutter. In the last five holes he dropped three strokes for a 68 and Baker, who had other things on his mind, like making sure of his place in the Johnnie Walker European Ryder Cup team, for which this was the last counting

Facing, David Feherty and left, Peter Baker, challenged for the title but had to give best to Bernhard Langer, above.

event, stole up on to his heels with seven birdies in his last 11 holes for a 66.

This semi-collapse by Langer continued in the third round for he took 37 to the turn, one of the shots he dropped to par being at the eighth where he took three putts from four feet. Then he made four birdies in the space of five holes and followed it by four-putting the 14th. It was easily done, other players agreed, on these glassy greens but there was also speculation that this could also have been the return of Langer's celebrated twitch. At once he called upon Peter Coleman, his caddie, to line up his putts just as Fanny

Sunesson does for Nick Faldo from a squatting position behind him, and in the putts started to flow again. Two more birdies in his last four holes, round in 70 and it was all over bar the size of the victory.

In the end it was five strokes but it should have been six. Langer, with a wry smile, took five at the last for his 66. It was, he suggested, 'one of the best ball-striking rounds I can recall' and his putting was pretty good again, too.

A cheque for £108,330 made Langer the leading qualifier in the Ryder Cup points table with £520,438 for the 12-month period of selection but the greater satisfaction was Baker's. He had come into the tournament in ninth place in the Ryder Cup rankings with the knowledge that, if he missed the cut, somebody could still overtake him, even David Feherty from 24th place in the table should the Irishman win and Baker miss the cut.

There were a number of other unlikely permutations that could have turned things around but Baker did not put a foot wrong. He was under par in every round and indeed promoted himself to seventh place in the final Ryder Cup batting order, ahead of both Mark James and Sam Torrance, whose convalescence with a chest injury took a decided turn for the better when he learned that he was still in the team on merit.

Joakim Haegmann, equal sixth in the tournament with Feherty, meanwhile packed his bags and left Hubbelrath convinced that he had not done enough to make the team against the Americans, even though he finished in tenth place. What he did not know was that Bernhard Gallacher had already made a note to ring him at 7.30 the following morning with the news of his selection.

Above, joint first round leader Johan Rystrom.

Bernhard Gallacher announces his European Ryder Cup team.

COURSE: GOLF-CLUB HUBBELRATH, DUSSELDORF						YARDAGE: 6777		PAR: 72
POS	NAME	CTY	1	2	3	4	TOTAL	PRIZE MONEY
1	Bernhard LANGER	Ger	65	68	70	66	269	£108330
2	Peter BAKER	Eng	68	66	71	69	274	56450
	Robert ALLENBY	Aus	71	70	65	68	274	56450
4	Colin MONTGOMERIE	Scot	68	71	70	66	275	30015
	Darren CLARKE	N.Ire	69	70	71	65	275	30015
6	David FEHERTY	N.Ire	67	69	69	71	276	21125
	Joakim HAEGGMAN	Swe	69	67	72	68	276	21125
8	Peter O'MALLEY	Aus	68	68	71	70	277	13930
	David GILFORD	Eng	69	74	65	69	277	13930
	Gary ORR	Scot	67	70	70	70	277	13930
	Johan RYSTROM	Swe	65	72	70	70	277	13930
12	Frank NOBILO	NZ	69	71	71	67	278	10058
	Olle KARLSSON	Swe	71	71	69	67	278	10058
	Sandy LYLE	Scot	69	69	71	69	278	10058
	Barry LANE	Eng	71	67	69	71	278	10058
	Costantino ROCCA	It	68	70	69	71	278	10058
17	Des SMYTH	Ire	70	71	70	68	279	8406
	Eduardo ROMERO	Arg	67	71	70	71	279	8406
	Howard CLARK	Eng	71	68	69	71	279	8406
20	André BOSSERT	Swi	66	69	72	73	280	7410
	Retief GOOSEN	SA	66	73	67	74	280	7410
	Ronan RAFFERTY	N.Ire	67	70	74	69	280	7410
	Wayne GRADY	Aus	70	67	73	70	280	7410
	Seve BALLESTEROS	Sp	72	69	68	71	280	7410
25	Stuart LITTLE	Eng	74	69	69	69	281	6435
	Alexander CEJKA	Ger	69	68	78	66	281	6435
	Greg TURNER	NZ	70	71	70	70	281	6435
	Mark JAMES	Eng	69	71	72	69	281	6435
	Tony JOHNSTONE	Zim	69	69	69	74	281	6435
30	Anders SORENSEN	Den	69	69	72	72	282	5752
	Glen DAY	USA	69	71	74	68	282	5752
32	Ruben ALVAREZ	Arg	72	71	72	68	283	5200
	Phillip PRICE	Wal	71	69	71	72	283	5200
	Manuel PINERO	Sp	72	71	69	71	283	5200
	Silvio GRAPPASONNI	It	72	70	68	73	283	5200
	Peter MITCHELL	Eng	71	71	70	71	283	5200
37	Ian PALMER	SA	66	70	77	71	284	4290
	Chris WILLIAMS	Eng	72	67	71	74	284	4290
	Roger CHAPMAN	Eng	68	74	69	73	284	4290
	Patrick HALL	Eng	73	70	71	70	284	4290
	Peter FOWLER	Aus	71	71	75	67	284	4290
	Mark DAVIS	Eng	70	70	74	70	284	4290
	Martin GATES	Eng	69	71	73	71	284	4290
	Paul BROADHURST	Eng	69	70	71	74	284	4290
	Paul EALES	Eng	70	69	71	74	284	4290
46	Eoghan O'CONNELL	Ire	72	69	72	72	285	3510
	Alberto BINAGHI	It	73	69	71	72	285	3510
	Santiago LUNA	Sp	70	71	73	71	285	3510
49	David CURRY	Eng	70	69	69	78	286	2925
	Domingo HOSPITAL	Sp	68	72	74	72	286	2925
	Stephen FIELD	Eng	69	74	69	74	286	2925
	Mike CLAYTON	Aus	71	70	74	71	286	2925
	Wayne WESTNER	SA	74	68	67	77	286	2925
	Paul AFFLECK	Wal	70	70	72	74	286	2925
55	José Maria CANIZARES	Sp	67	73	71	76	287	2275
	Steen TINNING	Den	69	73	72	73	287	2275
	Stephen AMES	T&T	67	72	72	76	287	2275
	Magnus SUNESSON	Swe	69	73	72	73	287	2275
59	Gavin LEVENSON	SA	69	73	74	72	288	1852
	Mats LANNER	Swe	70	72	71	75	288	1852
	Giuseppe CALI	It	70	73	72	73	288	1852
	Jean VAN DE VELDE	Fr	73	70	72	73	288	1852
	Pierre FULKE	Swe	70	73	70	75	288	1852
	Gordon BRAND Jnr	Scot	73	70	69	76	288	1852
65	José RIVERO	Sp	70	70	77	72	289	1136
	Gordon J BRAND	Eng	74	68	74	73	289	1136
	Torsten GIEDEON	Ger	69	74	71	75	289	1136
	Sven STRUVER	Ger	69	73	73	74	289	1136
69	José Manuel CARRILES	Sp	70	70	73	77	290	968
	Paul LAWRIE	Scot	68	72	78	72	290	968
71	Paul MAYO	Wal	68	74	71	78	291	965
72	Thomas LEVET	Fr	69	73	76	74	292	963

LANE IN PEAK FORM

High in the Swiss Alps, Barry Lane confirmed his standing as a new member of Europe's Ryder Cup team

It must be all that fresh, clear Alpine air. After all, the tired and weary have been travelling to Switzerland for rest, relaxation and recuperation for years. So it was not surprising to find the Canon European Masters, played 6,000 feet up in the Alps at Crans-sur-Sierre, rejuvenating the games of two men in varying needs of a tonic.

Barry Lane, with two previous Volvo Tour titles to his name, was the only automatic qualifier for Europe's Ryder Cup team who had not won in 1993. He had led the Johnnie Walker points table by a mile at the beginning of the year thanks to a blistering end to 1992, but had not been able to relax, knowing he was in the team, until he saw his name in print after the previous week's Volvo German Open.

Severiano Ballesteros, with 51 Tour titles and five major championships to his name, had not qualified to face the Americans at the Belfry. He was picked for his seventh appearance by captain Bernard Gallacher for his past record. Now was time to add some present form.

If anything could be described as tired and weary in 1993, it was Ballesteros's golf. Troubled for much of the time by persistent back trouble, the 36-year-old Spaniard was struggling to get the ball in play off the tee, and struggling to beat the cut seemingly every week. Not since his third place at the Dubai Classic in January had he reached the dizzying heights of a top ten finish.

Prior to the Volvo German Open he had had three weeks off, one of them

with bronchitis, and at some point he picked up a copy of his own teaching book, *Natural Golf*. 'It reminded me of the way I used to think,' he said. He also noticed his swing used to be more upright, something he was working on with the coach Simon Holmes. After a first round 71, Ballesteros shot a 66 on day two. 'My handicap is starting to come down,' he said. 'Today I hit shots that I have not hit in two years.'

He had been playing in the company of Lane. 'He is a different player,' Lane said of his new team-mate. 'He is stalking around the greens again.'

At halfway Ballesteros was six shots

behind Mats Lanner's 13-under-par lead. In past years Lanner had the chance to become Sweden's first Ryder Cup player but had seen that honour fall to his London flatmate, Joakim Haeggman earlier that week.

Lane was five back and the leader's closest challenger came from Ireland's Philip Walton, two behind, thanks to a hickory-shafted putter. Walton's troubles on the greens had got so bad he tried a broomhandle, anchored on this chest *à la* Sam Torrance, for three months before falling for a putter his father, a plasterer, found while doing a job in South Dublin. 'The first time I saw it I thought it was beautiful,' he said, though something was to go wrong over the weekend.

The only serious casualty at this stage was Bernhard Langer, fresh from his German win, but not fit following a recurrence of his neck injury which dated from the US Open. He retired after seven holes on day one.

Lane made his move on Saturday with an eight-under-par 64, though he still trailed by two from Spain's Miguel Angel Jimenez, whose 63 was the nearest anyone got to taking home the sponsor's 18-carat, £50,000 gold putter, to be awarded to the first man to break 60.

Miracles, though, are the preserve of another Spanish golfer and on Sunday Ballesteros obviously thought he was in Lourdes, not Crans. By the time he had got to the 18th tee he was 16 under par – thanks mainly to an eagle at the par five 14th and birdies at the 16th and the 17th. 'Even the Swiss are getting

Severiano Ballesteros works another miracle as he inspects his lie on the final hole, recovers from the trees to the front of the green, and reacts exultantly as he chips in for a birdie.

excited,' noted an American voice in the crowd as Seve put his wedge to three feet at the penultimate hole.

But at the 18th his drive went so far right he thought it had gone out of bounds. He hit a provisional before finding his original had hit a concrete wall protecting a swimming pool and was still in play. By common reckoning, including that of his caddie Billy Foster, he had to chip back to the fairway.

Instead, to the bewilderment of all, the man with the most imaginative mind in golf was considering playing a shot of breathtaking audacity. He was going for the green. To get there he had to go over the six-foot wall which stood five feet in front of him, under the branches of several trees, over the swimming pool, the press

tent, more trees and finally a greenside bunker.

Foster mentioned the word impossible. That got Seve going. 'I don't know why you think it is impossible,' he smarted. 'I think it is possible.' He swung and – miraculously – the next time he saw it, after fighting his way through the crowd to the fairway, there was the ball, just in front of the bunker, 18 yards from the hole. 'There was a small gap,' he said afterwards, 'but it was a big risk. I couldn't resist. I make more miracle shots because I try harder and take more risks.'

Of course the roar from the crowd was nothing compared to that when he holed the chip. Seve was pleased, too, pumping his arm as if he had won the Open.

But he wouldn't win the Canon

Mountainous backdrop at Crans.

European Masters. At the 15th Lane, in the process of birdieing the back-to-back par fives, heard the roar and thought Ballesteros had holed his second at the 18th . Never mind, he was in control even if it didn't feel like it. 'I was so nervous it was ridiculous.' he admitted.

'When I had won before I was three ahead with three to play. But this was really tight. My caddie said on the 14th tee that the tournament starts here.'

A three-putt at the 16th was claimed back with a birdie on the 17th, where Jimenez lipped out and when the Spaniard missed from seven feet at the last, Lane was home.

For Ballesteros, joint second, his best result since March 1992, there was now 'light at the end of the tunnel'. For Lane this was a timely Belfry confidence booster. 'There was a lot of pressure on me because I won so much money at the end of last year. Now I feel I deserve to be in the team.'

								PRIZE
POS	NAME	CTY	1	2	3	4	TOTAL	MONEY
1	Barry LANE	Eng	69	67	64	70	270	£102960
2	Seve BALLESTEROS	Sp	71	66	68	66	271	53640
	Miguel Angel JIMENEZ	Sp	67	68	63	73	271	53640
4	Per-Ulrik JOHANSSON	Swe	71	64	68	69	272	30900
5	Howard CLARK	Eng	67	70	66	70	273	26200
6	Darren CLARKE	N.Ire	69	66	71	68	274	20085
	Gary ORR	Scot	69	68	68	69	274	20085
8	Nick FALDO	Eng	65	70	69	71	275	13883
	Paul CURRY	Eng	69	70	65	71	275	13883
	Colin MONTGOMERIE	Scot	66	72	69	68	275	13883
11	Anders FORSBRAND	Swe	72	68	67	69	276	10650
	Robert KARLSSON	Swe	72	68	69	67	276	10650
	Torsten GIEDEON	Ger	68	69	69	70	276	10650
14	Glen DAY	USA	71	65	71	70	277	9080
	Des SMYTH	Ire	68	71	68	70	277	9080
	Wayne WESTNER	SA	68	72	69	68	277	9080
17	Eduardo ROMERO	Arg	71	65	68	74	278	8340
18	John McHENRY	Ire	69	70	68	72	279	7073
	Craig CASSELLS	Eng	67	70	72	70	279	7073
	Steen TINNING	Den	71	66	71	71	279	7073
	Domingo HOSPITAL	Sp	71	65	70	73	279	7073
	Mats LANNER	Swe	65	66	77	71	279	7073
	Tom PERNICE	USA	70	65	73	71	279	7073
	Bill MALLEY	USA	67	72	70	70	279	7073
	Philip WALTON	Ire	65	68	70	76	279	7073
	Jean VAN DE VELDE	Fr	68	72	68	71	279	7073
27	Roger CHAPMAN	Eng	69	69	73	69	280	5657
	Silvio GRAPPASONNI	It	68	72	70	70	280	5657
	Paul EALES	Eng	69	70	71	70	280	5657
	Mike CLAYTON	Aus	71	68	72	69	280	5657
	David A RUSSELL	Eng	68	70	72	70	280	5657
	Heinz P THUL	Ger	72	68	68	72	280	5657
33	Pierre FULKE	Swe	68	70	69	74	281	4757
	Paul McGINLEY	Ire	69	67	70	75	281	4757
	Mikael KRANTZ	Swe	71	69	71	70	281	4757
	Brian MARCHBANK	Scot	70	71	70	70	281	4757
	José Manuel CARRILES	Sp	70	69	71	71	281	4757
	Sandy LYLE	Scot	67	70	70	74	281	4757
39	Manuel PINERO	Sp	72	67	66	77	282	4257
	Chris MOODY	Eng	68	70	72	72	282	4257
41	David RAY	Eng	68	71	73	71	283	3945
	David WILLIAMS	Eng	70	68	74	71	283	3945
	Steven RICHARDSON	Eng	68	72	70	73	283	3945
44	Jamie SPENCE	Eng	67	72	74	71	284	3446
	Vicente FERNANDEZ	Arg	70	68	72	74	284	3446
	Justin HOBDAY	SA	69	71	73	71	284	3446
	Manny ZERMAN	It	72	68	73	71	284	3446
	Alberto BINAGHI	It	67	70	70	77	284	3446
49	Russell CLAYDON	Eng	69	69	76	71	285	2900
	Adam HUNTER	Scot	68	73	72	72	285	2900
	Gavin LEVENSON	SA	67	73	72	73	285	2900
	Martin GATES	Eng	70	71	73	71	285	2900
53	Michel BESANCENEY	Fr	71	69	72	74	286	2247
	Ove SELLBERG	Swe	71	69	73	73	286	2247
	Sven STRUVER	Ger	71	68	75	72	286	2247
	José COCERES	Arg	69	70	73	74	286	2247
	Stephen McALLISTER	Scot	69	67	80	70	286	2247
	José RIVERO	Sp	71	70	74	71	286	2247
	Santiago LUNA	Sp	68	72	71	75	286	2247
60	Steve BOWMAN	USA	73	68	73	74	288	1870
61	Robert LEE	Eng	70	71	71	77	289	1805
62	Ross DRUMMOND	Scot	72	69	74	75	290	1707
	Paul LAWRIE	Scot	68	73	76	73	290	1707
64	Jon ROBSON	Eng	68	71	77	76	292	1610
65	Stephen AMES	T&T	72	68	79	76	295	1545

COURSE: CRANS-SUR-SIERRE, SWITZERLAND   YARDAGE: 6745   PAR: 72

Photographer: Steve Munday

BEHIND EVERY GREAT APPROACH IS A COPIER AND A FAX.

Precise control, refined technique and a lifetime of preparation ... they can make all the difference on the course. Canon

shares this attitude, which is why we are proud to work behind the scenes at many major golf events. In 1993,

as official supplier of copiers and facsimile machines to both the Ryder Cup and PGA European Tour, we're helping

ease the flow of communications. So everyone can relax, enjoy the action and leave the worrying to the pros.

Canon

SUPPORTING THE WORLD OF SPORT

BRAND IS NATIONAL HERO

*Gordon Brand Junior
tamed the elements
and the East Sussex
National to record his
first Volvo Tour victory
for four years*

When the East Sussex National course was chosen as the 1993 venue for that most movable of golfing feasts, the GA European Open, the *cognoscenti* nodded approvingly.

Designed as Britain's first stadium golf course, East Sussex is, quite literally, tailor-made for big-time golf, its 400 acres easily accommodating any number of spectators as well as the corporate tentage plus public catering areas.

After years spent dodging between those pleasant home counties cousins, Walton Heath and Sunningdale, East Sussex came as a bit of a shock to many of the players. For the most part, however, the shock was a pleasant one. 'Great course, and the greens are the slickest we've played in Europe this year,' said Nick Faldo. There were no dissenting voices. Well, not until play actually began. For what no-one could have foreseen was the weather that suddenly struck Sussex in late September.

Until this GA European Open, the weather had been drier than a wombat's mouth in the middle of summer. In the weeks leading up to this event, we got used to seeing little clouds of dust spiralling into the air as golfers trudged over parched fairways. Of course a lack of rain was never a problem at East Sussex where technology means that, by pressing a button, one man can release enough water to accommodate several ocean going liners. So East Sussex was already green and lush when play began.

Unfortunately, this was also the day when whoever, or whatever, is in charge of The Really Big Button In The Sky decid-ed to end the drought. Suddenly an already dampish course was in danger of drowning as the heavens opened, the wind howled and anyone who didn't have to play golf for a living hurtled for cover.

It was the sort of disaster-laden scenario that is only too familiar to the sponsors, insurance giant General Accident, who must have feared their third and final year as title sponsor of the European Open was going to end with some expensive claims for damage.

The fact that it didn't, that four days later this European Open was heralded as a terrific event, is due generally to the fact that the Volvo Tour is now really efficient at keeping the show on the road, and more specifically to the brilliance of Gordon Brand Junior's golf.

Finally, after a season of almost getting it right, Brand found the secret of success, his game a thing of sublime beauty. Certainly his opening 65, seven under par, bore eloquent testimony to the oldest adage in town... the secret of success truly is timing.

While wind and rain worthy of *The Tempest* blasted across the downs, reducing the rest of the field to scurrying, bent figures, Brand Junior stood tall. Up at 5.45am for an 8am start off the tenth tee, Brand played into the teeth of the gale like a man possessed by the most positive of sporting demons. His 65 was quite simply a magnificent effort. Even he referred to it as 'a hell of a round of golf' while his fellow professionals queued to pay tribute to his seven under par score. 'That must be the best round of the year. I thought my 70 was pretty good but Gordon's is fantastic,' said Ian Woosnam. 'Unbelievable. It was just about as tough as it gets out there today.' chipped in Tony Jacklin.

What was truly staggering was the fact that Brand was eight under par after eleven holes. This was the sort of magical golf that could not last. And it didn't. Brand three putted his 12th hole, the

course's third, before finishing with a five at the horrendously difficult ninth, the only green he missed all day.

Nine single putts set up this score as Brand used his new Bullseye putter to magnificent effect. 'I used it for the first time in the pro-am,' he grinned. 'And it did quite well so I decided to keep it in my bag. I think it's got a good chance of staying with me for the rest of the week.'

Brand's start meant that he carried a three stroke advantage into the second day and though the gale reduced itself to no more than a stiff breeze, nobody managed to topple him from pole position. After the frustrations of the previous couple of years, he was determined to cash in on his near-miraculous start, his nerve as steady as his play over the next three days.

Indeed by the time Sunday arrived, Brand was still four shots clear of the chasing pack after adding rounds of 68 and 71 to that 65 for a total of 204, 12 under par. As far as the others were concerned, only a serious collapse, encouraged by nerves, by Brand could

Murky day for spectators and, below, Gordan Brand Junior.

give them any real hope of catching the leader.

It wasn't to be. Play was brought forward by three and a half hours after another storm warning and this was to be the only shock of the day. Brand sealed his victory by making birdies at the first two holes, setting up a barricade worthy of the SAS and winning his second European Open title.

By the time he came to the last hole, he was so far ahead he felt able to wander along, giving a radio interview. Victory by a stunning seven shots meant he could indulge in the most relaxed 18th fairway of the year.

Clearly, nothing reduces the strain of competition like facing a drive off the final tee, knowing the winner's £100,000 cheque already has your name on it. 'It's long overdue,' admitted the Kirkcaldy-born player. 'There were times during the last four years when I wondered if I'd ever win again. Yet this week I've played my best-ever golf. I just wish I'd reached this peak a few weeks ago and made the Ryder Cup side.'

It was the only way in which Gordon Brand Junior's timing was out at East Sussex National.

Phillip Price struck out for the largest cheque of his career.

POS	NAME	CTY	1	2	3	4	TOTAL	PRIZE MONEY
COURSE: EAST SUSSEX NATIONAL			YARDAGE: 7138				PAR: 72	
1	Gordon BRAND Jnr	Scot	65	68	71	71	275	£100000
2	Phillip PRICE	Wal	70	68	71	73	282	52110
	Ronan RAFFERTY	N.Ire	69	73	68	72	282	52110
4	Frank NOBILO	NZ	73	69	69	72	283	27700
	Olle KARLSSON	Swe	68	73	67	75	283	27700
6	Ian WOOSNAM	Wal	70	75	69	70	284	19500
	Paul LAWRIE	Scot	72	70	69	73	284	19500
8	Darren CLARKE	N.Ire	74	72	65	74	285	14220
	Steven RICHARDSON	Eng	72	70	70	73	285	14220
10	Sam TORRANCE	Scot	71	75	70	70	286	12000
11	Des SMYTH	Ire	73	75	71	68	287	10660
	Rodger DAVIS	Aus	72	77	69	69	287	10660
13	Seve BALLESTEROS	Sp	70	72	71	76	289	8322
	Jesper PARNEVIK	Swe	72	74	72	71	289	8322
	Mike McLEAN	Eng	71	71	72	75	289	8322
	Retief GOOSEN	SA	73	75	71	70	289	8322
	Miguel Angel JIMENEZ	Sp	74	73	74	68	289	8322
	Steen TINNING	Den	76	73	70	70	289	8322
	Jorge BERENDT	Arg	76	72	71	70	289	8322
	Santiago LUNA	Sp	75	73	71	70	289	8322
21	Paul McGINLEY	Ire	73	72	70	75	290	6300
	Sandy LYLE	Scot	72	74	76	68	290	6300
	José RIVERO	Sp	71	76	73	70	290	6300
	Rick HARTMANN	USA	72	73	71	74	290	6300
	Mats LANNER	Swe	73	71	73	73	290	6300
	Peter FOWLER	Aus	73	73	74	70	290	6300
	Paul EALES	Eng	75	72	71	72	290	6300
	Paul CURRY	Eng	71	73	71	75	290	6300
	Colin MONTGOMERIE	Scot	72	75	68	75	290	6300
30	Paul WAY	Eng	74	73	69	75	291	4758
	De Wet BASSON	SA	71	70	74	76	291	4758
	Mike CLAYTON	Aus	72	76	69	74	291	4758
	Peter BAKER	Eng	75	73	70	73	291	4758
	Brian MARCHBANK	Scot	71	73	73	74	291	4758
	Paul BROADHURST	Eng	76	72	70	73	291	4758
	Howard CLARK	Eng	73	73	72	73	291	4758
	Philip WALTON	Ire	68	75	73	75	291	4758
	Jeremy ROBINSON	Eng	69	74	74	74	291	4758
	Magnus SUNESSON	Swe	75	73	69	74	291	4758
40	Nick FALDO	Eng	76	71	69	76	292	3900
	Adam HUNTER	Scot	73	74	72	73	292	3900
	Greg TURNER	NZ	75	71	74	72	292	3900
	Stephen AMES	T&T	77	71	74	70	292	3900
44	Vicente FERNANDEZ	Arg	75	72	74	72	293	3240
	Michel BESANCENEY	Fr	74	71	75	73	293	3240
	Chris MOODY	Eng	76	70	72	75	293	3240
	Peter MITCHELL	Eng	76	71	69	77	293	3240
	Jean VAN DE VELDE	Fr	73	74	72	74	293	3240
	Brian BARNES	Scot	73	72	70	78	293	3240
	Eduardo ROMERO	Arg	74	75	70	74	293	3240
51	Tony JOHNSTONE	Zim	74	75	71	74	294	2460
	Robert KARLSSON	Swe	71	74	74	75	294	2460
	Mark JAMES	Eng	74	75	71	74	294	2460
	Andrew SHERBORNE	Eng	72	75	71	76	294	2460
	José COCERES	Arg	75	74	68	77	294	2460
	Jon ROBSON	Eng	72	75	69	78	294	2460
57	Gavin LEVENSON	SA	73	74	76	72	295	1940
	David FEHERTY	N.Ire	75	74	72	74	295	1940
	Haydn SELBY-GREEN	Eng	75	74	73	73	295	1940
60	Mark MOULAND	Wal	75	73	74	75	297	1770
	Peter O'MALLEY	Aus	74	72	74	77	297	1770
62	Steve BOWMAN	USA	75	71	74	78	298	1680
63	John McHENRY	Ire	71	78	74	76	299	1620
64	Jeff HAWKES	SA	71	76	71	82	300	1560
65	Derrick COOPER	Eng	73	75	76	77	301	1200
	Torsten GIEDEON	Ger	69	79	80	73	301	1200

WOOSNAM LEADS RYDER CUP PACK

Ian Woosnam captured his second Volvo Tour title in a month with a group of his Ryder Cup colleagues chasing him all the way

In 1987, 1989 and 1991, the Trophée Lancôme occurred the week before the Ryder Cup. It happened again this year, thus enhancing the appeal of the event that has always been held at the Saint-Nom-la-Bretèche course near Versailles.

Not that the tournament needs any enhancing. As one of the oldest on the Volvo Tour, it has a distinctive image generated in part by its eye-catching posters, its striking trophy of a torso, and the presence at the presentation of Isabella Rossellini, who is whisked in and out by helicopter.

Inevitably, though, much attention was paid to the players' form on the eve of the Ryder Cup by Johnnie Walker and it looked encouraging for Europe when Ian Woosnam won his second tournament within one month (he had not finished worse that sixth in his five previous events in Europe) and was chased home by a posse of his Ryder Cup colleagues.

Woosnam started with a crisp, six-under-par 64 and took a one-stroke lead. Gavin Christie, his new coach, had helped him hit the ball more penetratively, which gave him extra distance.

There was another reason, though. Since July Woosnam had been working with Dr John Allsopp, the sports psychologist whose other notable clients were Peter Baker (two tournament victories and a joint second place since the end of May) and Gordon Brand Junior, the winner of the GA European Open the previous week.

'I always thought I was mentally strong,' Woosnam said. 'The trouble was that one day I was so good, the next so bad. My confidence fell.' Never was a truer word spoken. Dominant in 1987 when he won the Order of Merit and seven events around the world and was world number one and US Masters champion in 1991, he fluctuated wildly in between. One minute he was at his wits' end about his putting, the next he was bubbly and eager for the fray.

'People who don't know anything about golf were giving me advice. That was happening all the time. I didn't think these sort of things were affecting me but John says they were. He has showed me how to work them out.'

Woosnam was overtaken by Mark James in the second round, another balmy day when most of Paris, dressed up to the neufs, was there. The scoring was as good as the weather – half the field scored par or better. Only three of the nine competing Ryder Cup men were over par. Costantino Rocca had a 71, and José Maria Olazabal and Colin Montgomerie both took 72s.

James, Woosnam's Ryder Cup teammate, added a 66 to his 65. He was one ahead of David Feherty, who having missed selection for the team, was anxious to finish as high as possible to get into the US Tour's final qualifying school where he hoped to win a card to play there next year. Peter Baker, about to make his debut at The Belfry, moved smoothly into joint third place with Peter Mitchell on 133.

Woosnam moved up a gear on

Left, Fred Couples was overshadowed

by Ian Woosnam, below, who wielded

a big stick.

Saturday, going round in 68. David Gilford, 63, José Rivero, 66, and Torrance, 68, all joined him on eight under par. However, they all trailed Fred Couples by two strokes and Feherty by one. No one actually said as much but everyone knew it would look bad if Couples, the only American Ryder Cup player in the field, were to win the tournament ahead of nine European Ryder Cup players.

It did not happen. Couples could do no better than a 71. Torrance led by two strokes with five holes remaining. As the pressure increased, Torrance made a couple of errors that he might not have made had he been fully match fit. It was his first tournament since recovering from injuring his sternum when sleepwalking the previous month. Torrance hooked his drive on the 14th for his first bogey of the

day and bogeyed the 15th as well. Woosnam, who had done no more than par both these holes, was now level.

On the 17th Torrance hit his drive a shade to the left and bogeyed the hole whereas Woosnam, after a better tee shot, flicked a nine iron to within a few feet of the cup and birdied it. The two-stroke swing was the margin of Woosnam's victory. He finished on 13 under par after a closing round of 65 and a total of 267.

The tournament had begun in doleful weather amid protests by French farmers who were beefing about EC regulations. Their notes of complaint were matched by José Maria Olazabal after rounds of 71, 72, 70 and 73, six over par. He was clearly at war with himself and suggested that if his form did not pick up in practice

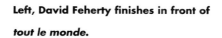

Left, David Feherty finishes in front of

tout le monde.

Below, joint third place finish for

Mark James.

the following week, Bernhard Gallacher should consider dropping him from the first two days of the Ryder Cup.

Four other members of Gallacher's team at The Belfry – Torrance, James, Lane and Nick Faldo – finished within four strokes of Woosnam, Faldo birdieing five of his last seven holes. They left Paris to make their way to Sutton Coldfield with optimism in their hearts.

Above, stars at the Lancôme, Ian Woosnam and Isabella Rossellini. Below, Sam Torrance let it go on the 71st.

POS	NAME	CTY	1	2	3	4	TOTAL	PRIZE MONEY
COURSE: ST NOM LA BRÉTECHE, PARIS					YARDAGE: 6756			PAR: 70
1	Ian WOOSNAM	Wal	64	70	68	65	267	£91500
2	Sam TORRANCE	Scot	69	65	68	67	269	61000
3	Barry LANE	Eng	71	66	66	67	270	28600
	Mark JAMES	Eng	65	66	72	67	270	28600
	David FEHERTY	N.Ire	69	63	69	69	270	28600
6	Fred COUPLES	USA	70	65	65	71	271	18000
	Nick FALDO	Eng	69	67	69	66	271	18000
8	Mark ROE	Eng	68	70	68	67	273	13750
9	José RIVERO	Sp	70	66	66	72	274	12250
10	Jesper PARNEVIK	Swe	71	67	70	68	276	10116
	Peter BAKER	Eng	66	67	73	70	276	10116
	David GILFORD	Eng	74	65	63	74	276	10116
13	Stephen AMES	T&T	72	68	68	69	277	8750
14	Peter FOWLER	Aus	72	69	68	69	278	8100
	Colin MONTGOMERIE	Scot	67	72	68	71	278	8100
16	Jamie SPENCE	Eng	72	71	68	68	279	7243
	Gordon BRAND Jnr	Scot	71	70	70	68	279	7243
	Darren CLARKE	N.Ire	71	71	66	71	279	7243
19	Gary ORR	Scot	72	74	69	65	280	6155
	Ronan RAFFERTY	N.Ire	69	69	73	69	280	6155
	Howard CLARK	Eng	67	70	71	72	280	6155
	Steven RICHARDSON	Eng	72	66	70	72	280	6155
	Miguel Angel JIMENEZ	Sp	65	76	70	69	280	6155
	Paul WAY	Eng	68	70	69	73	280	6155
	Peter MITCHELL	Eng	67	66	75	72	280	6155
26	Retief GOOSEN	SA	68	70	73	70	281	5252
	Roger CHAPMAN	Eng	70	70	70	71	281	5252
	Costantino ROCCA	It	70	71	72	68	281	5252
	Tony JOHNSTONE	Zim	73	67	72	69	281	5252
30	Rodger DAVIS	Aus	73	73	69	67	282	4810
	Steen TINNING	Den	73	68	70	71	282	4810
	Eduardo ROMERO	Arg	71	74	64	73	282	4810
33	De Wet BASSON	SA	73	68	71	71	283	4510
	Andrew SHERBORNE	Eng	73	73	70	67	283	4510
35	Paul BROADHURST	Eng	70	70	71	73	284	4270
	Per-Ulrik JOHANSSON	Swe	77	69	70	68	284	4270
37	Greg TURNER	NZ	72	74	70	70	286	3730
	Frank NOBILO	NZ	68	73	71	74	286	3730
	Mats LANNER	Swe	74	72	71	69	286	3730
	Ian PALMER	SA	73	72	70	71	286	3730
	Andrew OLDCORN	Eng	73	68	75	70	286	3730
	José Maria OLAZABAL	Sp	71	72	70	73	286	3730
	Jim PAYNE	Eng	69	76	69	72	286	3730
44	Jorge BERENDT	Arg	72	68	73	74	287	3130
	Peter O'MALLEY	Aus	68	76	74	69	287	3130
	Johan RYSTROM	Swe	71	73	72	71	287	3130
47	Ernie ELS	SA	69	73	74	72	288	2610
	Antoine LEBOUC	Fr	71	74	72	71	288	2610
	José COCERES	Arg	75	79	70	64	288	2610
	Carl MASON	Eng	75	71	70	72	288	2610
	Olle KARLSSON	Swe	72	68	72	76	288	2610
	Gary EVANS	Eng	75	72	71	70	288	2610
53	Jean VAN DE VELDE	Fr	69	72	75	73	289	2130
	Brian MARCHBANK	Scot	72	70	75	72	289	2130
	Paul LAWRIE	Scot	77	72	71	69	289	2130
	Santiago LUNA	Sp	71	73	72	73	289	2130
57	Des SMYTH	Ire	72	73	73	72	290	1950
58	Alberto BINAGHI	It	70	74	76	71	291	1860
	Thomas LEVET	Fr	74	75	71	71	291	1860
60	Jay TOWNSEND	USA	71	72	75	76	294	1770
61	Ove SELLBERG	Swe	80	71	76	73	300	1680
	Marc FARRY	Fr	72	77	77	74	300	1680
63	Gordon J BRAND	Eng	75	78	79	76	308	1600
64	Phillip PRICE	Wal	75	76	W/D		151	1500
	Vijay SINGH	Fij	73	75	W/D		148	1500
	Wayne WESTNER	SA	77	W/D				1500

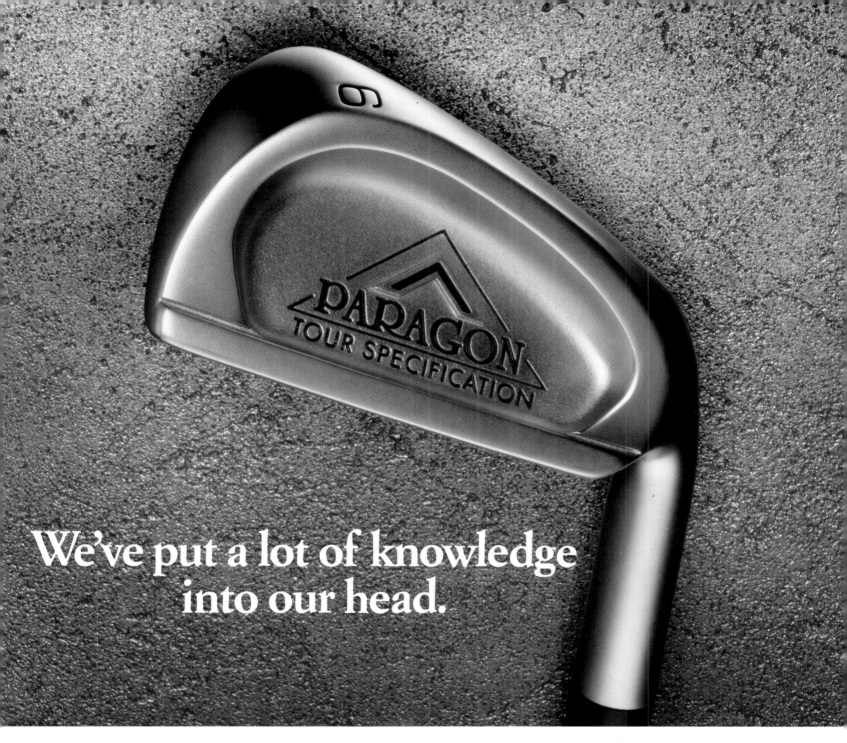

We've put a lot of knowledge into our head.

Introducing our new revolutionary game improvement club. The Paragon – for golfers of all handicaps.

Never before has so much knowledge been put into a golf club. Knowledge which comes from our unique position on the PGA European Tour, with our official mobile workshop for the professionals.

The world's finest craftsmen, together with the top tour players, have developed Paragon's unique design, with its eye-catching nickel cobalt chrome finish.

> "A big divot is a waste of energy. The perfect iron would help re-channel all that energy into the ball."
>
> ———— SANDY LYLE

The principal feature of this design is that the angle of the sole becomes more rounded as the irons get shorter.

This enables you to make a sweeter contact, striking the ball first, divot second. Squeezing the ball from the turf in this way minimises energy loss.

Paragon also boasts a larger sweet spot, a recognised feature of cavity back clubs.

The Dynaflex Light CT40 shaft is the first of its kind with a high kick point and a high launch angle, whilst the Lamkin Perma-tac grip ensures an excellent performance in even

the worst of conditions. We think Paragon, also available with titanium face inserts and a choice of alternative shafts, is the most exciting development in game improvement clubs.

Now the knowledge in our head is in your hands.

WHEN GOLF GETS SERIOUS

For further information, please return this coupon to Mizuno (UK) Limited, Mizuno House, 612 Reading Road, Winnersh, Wokingham, Berks RG11 5HE.

NAME

ADDRESS

POSTCODE

HANDICAP   VOLVO

AMERICA TAKES A BOW IN THE ULTIMATE AMPHITHEATRE

In its brief history of time, the 18th at The Belfry has accumulated enough drama to make it the ultimate amphitheatre in golf. When the stands are packed and the issue is in doubt, there is no finer arena for triumph and tragedy to be enacted.

The 1993 Ryder Cup by Johnnie Walker saw the 18th again provide the setting for a rousing finish of three days of golf in which the nerve and skill of 24 players was tested to new limits. The record books will show that the 30th staging of the encounter resulted in victory for America over Europe by 15 points to 13 but that prosaic statistic cannot convey the standard this contest set to the rest of the sporting world.

For several months before the match, the two captains, Bernard Gallacher and Tom Watson, had embarked on an extensive PR campaign to take the nationalistic sting out of the Ryder Cup. Aware of the excesses of 1991, they took pains to defuse any potential explosive areas and their constant message that the spirit of the game must be upheld struck home in the hearts and minds of the people.

They don't come any better than this. From the moment Corey Pavin struck the opening tee shot at 10.30am on a misty Midlands morning, the galleries responded and revelled in a display of golf hitherto unseen on these shores.

The reason for that late start on the first day was because thick fog reduced visibility to just a few yards. When the fog lifted, the first set of foursomes were due to go out thus: Pavin and Lanny Wadkins

Once again the 18th at The Belfry was the setting for unparalleled drama as America triumphed in the Ryder Cup by Johnnie Walker

against Sam Torrance and Mark James; Paul Azinger and Payne Stewart against Ian Woosnam and Bernhard Langer; Tom Kite and Davis Love against Severiano Ballesteros and José Maria Olazabal; and Ray Floyd and Fred Couples against Nick Faldo and Colin Montgomerie.

The European foursomes record is strangely inconsistent and under the present format, established in 1979, they have yet to win the first day set.

They didn't improve on that this time but still made a pretty good fist of things. The top game saw Pavin and Wadkins in reasonable form and Torrance and James not. The Europeans lost five holes in a row from the eighth, four of them to pars and that was that as the Americans won 4 & 3. The situation was reversed in the second match with two of America's big guns muffled by their inability to gel and Woosnam and Langer's brilliance. Three opening bogeys by Azinger and Stewart put them on the back foot and although Stewart holed a full wedge shot at the fourth for an eagle, further birdies at the fifth and seventh from the Europeans put them five up at the turn and beyond reach.

In the bottom game, Faldo and Montgomerie took an early grip on Floyd and Couples. Montgomerie's chip in for a birdie on the eighth followed by a missed short putt from Floyd on the ninth put the Europeans three up and steady play thereafter clinched the point.

It was the third game which provided the upset. Ballesteros and Olazabal, unbeaten in foursomes since they came together in 1987, were always up against it with Kite and Love. The Europeans trailed from the second and despite some outstanding figures from the Americans, remained only one down at the turn. The turning point came at the 10th where Kite struck a sumptuous shot over the water to within a few feet of the pin after Ballesteros had laid up. The Europeans made a birdie but the

Tom Kite moves off as Jose Maria Olazabal and Joakim Haeggman celebrate winning the tenth.

Americans made an eagle and their two up margin was preserved until the 17th.

So with honours even it was time for some blooding in the afternoon four-balls. In came Peter Baker with Ian Woosnam, Barry Lane with Bernhard Langer, and in came Jim Gallagher and Lee Janzen for America. Love, who had been blooded with Kite in the morning, stayed with the senior man and they again faced the Spanish duo in the final game.

Woosnam and Baker took on the rookies, Gallagher and Janzen, and what a battle they had. There was never more than a hole in it and it was Baker who did the damage, holing outrageously for a two on the 14th to go one up and then clinching the match with a four iron to the final green and a putt from 25 feet. It was Baker's fifth birdie on the day to Woosnam's one.

Lane and Langer faced a blistering attack from Pavin and Wadkins and eventually succumbed while Ballesteros and

Severiano Ballesteros in positive frame of mind.

Flat out finish as Corey Pavin misses a putt.

Peter Baker charges home a putt on the 10th as Barry Lane watches.

Paul Azinger salutes his final green birdie to halve with Nick Faldo.

Olazabal were back to their imperious best in their 11-under par destruction of Kite and Love.

It was the Faldo/Montgomerie versus Azinger/Couples game which was the real humdinger. The Europeans were behind on four different occasions but hung on. Faldo was a giant, birdieing the 13th, 14th and 15th to keep in the game – his chip in on the 14th being a real life-saver as Azinger had already holed for a birdie. Because of the late start, the light was fading fast but through the gathering gloom strode Faldo to birdie the 17th and draw level again. It was now virtually dark and it was decided that the four players would have to return at 8am the following morning to play the final hole.

This is execution hour and all four men must have felt like death when they turned up on a chilly morning to complete matters. Couples drowned his ball from the tee, Montgomerie did likewise with his second shot. Faldo hit the green but his ball ran back down the slope, a tier too short. Azinger thumped an eight iron to 15 feet. Faldo putted up but the ball crept to a standstill some 12 feet short of the hole. Azinger lagged up safely for a par leaving Faldo with his putt for the half. Not for nothing is Faldo rated the best player in the world for with a sure, measured stroke he delivered the ball into the heart of the hole. The crowd, and there were plenty of them even at that ungodly hour, went berserk. It was wonderful stuff, the essence of the Ryder Cup encapsulated in that one moment.

Now enjoying a one point lead, the Europeans went out for the second day

Packed crowds watch as Olazabal drives from the 17th.

foursomes in buoyant mood. Faldo and Montgomerie again did their stuff and put a stop to the Pavin/Wadkins bandwagon. Langer and Woosnam were equally effective against Couples and Azinger and Ballesteros and Olazabal gained further revenge on Kite and Love. Only Baker and Lane went down, losing to Floyd and Stewart.

Lunching on a three-point lead should have put the Europeans in a confident frame of mind for the afternoon four-balls but then things started to go wrong. Faldo and Montgomerie suddenly found that could not buy a putt and went down on the final green to Chip Beck and John Cook, the latter making their first outing.

Mark James was brought back to pair up with Costantino Rocca but they ran into Pavin. The Europeans were one under par after six holes and four down as the slim American with the Charlie Chaplin looks rattled in the putts and then on the fifth holed his second shot with a nine iron just when the Europeans looked like they might get one back. There was no further response from James or Rocca and they went quietly.

In the third game, Baker again showed why he was the 'find' of the European team. Partnering Woosnam against Couples and Azinger, Baker fully lived up to all that had been expected of him. Having collected five birdies in his first four-ball outing over 18 holes, this time he racked up six in just 13 holes with putts ranging from between ten and 35 feet. The Americans reeled under this onslaught and were beaten 6 & 5.

The final game saw José Maria Olazabal make his fourth appearance in two days but this time he was without Ballesteros who had asked to be rested because of his poor form. Into the breach stepped Joakim Haeggman to line up against Stewart and Floyd. Four down after six holes, the Europeans seemed to be sunk. Still three down with four to play, the Europeans looked certain to win the 15th when Floyd missed from a few feet to halve Haeggman's birdie. Stewart had hit the green on this par five in two but his first putt from miles away had finished 30 feet short. He then holed to preserve the

American lead. On the 16th, Olazabal holed from a bunker to take the match on to the 17th and here both Europeans were close with their third shots but again Stewart provided the heartbreak when he holed from further away for a birdie and the match by 2 & 1.

The margin was now only one point and the Americans had their tails up for the final series of 12 singles. Actually, it turned out to be only 11, as for the second Ryder Cup running, injury caused the envelope system to be used. This time it was Torrance who had to withdraw due to an infected toe and his name was matched with Wadkins.

Fortunes fluctuated dramatically on that final afternoon. At one stage, Europe were ahead on the first five games but then gradually the balance swung towards America. In the top game, Couples fought back from a two-hole deficit against Woosnam and in the end

The 17th and 18th acted as a magnet for the crowds.

the Welshman had to hole a terrifying putt of four feet on the final green to halve. Lane was three up with five to play against Beck but then lost three holes in a row from the 14th and reached the 18th all square. Here, Lane drove too straight into the bunker, had to go for the green and put his second in the water. Beck's cast iron four gave him the match by one hole.

The next three games all went Europe's way. Montgomerie accounted for Janzen in a thoroughly sporting contest; Baker out-putted the arch-putter Pavin for a two up victory and Haeggman beat Cook on the 18th after the American found water with his second shot from the same bunker

Faldo kept a close watch on Azinger during the first day four-balls.

Ray Floyd showed that age is no handicap.

Singles success for Sweden's Haeggman.

Above right, Baker's moment of glory as he beats Pavin on the last green.

that had trapped Lane.

James was always trailing Stewart and so the game between Rocca and Love became crucial. Rocca came to the 17th one up and had a putt of some twenty feet to win the hole and the match. It was a lightning fast putt and he ran it four feet past the cup, missed the return and the match was all square. Davis drove long and in perfect position on the last, Rocca drove too straight and finished in heavy rough. From there he did well to get the ball over the water to the front of the

green. Love's second pitched short of the pin and ran back down the hill to finish some 30 feet away. Rocca's chip was strong and ran 12 feet above the hole. Love's first putt was eight feet short and when Rocca missed Love had his putt for

American captain Tom Watson is swamped by the press after victory.

the win. To his eternal credit he holed it and that was another point snatched back.

At the back of the field however, the engine room of the European team was spluttering. Ballesteros' poor form was still with him and having gone out in 42 against Gallagher, faced a hopeless task. Floyd always had the measure of Olazabal and Kite was in impregnable form against Langer.

In the final game, Faldo continued his superhuman feats against Azinger but the American refused to wilt. Even when Faldo holed in one at the 14th, the second time this had been done in the Ryder Cup, it only gave him a one up lead which Azinger immediately clawed back with a birdie at the next. Faldo birdied the 17th to go one up again and so to the 18th.

By this time the Americans had retained the Cup but for Faldo and Azinger, pride and reputation was still at stake. Both players hit the green and it was Azinger who holed for a birdie and a half to provide a fitting climax.

Altogether, eight of the 11 games came down the final fairway to enter that ultimate amphitheatre. Some rose to the occasion, other found the experience overwhelming but all of them contributed magnificently to a great moment in sport.

As American captain, Tom Watson received the Ryder Cup from HRH The Duke of York, the applause for him and his team was genuine in its appreciation. The Ryder Cup will continue to be sponsored by Johnnie Walker up to and including the 1997 match in Spain, therefore it will not return to Britain until 2001 at the earliest.

In the meantime, the 18th at The Belfry will have to return to the more mundane business of dealing with the thousands of ordinary golfers who will play it, most of them imagining that they too are part of the enduring tradition of the Ryder Cup. And in a way they are, for the challenge remains eternal.

Left, Colin Montgomerie lets his emotions run free. Far left, Davis Love and Tom Kite enjoyed a successful first morning partnership.

The European team and caddies.

INDIVIDUAL RECORDS

EUROPE

	P	W	H	L
Woosnam	5	4	1	0
Montgomerie	5	3	1	1
Baker	4	3	0	1
Faldo	5	2	2	1
Langer	4	2	0	2
Ballesteros	4	2	0	2
Olazabal	5	2	0	3
Haeggman	2	1	0	1
Rocca	2	0	0	2
Lane	3	0	0	3
James	3	0	0	3
Torrance	1	0	1	1

UNITED STATES

	P	W	H	L
Floyd	4	3	0	1
Stewart	4	3	0	1
Pavin	5	3	0	2
Beck	2	2	0	0
Wadkins	3	2	1	1
Gallagher	3	2	0	1
Kite	4	2	0	2
Love	4	2	0	2
Cook	2	1	0	1
Azinger	5	0	2	3
Couples	5	0	2	3
Janzen	2	0	0	2

The victorious American team.

COURSE: BRABAZON COURSE, THE BELFRY			YARDAGE: 7182	PAR: 72	

FIRST DAY FOURSOMES: MORNING

EUROPE	RESULT	USA	SCORE	EUROPE	USA
S Torrance M James	Lost to	L Wadkins C Pavin	(4 & 3)	0	1
I Woosnam B Langer	Beat	P Azinger P Stewart	(7 & 5)	1	0
S Ballesteros J M Olazabal	Lost to	T Kite & D Love III	(2 & 1)	0	1
N Faldo & C Montgomerie	Beat	R Floyd & F Couples	(4 & 3)	1	0
				2	2

FIRST DAY FOURBALLS: AFTERNOON

EUROPE	RESULT	USA	SCORE	EUROPE	USA
I Woosnam & P Baker	Beat	J Gallagher Jnr L Janzen	1 Hole	1	0
B Langer B Lane	Lost to	L Wadkins & C Pavin	4 & 2	0	1
N Faldo C Montgomerie	Halved with	P Azinger F Couples		½	½
S Ballesteros J M Olazabal	Beat	D Love III T Kite	4 & 3	1	0
				2½	1½

SECOND DAY FOURSOMES: MORNING

EUROPE	RESULT	USA	SCORE	EUROPE	USA
N Faldo C Montgomerie	Beat	L Wadkins C Pavin	3 & 2	1	0
B Langer I Woosnam	Beat	F Couples P Azinger	2 & 1	1	0
P Baker B Lane	Lost to	R Floyd P Stewart	3 & 2	0	1
S Ballesteros J M Olazabal	Beat	D Love III T Kite	2 & 1	1	0
				3	1

SECOND DAY FOURBALLS: AFTERNOON

EUROPE	RESULT	USA	SCORE	EUROPE	USA
N Faldo C Montgomerie	Lost to	J Cook C Beck	2 holes	0	1
M James C Rocca	Lost to	C Pavin J Gallagher Jnr	5 & 4	0	1
I Woosnam P Baker	Beat	F Couples P Azinger	6 & 5	1	0
J M Olazabal J Haeggman	Lost to	R Floyd P Steward	2 & 1	0	1
				1	3

FINAL DAY SINGLES

EUROPE	RESULT	USA	SCORE	EUROPE	USA
I Woosnam	Halved with	F Couples		½	½
B Lane	Lost to	C Beck	1 Hole	0	1
C Montgomerie	Beat	L Janzen	1 Hole	1	0
P Baker	Beat	C Pavin	2 Holes	1	0
J Haeggman	Beat	J Cook	1 Hole	1	0
M James	Lost to	P Stewart	3 & 2	0	1
C Rocca	Lost to	D Love III	1 Hole	0	1
S Ballesteros	Lost to	J Gallagher Jnr	3 & 2	0	1
J M Olazabal	Lost to	R Floyd	2 Holes	0	1
B Langer	Lost to	T Kite	5 & 3	0	1
N Faldo	Halved with	P Azinger		½	½
S Torrance*	Halved with	L Wadkins		½	½
				4½	8½
				13	**15**

*Torrance withdrawn injured

Savour that wonderfully warm glow as a Johnnie Walker Black Label goes down in **O**ne

RICHARDSON TAKES A RIDE TO THE TOP

It's been a rollercoaster career for Steven Richardson so far. Just pipped for Rookie of the Year honours in 1990, he won twice early in 1991. He would finish his second year on the Volvo Tour second behind none other than Severiano Ballesteros in the Volvo Order of Merit and make his Ryder Cup debut at Kiawah Island. A star in the ascendance.

But come the latest re-make of the transatlantic classic, Richardson was not in the cast. Ryder-less, he was instead on the rides. The rollercoaster career was continuing, not under the unbearable pressure of singles (and foursomes and four-balls) armed action at The Belfry, but on the Corkscrew, Wild Beast, Black Hole and Loop-the-loop of Alton Towers theme park. Stars before the eyes, more like.

'In some ways you're glad not to be at the Ryder Cup because there is so much pressure,' Richardson said. 'But when we drove past and saw the queues for the first day's play,' he added, 'I missed not being there.'

That Richardson had taken five days off with his girlfriend Helen is remarkable enough. Having a weekend off when missing the cut is usually the longest he spends away from the Tour. So far in 1993 he had played in 30 out of 34

A visit to Alton Towers during Ryder Cup week allowed Steven Richardson to return refreshed for victory in Stuttgart

events, but he intends to take more regular weeks off next year after winning the Mercedes German Masters in Stuttgart.

Rested and relaxed, which could not be said for those returning from Ryder combat (including Americans Chip Beck, Tom Kite and their captain Tom Watson), Richardson shot rounds of 67, 66 to lead at halfway, then 70, 68 to take his third Volvo Tour title. Robert Karlsson, the tall Swede, trailed in two shots behind with

Beck one shot further back.

It was the 27-year old Hampshire's man first win for two-and-half years. In the meantime he seems to have been re-learning to cope with pressure — something which seemed to come so naturally when he won the 1989 English Amateur title and during his early Tour successes.

'I was getting desperate,' Richardson said. 'I got to the stage where I didn't think I was going to do well under pressure. I was reacting badly to good situations. My dad, John [the pro at Lee-on-the-Solent where the son learnt his golf], told me to just go out and try and enjoy myself. But is is easy to say, hard to do. For the first two days I was really relaxed, but I got nervous over the weekend.'

Summer had turned to autumn at the Stuttgarter Golf Club but the only Frost in the air was the South African David, hot-foot from back-to-back wins on the US Tour, who led the first round with a 66 thanks to a 1am transatlantic call to his coach David Leadbetter.

The course could have been made for Richardson's game. The autumn colours of the leaves made a pleasant backdrop, far enough removed from the fairways to allow him to unleash his 280-yard plus drives. 'You can give it a good whack off the tee.' as Richardson said.

His halfway lead was threatened by

Beck who turned in a nine-under-par 63 on Friday, one outside Ian Woosnam's course record. Since preferred lies were in operation all week, it wouldn't have counted anyway. Beck won the two matches he played at The Belfry after altering his posture – Richardson had been struggling with a problem of a similar nature until recently – and was still raring to go. Bernhard Langer put in a second day 64 after a quick session with his mentor Willi Hoffman the night before to put him back where his home supporters expect to see him.

Langer had been drawn with Watson and Costantino Rocca for the first two days, but coincidental scores brought a re-match with Tom Kite on Saturday. Kite had won their vital singles the weekend before 5 & 3, but Langer got revenge with a 2 & 1 win. Not that it mattered. 'I wasn't thinking matchplay,' he said. 'I just played better. We chatted a little but it was difficult with the rain; we were trying to keep everything dry.'

It pelted down all afternoon and the greens on the seventh and 15th were beginning to look like Scottish lochs rather than the German versions, but the squeegee men kept play going. Richardson, waterprooftop-less, was not fussed. Not even after a double-bogey at the fourth which let Beck into the lead. He birdied the 12th and 13th and 14th and the 18th from no more than four feet to lead Beck by one. 'I don't think I have ever hit it closer,' he said, nominating the inward half as his best ever nine holes.

On Sunday he simply had to hold off the tenacious Beck and Langer, wearing his famous red trousers. As it turned out the worst thing he had was his name being transposed to Richard Stevenson in the local paper. He birdied two of the first three holes, while Beck bogeyed the first to allow Richardson to lead by four. A couple of bogeys were repaired by an eagle at the long seventh, where he holed from 40 feet, one of four putts over 15 feet that day. One bogey and eight solid pars saw him home comfortably.

Karlsson, swing surgery explaining his quiet year after two seconds in 1992, was charging round with a 66 but couldn't get close enough. On day one his approach to the 12th had hit the cup and spun back into the water – from a two to a six. What would he have given for those shots on Sunday?

Richardson, meanwhile, had been hoping to take eight weeks off over the winter but now would have to put those plans on hold. The win meant a trip to the Johnnie Walker World Championship in Jamaica just before Christmas. 'I will have to put in some practice,' he promised.

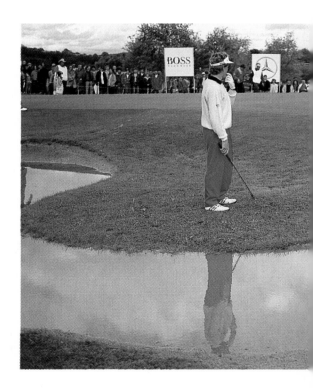

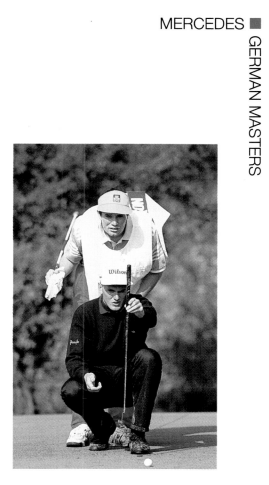

Above, Robert Karlsson revelled in the conditions and, below, his eventual runner-up spot was witnessed by Tom Watson.

Chip Beck's second round 63 was the lowest of the week.

Richardson took everything in his stride.

								PRIZE
POS	NAME	CTY	1	2	3	4	TOTAL	MONEY
1	Steven RICHARDSON	Eng	67	66	70	68	271	£100000
2	Robert KARLSSON	Swe	68	69	70	66	273	66660
3	Chip BECK	USA	72	63	69	70	274	37560
4	Bernhard LANGER	Ger	73	64	70	69	276	27700
	Jesper PARNEVIK	Swe	70	72	68	66	276	27700
6	José Maria OLAZABAL	Sp	69	69	72	67	277	21000
7	Tom WATSON	USA	74	67	69	68	278	16500
	David FROST	SA	66	70	71	71	278	16500
9	Frank NOBILO	NZ	68	71	71	69	279	13440
10	Glen DAY	USA	69	71	70	70	280	10740
	Russell CLAYDON	Eng	68	72	71	69	280	10740
	Sandy LYLE	Scot	73	70	73	64	280	10740
	Ernie ELS	SA	67	73	69	71	280	10740
14	Per-Ulrik JOHANSSON	Swe	70	71	73	67	281	8820
	Costantino ROCCA	It	72	73	69	67	281	8820
	Mark ROE	Eng	68	74	71	68	281	8820
17	Andrew OLDCORN	Eng	70	74	70	68	282	7620
	Phillip PRICE	Wal	71	73	69	69	282	7620
	Robert ALLENBY	Aus	71	74	69	68	282	7620
	Tom KITE	USA	71	67	73	71	282	7620
21	Gary ORR	Scot	71	72	69	71	283	6840
	Andrew SHERBORNE	Eng	70	68	76	69	283	6840
	Seve BALLESTEROS	Sp	70	73	71	69	283	6840
24	Miguel Angel JIMENEZ	Sp	68	73	70	74	285	5940
	Jim PAYNE	Eng	72	71	72	70	285	5940
	Rodger DAVIS	Aus	68	75	70	72	285	5940
	Mark DAVIS	Eng	71	69	72	73	285	5940
	Jeff HAWKES	SA	71	72	68	74	285	5940
	Gary EVANS	Eng	72	70	76	67	285	5940
	Paul CURRY	Eng	76	69	69	71	285	5940
31	José RIVERO	Sp	70	71	75	70	286	4808
	Glenn RALPH	Eng	74	71	69	72	286	4808
	Miguel Angel MARTIN	Sp	68	75	73	70	286	4808
	Mark McNULTY	Zim	71	70	73	72	286	4808
	Alexander CEJKA	Ger	72	73	73	68	286	4808
	Manny ZERMAN	It	72	72	69	73	286	4808
	Wayne WESTNER	SA	68	72	74	72	286	4808
38	Mats HALLBERG	Swe	68	76	76	67	287	4020
	Jay TOWNSEND	USA	70	71	73	73	287	4020
	Philip WALTON	Ire	70	71	74	72	287	4020
	Jean VAN DE VELDE	Fr	70	72	77	68	287	4020
	Manuel PINERO	Sp	69	75	70	73	287	4020
	Barry LANE	Eng	73	71	72	71	287	4020
44	Olle KARLSSON	Swe	71	67	76	74	288	3420
	Ian PALMER	SA	75	68	73	72	288	3420
	Martin POXON	Eng	71	73	70	74	288	3420
	Magnus SUNESSON	Swe	73	72	73	70	288	3420
48	Silvio GRAPPASONNI	It	73	70	73	73	289	2820
	Andrew MURRAY	Eng	71	67	76	75	289	2820
	Fredrik LINDGREN	Swe	71	70	73	75	289	2820
	Peter O'MALLEY	Aus	73	72	70	74	289	2820
	Sven STRUVER	Ger	70	70	74	75	289	2820
	Johan RYSTROM	Swe	71	74	74	70	289	2820
54	David FEHERTY	N.Ire	69	71	75	75	290	2280
	Stephen McALLISTER	Scot	70	74	74	72	290	2280
	Mats LANNER	Swe	71	72	74	73	290	2280
57	Vijay SINGH	Fij	71	71	76	73	291	1980
	Mike McLEAN	Eng	75	71	73	72	291	1980
59	Gordon BRAND Jnr	Scot	69	74	75	74	292	1800
	Jamie SPENCE	Eng	69	70	77	76	292	1800
	Stephen FIELD	Eng	73	73	77	69	292	1800
62	José Manuel CARRILES	Sp	73	73	74	73	293	1650
	Mark MOULAND	Wal	71	71	76	75	293	1650
64	Gordon J BRAND	Eng	70	75	77	72	294	1530
	Torsten GIEDEON	Ger	73	73	75	73	294	1530
66	Marc FARRY	Fr	73	73	76	73	295	899
	Danny MIJOVIC	Can	72	70	75	78	295	899

COURSE: MONSHEIM, STUTTGART   **YARDAGE: 6839**   **PAR: 72**

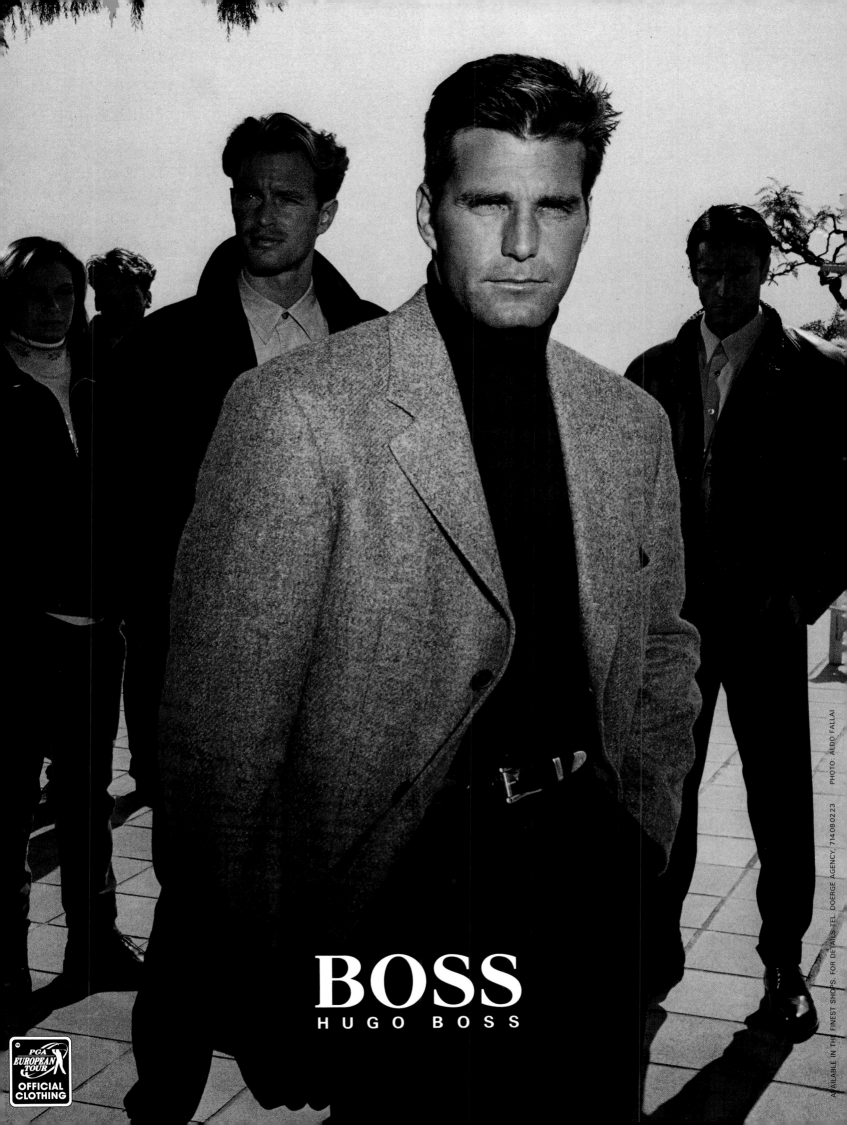

BOSS

HUGO BOSS

CLARKE SPIKES THE BIG GUNS

Jack Nicklaus was an inspiration to the young Nick Faldo whose appetite for golf was whetted when he watched a telecast of the US Masters from Augusta and televised golf was also where Darren Clarke got his early inspiration.

In the case of the 25-year old from Bushmills near Dungannon in County Antrim, a village which, until now, has been noted internationally for having the oldest distillery in the world, the star who gave Clarke all his early incentive to stick at golf was Severiano Ballesteros.

In the Alfred Dunhill Open, which incorporates the long established Belgian Open, Clarke became the ninth first-time winner of the season and, ironically, foiled his idol Ballesteros' bid on this occasion to extend his winning run in Europe by a further year.

At Royal Zoute, Clarke, who as a plus four amateur won everything there was to win in Ireland, not only played the last two rounds with Seve, he also outscored him using the graphite-shafted clubs he had switched to earlier in the year to protect an injured wrist. The graphite cushions the impact when the club hits the ground.

Seve led by four shots at halfway, playing with all his old flair and confidence. After opening rounds of 67 and 65 he had a comfortable cushion over a chasing group of golfers including Clarke, Bernhard Langer who equalled the record of 64 on the second day, and Nick Faldo.

The Royal Zoute course, designed

Darren Clarke held off the might of the Volvo Tour to become the ninth first-time winner of the season

by Harry Colt, who also gave us Wentworth's famous West course, Moor Park and Sunningdale New to name just three, always brings out the best in the best.

In such a strong field the likelihood was that one of the big names would land the £100,000 first prize and the favourite, as always, was Faldo, determined to erase the memory of his 42 home in the last round the previous year when he lost to Miguel Angel Jiminez of Spain. Clarke, a 16-stone trencherman

who, in fairness, is making a big effort to take off weight, was a somewhat generous 66-1 before the start with William Hill, the Tour's official bookmaker.

His odds reflected the fact that the best he had done in three years was second in the 1992 Honda Open but the bookmaker's assessment of the big-hitter's chances in such a strong field did not accurately take into account that in four of his previous six outings he had finished fourth twice, sixth and eighth.

That kind of form earlier in the year would have helped him make the Irish side for the Alfred Dunhill Cup and maybe even the Irish side for the Heineken World Cup of Golf. When the season began he was even being talked of as a possible newcomer in the European team for the Ryder Cup by Johnnie Walker, but it was not to be.

Instead he is content to wait in the sure knowledge that he has the ability to fulfil his every dream in golf if he has the desire, the discipline and determination to do so. There is little doubt he has all three qualities plus a wry sense of humour and innate sense of perspective that helps him cope with the many disappointments of professional golf.

He is single-minded. His manager Andrew Chandler, himself a former professional whose own experiences have proved a valuable text book for Clarke, recalled in Belgium how they teamed up. Dougie Heather, an Irish international whose corporate law career makes him a regular contact for young Irish amateurs

Above, Sam Torrance and David Feherty ham it up.

Ian Woosnam's clinical assessment of a rather steep attack from Nick Faldo.

Above, Darren Clarke and Severiano Ballesteros on the ninth green.

turning professional, had phoned Chandler in 1990 suggesting Clarke's potential was such that he could make a real go of it as a professional.

Unlike close friends Eoghan O'Connell and Paul McGinlay, who waited another year before joining the paid ranks in order to play Walker Cup against America's amateurs, Clarke decided he would forego that honour. He would have been a certainty for the team and the temptation to delay making the switch was all the greater because the Walker Cup in 1991 was a certain sell-out at Portmarnock.

Clarke not only gave all that up to turn professional, he also spurned a late advance by the management giant IMG

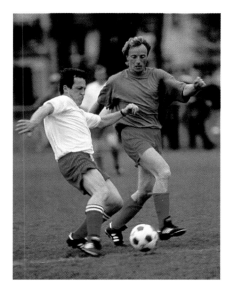

Bernhard Langer probes the defence in the Gatorade soccer match.

headed by Mark McCormock and stuck with the smaller, more personal organisation. Chandler handles all business matters while Bob Torrance is his on-course guru having helped him, in the short space of two months, to make the swing changes in 1991 that turned a loose 'amateur' swing into a solid professional one in which he has total confidence.

Maybe the fact that he was up against so many big names with credentials far greater than his, helped him score his break-through victory. He wanted to win but because he did not expect to do so with so many established winners around he remained relaxed throughout, although the smile was beginning to look a bit strained as he turned into the back nine on the final day and faced up to his greatest challenge yet.

Despite his cast-iron performance on the final day, it could be argued that he won the title on the Saturday when he outshot playing companion Ballesteros by

five shots to move one ahead. Seve had summed up his round that day by saying he had 'survived' but only just as his long game turned cruelly crooked on him. Clarke admitted he had not played well but had been 'saved' by his putter.

On the Sunday, in front of record crowds, Clarke was never headed although Vijay Singh, who shot a record equalling 64 in which he stormed home in 30 with five birdies and an eagle, caught him. Then so did Langer who almost matched his own second round record-equalling 64. On the final day he took 65.

Faldo, desperately unlucky on the greens, never quite drew level, although two closing birdies which tied him with Singh in the clubhouse, one clear of Langer, kept the pressure on Clarke. Gordon Brand Junior and Rodger Davis, his form improved by daily pep talks from graphologist Irve Salburg, acting as lady starter for the week, had their chances

**Ballesteros was up against it on the
17th in the third round.**

too, but Clarke kept his head.

The clincher came at the 15th, a
par-five reduced by 70 yards to give the
players the incentive to go for it. Clarke
missed the green but got up and down
from thick rough lobbing the ball over the
bunker to a pin cut close to it with, it
seemed, all the confidence in the world.

In fact he admitted later he rather
mishit the ball as it lay in the saturated
grass but the result was good and he
made his birdie to move clear on his
own, then rolled in a putt from 12 feet for
a birdie on the 17th that all but settled
the issue.

Seve, destructively wild off the tee was
beaten; Faldo, who should have won in
1992 was relegated to joint runner-up
which was at least two places better than
the year before.

On a week when both Barry Lane and
Ove Sellberg had holes in one, Clarke
was the real ace at Royal Zoute and
everyone back home certainly agreed.
No sooner had he collected the cheque
than the Volvo Tour's newest winner was
on the telephone ordering drinks all round
for the members of his home club.

COURSE: ROYAL ZOUTE, KNOKKE-LE-ZOUTE, BELGIUM YARDAGE: 6882 PAR: 71								
POS	NAME	CTY	1	2	3	4	TOTAL	PRIZE MONEY
1	Darren CLARKE	N.Ire	68	68	66	68	270	£100000
2	Nick FALDO	Eng	68	68	69	67	272	52110
	Vijay SINGH	Fij	68	69	71	64	272	52110
4	Gordon BRAND Jnr	Scot	66	71	68	68	273	23600
	Rodger DAVIS	Aus	74	67	64	68	273	23600
	Bernhard LANGER	Ger	72	64	72	65	273	23600
	Seve BALLESTEROS	Sp	67	65	71	70	273	23600
8	Jean VAN DE VELDE	Fr	70	68	66	70	274	15000
9	Barry LANE	Eng	71	69	69	66	275	13440
10	Eduardo ROMERO	Arg	70	69	69	68	276	11510
	Greg TURNER	NZ	70	68	72	66	276	11510
12	Tom PERNICE	USA	70	66	72	69	277	9706
	David FEHERTY	N.Ire	69	69	69	70	277	9706
	Sam TORRANCE	Scot	71	68	67	71	277	9706
15	Gary EVANS	Eng	68	75	68	67	278	8460
	José COCERES	Arg	70	69	70	69	278	8460
	Costantino ROCCA	It	67	71	71	69	278	8460
18	David FROST	SA	69	68	71	71	279	7248
	José Maria CANIZARES	Sp	68	69	71	71	279	7248
	Magnus SUNESSON	Swe	75	68	70	66	279	7248
	Wayne WESTNER	SA	70	67	71	71	279	7248
	Ian WOOSNAM	Wal	72	70	72	65	279	7248
23	Joakim HAEGGMAN	Swe	72	70	65	73	280	6030
	Vicente FERNANDEZ	Arg	72	72	68	68	280	6030
	Robert KARLSSON	Swe	71	71	67	71	280	6030
	David WILLIAMS	Eng	66	72	71	71	280	6030
	Miguel Angel MARTIN	Sp	69	71	72	68	280	6030
	Paul WAY	Eng	71	72	70	67	280	6030
	Philip WALTON	Ire	73	71	71	65	280	6030
	Ian PALMER	SA	69	70	71	70	280	6030
31	Frank NOBILO	NZ	73	70	71	67	281	4870
	Gordon J BRAND	Eng	69	71	67	74	281	4870
	Tony JOHNSTONE	Zim	72	72	68	69	281	4870
	Roger CHAPMAN	Eng	72	66	75	68	281	4870
	Miguel Angel JIMENEZ	Sp	68	71	70	72	281	4870
	Jay TOWNSEND	USA	76	68	70	67	281	4870
37	Ernie ELS	SA	72	68	72	70	282	4260
	Ronan RAFFERTY	N.Ire	72	67	71	72	282	4260
	Colin MONTGOMERIE	Scot	72	71	67	72	282	4260
	Richard BOXALL	Eng	71	70	71	70	282	4260
41	Peter FOWLER	Aus	72	70	72	69	283	3660
	Sven STRUVER	Ger	68	71	72	72	283	3660
	Peter MITCHELL	Eng	75	67	68	73	283	3660
	Jesper PARNEVIK	Swe	70	70	71	72	283	3660
	Paul LAWRIE	Scot	71	69	71	72	283	3660
	Jeff HAWKES	SA	68	70	73	72	283	3660
47	Howard CLARK	Eng	70	69	69	76	284	3120
	Andrew MURRAY	Eng	72	69	70	73	284	3120
	Anders FORSBRAND	Swe	67	74	72	71	284	3120
50	Carl MASON	Eng	68	73	70	74	285	2760
	Ricky WILLISON	Eng	67	74	71	73	285	2760
	Marc FARRY	Fr	70	71	74	70	285	2760
53	Glen DAY	USA	70	74	70	72	286	2400
	Mark ROE	Eng	71	72	70	73	286	2400
	Paul BROADHURST	Eng	68	72	72	74	286	2400
56	Craig CASSELLS	Eng	74	68	72	73	287	1920
	Juan QUIROS	Sp	72	71	73	71	287	1920
	Martin GATES	Eng	75	69	74	69	287	1920
	Mats LANNER	Swe	70	73	69	75	287	1920
	Justin HOBDAY	SA	69	70	77	71	287	1920
	Mark McNULTY	Zim	71	72	73	71	287	1920
62	José RIVERO	Sp	70	70	76	72	288	1590
	Russell CLAYDON	Eng	72	71	70	75	288	1590
	Stephen FIELD	Eng	71	73	72	72	288	1590
	Derrick COOPER	Eng	74	69	72	73	288	1590
	N. VANHOOTEGEM (AM)	Bel	72	71	74	71	288	–
66	Roger WINCHESTER	Eng	73	69	73	74	289	900
67	Chris MORTON	Eng	67	76	73	74	290	897
	Keith WATERS	Eng	70	71	73	76	290	897
69	Retief GOOSEN	SA	71	73	77	72	293	893
	Boris JANJIC	Aus	70	72	80	71	293	893

We're happy to be way over par.

At Kleinwort Benson Private Bank we consider our service to be more personal than the conventional bank/client relationship.

We make it our priority to meet you face to face so that we can explore your individual circumstances and requirements.

Then we can select from a range of skills and services a package that exactly matches your needs.

If you would like to find out more please talk to Jacqui Brabazon on 071 956 6091.

You may find us a little different from a normal bank, but you'll soon get into the swing of things.

Kleinwort Benson
PRIVATE BANK

Kleinwort Benson Private Bank
PO Box 191 10 Fenchurch Street London EC3M 3LB

UNITED STATES BLOWS
HOT IN THE COLD

Wrapped up in thermals and topped off in bobble hats, a hardy USA trio of Payne Stewart, John Daly and Fred Couples won the Alfred Dunhill Cup over a frostbitten Old Course during a week of icy autumnal glow at St Andrews.

The beauty of this event came in learning to expect the unexpected. Maybe the eventual victors weren't the greatest of surprises, but normality by then was long overdue: Australia had been thumped by Japan and Canada, Nick Faldo had lost to one Chen Liang-Hsi and, worst of all if you were a native, the Scots had gone down to Paraguay in an affair that warranted some inglorious front-page headlines.

If you could have somehow been immunised against cold, St Andrews was a picture of lights and shades to behold. This tournament had a backdrop that could not have been more inspired. 'It's amazing here,' said Faldo. 'I stood on my balcony and watched the sun come up, and it was quite brilliant, I got a real buzz just being here.'

That was earlier in the week. As the days wore on, something just as dramatic as nature arousing itself befell Faldo and quite a few others, before England and the USA beat frosted paths to the final.

John Daly breezed into town, headed straight up for a first day practice, and

Despite freezing conditions, the Alfred Dunhill Cup provided the United States team with a warm glow at St Andrews

promptly dumped his drive off the first into the Swilcan Burn. It was a misleading moment of brashness. As the competition unfolded, Daly developed a velvety feel for every windswept hump and hollow, ending up with four victories from five

matches and becoming a talisman of American success.

The USA teed off with a 3-0 win over Wales, while England saw off Mexico with similar ease. On that gloriously azure Thursday it was the Scots that truly suffered, going down 2-1 to the Paraguayans after Colin Montgomerie witnessed his three-shot advantage with five to play being whittled away by Raul Fretes in the third and decisive match.

When it came down to the final green, Fretes watched his snaking 30 foot putt disappear into the ground before Montgomerie failed to find redemption from 15 feet. Here was a South American, from a land with fewer courses than in St Andrews itself, having boarded three airplanes to come to this place of homage, suddenly sensing something beyond mere sport. 'I've never been a religious man, but right at this moment I feel close to God,' he said with some feeling. Montgomerie uttered some other, less theological remarks.

We thawed out, and wrapped up again for Friday. The USA beat Paraguay to maintain their momentum, while the Scots took out their vengeance with a 3-0 win over Wales. In England's 2-1 defeat of Chinese Team Taipei, however, came the unlikeliest score of the week: Faldo's 72-73 slump to Liang-Hsi. 'I volunteered to play Mr Faldo because it was a once in a lifetime chance to meet the world's number one,' said the Taipei player. 'But I didn't think I had a hope.'

The week froze out a few other expectations. Having lost to Canada, Australia's trio of Craig Parry, Peter Senior and Rodger Davis then went down 2-1 to Japan, with Senior putting together a six-over-par 78 which suggested it would be neither his nor his side's week. Indeed, the Aussies bowed out on Saturday evening without a victory to their name.

Ireland and Sweden emerged as the two others who would contest the semi-finals. In a group of fraught nerves and slightly bemusing arithmetic, the Irish finished ahead of Spain and Zimbabwe in Group One, despite losing their opening matches to the Spaniards, while the Swedes dominated Group Four with straight wins over Canada, Japan and Australia.

The skies remained clear as crystal, the ground hardened up with frost on each new dawn, and by the time the delayed starts and group matches were over in readiness for Sunday morning's semi-finals Freddie Couples had decided this should be a week of all-consuming excellence.

Couples faced Anders Forsbrand, shot

Right, Paraguay's Angel Franco drives from the 12th.

American-style snack for John Daly.

Left, Nick Faldo bathed in

clubhouse glow.

Below, Anders Forsbrand faltered on

the 17th against the USA.

Cold comfort for Peter Baker.

a 67 to the Swede's 69, and completed four wins out of four. It was just as well for Uncle Sam, since Payne Stewart's loss to Jesper Parnevik and John Daly's defeat of Joakim Haeggman meant it all came down to the third match. England's 3-0 defeat of Ireland in the other semi-final promised a mouth-watering showdown.

Even the final twisted all logic and expectation. It hadn't been a great weekend for Mark James, who had shot a 79 against Fulton Allem on Saturday; Payne Stewart, on the other hand, had only lost to Parnevik's brilliant 66. Yet James duly beat Stewart, 70 to 74.

The second of the final matches, between Couples and Faldo, bore every distinction of a classic, pitting Faldo's mechanised brilliance against Couples's

languid talents. The American excelled once more, carrying a two-shot lead from the turn, having it cut to one brilliantly but without consequence by Faldo on the 18th, and completing five memorable rounds of the Old Course in 15-under-par. Couples was unquestionably the player of the tournament.

John Daly's 70 against Peter Baker's 73 ensured that the USA hugged the silver trophy as dusk came down like a blanket around them. So the week finished where it had started: with a bang for Daly, a feast of golf for the spectators, and an icy blast whistling down through the spires of the 'auld grey toon' to remind all of us that this game of golf is first and foremost about an intricate marriage with nature.

FINAL

	USA 2	ENGLAND 1	
Payne Stewart	74	70	Mark James
Fred Couples	68	69	Nick Faldo
John Daly	70	73	Peter Baker

SEMI-FINAL

ENGLAND 3 IRELAND 0

Mark James	67	70	Ronan Rafferty
Peter Baker	72	73	David Feherty
Nick Faldo	70	74	Paul McGinley

USA 2 SWEDEN 1

Payne Stewart	68	66	Jesper Parnevik
John Daly	68	71	Joakim Haeggman
Fred Couples	67	69	Anders Forsbrand

GROUP ONE

	Matches Played	Matches Won	Ind. Games Won
Ireland	3	2	7
Spain	3	2	5
Zimbabwe	3	2	4
Argentina	3	0	2

(Ireland win on individual victories)

DAY 1

IRELAND beat ZIMBABWE 3-0
Ronan Rafferty	74	beat	Tony Johnstone	75
Paul McGinley	74	beat	Mark McNulty	74
David Feherty	71	beat	Nick Price	72

SPAIN beat ARGENTINA 2-1
José-Maria Olazabal	69	beat	José Coceres	72
Miguel Angel Jiménez	78	lost to	Vicente Fernandez	74
José Rivero	73	beat	Eduardo Romero	76

DAY 2

ZIMBABWE beat ARGENTINA 2-1
Nick Price	71	lost to	Eduardo Romero	71
Mark McNulty	69	beat	Vicente Fernandez	74
Tony Johnstone	76	beat	José Coceres	76

SPAIN beat IRELAND 2-1
Miguel Angel Jiménez	74	lost to	David Feherty	72
José Rivero	72	beat	Paul McGinley	73
José Maria Olazabal	71	beat	Ronan Rafferty	74

DAY 3

IRELAND beat ARGENTINA 3-0
Ronan Rafferty	74	beat	José Coceres	77
Paul McGinley	75	beat	Vicente Fernandez	78
David Feherty	72	beat	Eduardo Romero	76

ZIMBABWE beat SPAIN 2-1
Nick Price	77	lost to	José Maria Olazabal	73
Tony Johnstone	74	beat	José Rivero	74
Mark McNulty	76	beat	Miguel Angel Jiménez	77

GROUP TWO

	Matches Played	Matches Won	Ind. Games Won
England	3	2	6
S Africa	3	2	5
Taipei	3	1	4
Mexico	3	1	3

(England win on individual victories)

DAY 1

SOUTH AFRICA beat CHINESE TEAM TAIPEI 2-1
Fulton Allem	71	beat	Chung Chun-Hsing	80
Ernie Els	71	beat	Chen Liang-Hsi	77
David Frost	77	lost to	Yuan Ching-Chi	73

ENGLAND beat MEXICO 3-0
Peter Baker	73	beat	Carlos Espinoza	75
Nick Faldo	72	beat	Rafael Alarcon	75
Mark James	75	beat	Juan Brito	80

DAY 2

MEXICO beat SOUTH AFRICA 2-1
Rafael Alarcon	72	beat	Ernie Els	73
Carlos Espinoza	72	beat	Fulton Allem	72
Juan Brito	75	lost to	David Frost	70

ENGLAND beat CHINESE TEAM TAIPEI 2-1
Peter Baker	71	beat	Yuan Ching-Chi	76
Nick Faldo	73	lost to	Chen Liang-Hsi	72
Mark James	71	beat	Chung Chun-Hsing	77

DAY 3

SOUTH AFRICA beat ENGLAND 2-1
Ernie Els	72	lost to	Peter Baker	71
Fulton Allem	71	beat	Mark James	79
David Frost	70	beat	Nick Faldo	74

CHINESE TEAM TAIPEI beat MEXICO 2-1
Chen Liang-Hsi	76	lost to	Rafael Alarcon	73
Chung Chun-Hsing	79	beat	Carlos Espinoza	87
Yuan Ching-Chi	81	beat	Juan Brito	82

GROUP THREE

	Matches Played	Matches Won	Ind. Games Won
USA	3	3	8
Paraguay	3	2	5
Scotland	3	1	4
Wales	3	0	1

DAY 1

PARAGUAY beat SCOTLAND 2-1
Carlos Franco	70	beat	Sam Torrance	74
Angel Franco	77	lost to	Gordon Brand Jnr	71
Raul Fretes	74	beat	Colin Montgomerie	75

USA beat WALES 3-0
John Daly	72	beat	Mark Mouland	77
Payne Stewart	78	beat	Paul Mayo	80
Fred Couples	71	beat	Ian Woosnam	72

DAY 2

USA beat PARAGUAY 2-1
John Daly	76	lost to	Angel Franco	76
Payne Stewart	70	beat	Raul Fretes	73
Fred Couples	70	beat	Carlos Franco	73

SCOTLAND beat WALES 3-0
Colin Montgomerie	67	beat	Ian Woosnam	70
Sam Torrance	73	beat	Paul Mayo	78
Gordon Brand Jnr	72	beat	Mark Mouland	75

DAY 3

PARAGUAY beat WALES 2-1
Carlos Franco	74	lost to	Ian Woosnam	70
Raul Fretes	77	beat	Paul Mayo	78
Angel Franco	74	beat	Mark Mouland	75

USA beat SCOTLAND 3-0
John Daly	73	beat	Sam Torrance	78
Payne Stewart	74	beat	Gordon Brand Jnr	80
Fred Couples	69	beat	Colin Montgomerie	73

GROUP FOUR

	Matches Played	Matches Won	Ind. Games Won
Sweden	3	3	7
Canada	3	2	5
Japan	3	1	3
Australia	3	0	3

DAY 1

CANADA beat AUSTRALIA 2-1
Richard Zokol	70	beat	Peter Senior	77
Jim Rutledge	71	beat	Rodger Davis	71
Dave Barr	73	lost to	Craig Parry	73

SWEDEN beat JAPAN 3-0
Jesper Parnevik	68	beat	Tetsu Nishikawa	80
Joakim Haeggman	71	beat	Yoshinori Mizumaki	73
Anders Forsbrand	73	beat	Tsuyoshi Yoneyama	74

DAY 2

JAPAN beat AUSTRALIA 2-1
Yoshinori Mizumaki	73	beat	Rodger Davis	74
Tsuyoshi Yoneyama	74	lost to	Craig Parry	74
Tetsu Nishikawa	75	beat	Peter Senior	78

SWEDEN beat CANADA 2-1
Jesper Parnevik	72	lost to	Richard Zokol	71
Joakim Haeggman	71	beat	Jim Rutledge	73
Anders Forsbrand	69	beat	Dave Barr	71

DAY 3

CANADA beat JAPAN 2-1
Dave Barr	74	beat	Tetsu Nishikawa	76
Jim Rutledge	81	lost to	Tsuyoshi Yoneyama	75
Richard Zokol	72	beat	Yoshinori Mizumaki	77

SWEDEN beat AUSTRALIA 2-1
Jesper Parnevik	75	beat	Rodger Davis	77
Anders Forsbrand	72	beat	Peter Senior	82
Joakim Haeggman	82	lost to	Craig Parry	74

PRIZE MONEY

	Team £	Player £	Total £
WINNERS			
USA	300,000	100,000	300,000
RUNNERS-UP			
ENGLAND	150,000	50,000	150,000
LOSING SEMI-FINALISTS			
IRELAND	95,000	31,666	
SWEDEN	95,000	31,666	190,000

	Team £	Player £	Total £
GROUP 1			
IRELAND			
SPAIN(8)	45,000	15,000	
ZIMBABWE(1)	25,500	8,500	
ARGENTINA	19,500	6,500	90,000
GROUP 2			
ENGLAND(5)			
SOUTH AFRICA	45,000	15,000	
CHINESE TEAM TAIPEI	25,500	8,500	
MEXICO	19,500	6,500	90,000

	Team £	Player £	Total £
GROUP 3			
USA(6)			
PARAGUAY	45,000	15,000	
SCOTLAND(3)	25,500	8,500	
WALES	19,500	6,500	90,000
GROUP 4			
SWEDEN(7)			
CANADA	45,000	15,000	
JAPAN	25,500	8,500	
AUSTRALIA(2)	19,500	6,500	90,000

Nos. in parentheses indicate seeds

THE ALFRED DUNHILL CUP.

The Alfred Dunhill Open, Knokke, Belgium, 2nd-5th June 1994

The Alfred Dunhill Cup, St. Andrews, Scotland, 6th-9th October 1994

Sought after since 1893.

PAVIN ENDS AMERICAN DROUGHT

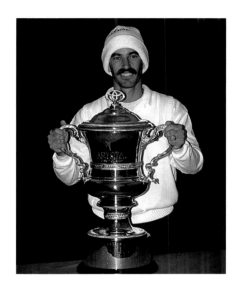

'An unbelievable final.' Corey Pavin said it, we all said it, after Nick Faldo had uncharacteristically let his Toyota World Match-Play title slip away in a denouement as dramatic as the eagle winner he had sunk to beat Ian Woosnam on the same 36th green four years earlier.

Unbelievable, because no fewer than 20 of the last 25 holes had been swapped, punch for punch, in as thrilling an exhibition of the match-play art as this unique tournament can have witnessed in its rich 30-year history. Of the dozen Wentworth finals that have gone 36 holes and beyond, this one ranks right up there with the best of them.

A poor drive, a bad three-wood into the rhododendrons, a penalty shot, an eternity of waiting, a recovery that hit the last branch, a last-ditch putt for the bogey six still, incredibly, left Faldo with a faint glimmer of survival.

Pavin, that tough little Californian with the Mexican bandido moustache, had, after all, run his 'lag' putt from 25 feet a good five feet past the hole, fooled by the fading light. It was fast becoming a comedy of errors, but in went the winning par putt that put Faldo, and the enraptured crowd, out of their misery.

Fourteen years earlier, Bill Rogers, a similarly frail-looking short hitter far removed from the normal image of the all-American athlete, holed a putt from not much further on the same green to beat Isao Aoki for the last previous US success

Corey Pavin ended a 14-year spell without an American victory when he defeated Nick Faldo in an epic final at Wentworth

in what for six years had since become an exclusively European preserve.

The Ryder Cup should have warned us and the Alfred Dunhill Cup underlined it: it was America's year on British soil and how impatiently they had waited for it. Pavin's win was the first in Britain since Mark Calcavecchia captured the 1989 Open at Royal Troon and the first in England since Mark O'Meara's in the

Lawrence Batley International at Royal Birkdale in 1987. Pavin was also the first player since Woosnam in 1987 to play through all four days of the World Match-Play and emerge the victor, coincidentally requiring the same number of holes, 141, to shunt out the entire British contingent of Peter Baker, Colin Montgomerie and Faldo, plus third seed Nick Price. Price, it was, licking his wounds after playing well enough to have beaten anyone else in the field, yet finding himself on the wrong end of a 2 & 1 verdict, who best summed up Pavin's gifts: 'Corey gets more from his game than anyone else I have ever seen. If I had a golfing son, I'd send him to Corey for lessons. He's the supreme strategist, but to be a great strategist you also have to be a great putter, which Pavin is.'

Baker, conqueror of Pavin at The Belfry was worn down 4 & 3, unable to match his Ryder Cup victim's expertise on the greens and missing three short birdie chances in a row in the afternoon, one from only a yard that would have put him back in with a shout.

Montgomerie, after edging past a more-stubborn-than-usual Japanese in Yoshinori Mizumaki and blowing away second seed Bernhard Langer, looked like doing the same to Pavin when strolling into a three-up lead, but the slight American, giving away the best part of five stone and 25 yards, rallied to such good effect that he stood three ahead with four to play. Montgomerie squared

brilliantly, then tossed it all away in extra
time, tugging his approach to the first
green into no-man's-land. Exit one Briton,
enter another. Faldo had already dis-
posed of two US Tour regulars in Steve
Elkington and David Frost, although the
South African, who had beaten Faldo in
the Alfred Dunhill Cup, predictably gave
him a very good run for his money before
going down 2 & 1. Elkington, first-round
conqueror of John Daly, the man surely
responsible for the 21 per cent increase
in opening-day crowd figures of a record
9,590, had a memorable phrase for his
upcoming clash with the favourite.
'Playing Faldo on his home course,' he
said, 'is like looking forward to falling off
a cliff.' He played a bit like that, committing suicide with his putter.

The Elkington-Daly match, incidentally,
must have been the fastest in Match-Play
history, the pair covering the first 18 in
two hours 43 minutes and needing only a
further one hour 58 minutes for the 14
more needed to bring the duel to its 5 &
4 conclusion.

The quick defeats of Daly and Seve
Ballesteros, a 7 & 6 victim of Frost, meant
much of the light had been snuffed out of
the tournament on day one. Only a
supreme romantic would have backed the
struggling Spaniard to achieve a record-
breaking sixth title, yet it was a great
sadness that the inevitable should occur
with such indecent haste, and accentuat-
ed by an absent-minded Rules breach by
Seve at the 20th.

And so to the final. Nick and tuck all
the way, highlighted by one astonishing
ten-hole spell from the 12th in the morning
to the fourth in the afternoon where not a
single hole was shared.

On a clear, cool October morning, the
early skirmishes gave little hint of the
excitement to come. Both out in level-par
35 and all square. Then Pavin rolled one
in from 40 feet at the tenth and Faldo followed him in from 12 feet. At the 16th, it
was the champion's turn to ram in a long
putt to sneak ahead. Then, for no appar-
ent reason, he pulled his second shot out
of bounds at the 17th. The swing was
less than immaculate but Faldo managed

to squeeze a birdie out of the last to lunch
one up, then it was on to the practice
ground with David Leadbetter for repairs.

The treatment resulted in a new-look
Nick for the afternoon and a super iron to
five feet at the first gave him a two-hole
lead for the first time. This, we thought
was the conclusive break, especially
when he wafted an eight iron to eight feet
at the short second. Little did we think he
would lose that hole to Pavin's even-better
eight-iron, a double swing which Pavin
later confirmed was the turning point of
the match. When Faldo overshot the next
green and chipped too strongly, it was
suddenly square again.

An outrageous downhill putt from 40
feet at the second short hole put Pavin
ahead and four more birdies in five holes
from the 25th, the pair having again
halved the tenth in twos, appeared to put
the issue beyond doubt. Faldo fell just
three inches short of an albatross two at

Left, David Frost takes the trunk road.
Below, Pavin prays for some warmer
weather.

Yoshinori Mizumaki escapes

from trouble.

COURSE: WENTWORTH CLUB (WEST COURSE)				YARDAGE: 6957	PAR: 72
NAME	CTY		NAME	CTY	TOTAL	PRIZE MONEY
FIRST ROUND						
Steve Elkington	Aus	beat	John Daly	USA	5 & 4	£25,000
David Frost	SA	beat	Seve Ballesteros	Sp	7 & 6	£25,000
Corey Pavin	USA	beat	Peter Baker	Eng	4 & 3	£25,000
Colin Montgomerie	Scot	beat	Yoshinori Mizumaki	Jap	at 37th	£25,000
						£100,000
SECOND ROUND						
Nick Faldo	Eng	beat	Steve Elkington	Aus	4 & 3	£35,000
David Frost	SA	beat	Ian Woosnam	Wal	2 & 1	£35,000
Corey Pavin	USA	beat	Nick Price	Zim	2 & 1	£35,000
Colin Montgomerie	Scot	beat	Bernhard Langer	Ger	6 & 4	£35,000
						£140,000
SEMI-FINALS						
Nick Faldo	Eng	beat	David Frost	SA	2 & 1	
Corey Pavin	USA	beat	Colin Montgomerie	Scot	at 37th	
PLAY-OFF FOR THIRD & FOURTH PLACES						
David Frost	SA	beat	Colin Montgomerie	Scot	2 & 1	£60,000 (3th) £50,000 (4th)
						£110,000
FINAL						
Corey Pavin	SA	beat	Nick Faldo	Eng	1 hole	£160,000 (1st) £90,000 (2nd)
						£250,000
TOTAL PRIZE MONEY						£600,000

Toyota World Match-Play top trio

Frost, Faldo and Pavin.

the long 30th, yet time was running out. Two down with three to play. Now the American made a mess of the 16th for the second time. Faldo needed no second bidding and despite a miserable drive up the 17th, he memorably levelled the match with a birdie on that notorious hole. All square, advantage Faldo. Then a nightmare, a forced smile, a warm handshake. Great match, great tournament.

'A long way to walk for that to happen,' was the loser's summing-up. 'I made an eagle to win the title on that hole four years ago; this time I didn't.' Pavin, winner by 139 shots to 140, suddenly found himself rating the tournament 'next in line' to the majors. 'Match-play is much more stressful than stroke-play but much more enjoyable, every hole is a tournament in itself,' he said, relishing his first victory for 18 months.

No one casts their network wider than Cellnet.

Cellnet's network covers 98% of the UK population with a choice of affordable tariffs.

Around the country, around the clock, no other company casts its network wider.

Cellnet, official supplier of cellular communications to the PGA European Tour, would like to wish everyone involved the very best of luck in the coming season.

PGA EUROPEAN TOUR OFFICIAL SPONSOR

✴ cellnet

The big network for small phones. 0800 21 4000.

SMYTH BACK IN THE FOLD

In the main, the pain waiting for the rain in Spain to drain was worth the gain for Des Smyth. When you have waited five years, a few more hours, well, a whole day in fact, doesn't matter that much. Even if it felt like the opposite at the time.

The Madrid Open, the tournament that almost never happened, became the tournament that went on until Monday – for the first time anyone could remember outside the 1988 Open and World Match-Play. Smyth, becoming perhaps the longest first day to last day leader but in a fashion which would get the approval of specialists in Chinese torture, hardly slept on Sunday night.

By then he should have been on his way home to Drogheda, Ireland. Instead, due to a storm that held up play when a significant number of greens flooded, he had to come back at eight o'clock the next morning to complete the final day's play. 'This was the worst day in ten years. I was so nervous starting out for a fifth time.' Smyth said of his feelings early on Monday morning. Two hours later he could add: 'It is a great relief to win again. When you haven't won for so long you don't believe it is going to happen again.'

Previously, as they say when all good mini-series are continued in their next instalment, David Feherty, the defending champion, had closed with a 66, including birdies at four of the last six holes, to finish on 12 under par. He was then joined on that mark a few minutes after sunset on Sunday evening by David

Des Smyth ended a five year spell without victory when he captured an extended Madrid Open

J Russell, belying his 23 missed cuts including the last eight.

The leaders in the clubhouse were in their own houses by the time the tournament resumed the following day, but fortunately a 'teleconference' play-off would not be needed. Smyth had led since his first day 65, a round he described as 'easy'. Two rounds of 68 kept him in front. On Monday morning he was on 16 under after ten holes and led by three shots from Jose Rivero, who had played a hole more.

The Spaniard was to drop a shot at the 12th before eventually rallying to finish second. But his countrymen were there in force. Santiago Luna picked up a birdie at the long 15th to get within one shot of Smyth, when the Irishman wobbled with two three-putts at the 13th and 14th. Of the second putt at the latter, from just two feet, Smyth said: 'It was a very bad putt. I quit on it. Now I was really worried because I wasn't sure what was going on ahead. I assumed someone was making a move.'

But no-one could get past Rivero's mark of 13 under. Mark Roe, who had earlier in the week been supported by his snooker star chum Willie Thorne, picked up two birdies, as did South African Wayne Westner, having just learnt that the Department of Immigration had refused to let his family take up temporary residency in England. Another local, Domingo Hospital, produced an eagle at the 15th and a birdie at the last to join the four-way tie for second.

Smyth, though, had recovered to birdie the 15th, and then ripped a five-iron at the short 17th which pitched eight feet past the pin and spun back to a foot. 'That relieved the pressure,' Smyth said. 'I didn't want to go to the last needing to make a four to win.' In fact he had a three-shot lead and a small, but delighted gallery could soon give its appreciation of Smyth's seventh Tour title.

Despite the wobble on Monday, Smyth's putting was solid thanks to his employment of the Langer method, which he had been using since the Open. If there was one moment when he thought it might be his week it came on the 15th on Saturday. His second shot finished in

scrubland to the left of the green and he had to go to the left of a scoreboard, bounce it on a dirt path so that it could skip between to two trees and through the semi rough. He got it onto the green and holed the putt from 25 feet for an improbable birdie.

It was that kind of extraordinary week. Gordon Brand Junior holed a three wood from 247 yards at the fifth for the second albatross of the season on Friday, then holed a wedge shot from 108 yards for eagle at the 18th on Saturday. At the ninth on Friday, Barry Lane holed out with a nine-iron from 154 yards, the same club and yardage as when he holed in one at the Alfred Dunhill Open.

Then, there was the tournament itself, saved from extinction after the loss of sponsors Iberia by the Spanish Sports Ministry, Puerta de Hierro and the PGA European Tour. So it was natural that when a storm hit on Sunday it was all hands on deck and the show must go on. The scoring was still superb and 49 players got round, leaving only 19 to resume on Monday. 'The players were very positive.' said Tournament Director

Andy Stubbs,' and said the decision to play was the right one.'

Especially for those trying to secure their cards, although no-one outside the top 120 on the Volvo Order of Merit managed to move high enough up. Robert Lee, the 32-year-old Londoner, closed with a 68, with four birdies and no bogeys, to finish in a tie for 22nd place, which still left him £445, or one more birdie, adrift of 120th place. Earlier Martin Poxon's hopes were crushed when he was disqualified on the first day when he took relief from casual water on the 17th green and dropped off the green, when he should have placed.

Smyth, though, showed the virtue of never giving up: 'I am 40 now, and it is great to win a tournament at 40. When you are doing well, everything seems very easy. Like all the guys, I work on my game very hard. You are always hoping to find a bit of form and confidence. Ray Floyd is an inspiration for all those of us who are getting on. I have put on a bit of weight recently, but I am in really good condition. I feel I can still compete. When I feel I can't compete any more, I'll stop.'

Above, extra time victory for Des Smyth. Below, Santiago Luna in conference.

Above, Jose Rivero and Mark Roe
shared second place. Below, mopping
up gets underway.

COURSE: REAL CLUB DE LA PUERTA DE HIERRO		YARDAGE: 6940					PAR: 72	
POS	NAME	CTY	1	2	3	4	TOTAL	PRIZE MONEY
1	Des SMYTH	Ire	65	68	68	71	272	£66660
2	José RIVERO	Sp	68	72	66	69	275	26605
	Domingo HOSPITAL	Sp	68	69	68	70	275	26605
	Mark ROE	Eng	69	66	71	69	275	26605
	Wayne WESTNER	SA	70	65	68	72	275	26605
6	David FEHERTY	N.Ire	68	72	70	66	276	11230
	Eduardo ROMERO	Arg	73	66	68	69	276	11230
	Santiago LUNA	Sp	70	70	67	69	276	11230
	David J RUSSELL	Eng	74	67	68	67	276	11230
10	Gordon BRAND Jnr	Scot	75	65	68	69	277	7680
	David GILFORD	Eng	68	67	70	72	277	7680
12	Andrew OLDCORN	Eng	70	71	70	67	278	6330
	De Wet BASSON	SA	70	72	67	69	278	6330
	Greg TURNER	NZ	69	70	68	71	278	6330
	Sven STRUVER	Ger	72	70	67	69	278	6330
16	Mark JAMES	Eng	71	69	68	71	279	5106
	Peter FOWLER	Aus	68	70	71	70	279	5106
	Fredrik LINDGREN	Swe	74	68	69	68	279	5106
	Barry LANE	Eng	69	66	73	71	279	5106
	Mark DAVIS	Eng	68	72	69	70	279	5106
	Anders FORSBRAND	Swe	73	68	70	68	279	5106
22	Robert LEE	Eng	70	71	71	68	280	4320
	José Manuel CARRILES	Sp	71	70	68	71	280	4320
	José COCERES	Arg	70	69	68	73	280	4320
	Patrick HALL	Eng	73	68	68	71	280	4320
	Keith WATERS	Eng	69	72	67	72	280	4320
27	Anders SORENSEN	Den	68	72	70	71	281	3780
	Paul WAY	Eng	70	70	72	69	281	3780
	Ronan RAFFERTY	N.Ire	72	71	66	72	281	3780
	Ignacio GARRIDO	Sp	72	67	70	72	281	3780
31	Haydn SELBY-GREEN	Eng	71	72	70	69	282	3246
	Steven RICHARDSON	Eng	69	69	73	71	282	3246
	Jeremy ROBINSON	Eng	71	70	69	72	282	3246
	Paul EALES	Eng	72	71	69	70	282	3246
	Andrew MURRAY	Eng	69	71	67	75	282	3246
	Derrick COOPER	Eng	72	67	71	72	282	3246
37	Manuel PINERO	Sp	69	70	71	73	283	2800
	Alfonso PINERO	Sp	70	70	73	70	283	2800
	Yago BEAMONTE	Sp	68	72	73	70	283	2800
	Chris MOODY	Eng	73	69	72	69	283	2800
	Michel BESANCENEY	Fr	69	72	68	74	283	2800
42	John McHENRY	Ire	72	70	71	71	284	2320
	Silvio GRAPPASONNI	It	71	71	69	73	284	2320
	Jay TOWNSEND	USA	73	67	71	73	284	2320
	Giuseppe CALI	It	68	75	68	73	284	2320
	Antonio GARRIDO	Sp	71	71	73	69	284	2320
	Brian MARCHBANK	Scot	69	72	68	75	284	2320
49	Richard BOXALL	Eng	72	70	70	73	285	1880
	Mikael KRANTZ	Swe	71	69	69	76	285	1880
	Miguel Angel JIMENEZ	Sp	74	69	71	71	285	1880
	David R JONES	Eng	73	70	69	73	285	1880
	Luis GABARDA (AM)	Sp	66	73	73	73	285	—
53	Jim PAYNE	Eng	71	71	73	71	286	1520
	José ROZADILLA	Sp	72	71	72	71	286	1520
	Ross MCFARLANE	Eng	71	70	73	72	286	1520
	Miguel Angel MARTIN	Sp	72	68	74	72	286	1520
	Juan QUIROS	Sp	67	72	74	73	286	1520
58	Carl MASON	Eng	74	68	71	74	287	1260
	Mark MOULAND	Wal	74	68	72	73	287	1260
60	Diego BORREGO	Sp	70	73	73	72	288	1180
	Phillip PRICE	Wal	74	67	73	74	288	1180
62	Manuel MORENO	Sp	69	74	74	72	289	1120
63	Peter MITCHELL	Eng	68	74	74	74	290	1060
	Mats HALLBERG	Swe	72	71	75	72	290	1060
65	Philip WALTON	Ire	71	72	76	74	293	1000

MONTGOMERIE SURGES TO THE TOP

An outstanding performance at Valderrama enabled Colin Montgomerie to capture the Volvo Order of Merit

Colin Montgomerie has never been short of talent. As a promising Scottish amateur, he won a scholarship to Baptist University in Houston, Texas. No sooner had he turned professional than he demonstrated that he was a fast learner. He improved his position in the Volvo Order of Merit each year, represented Europe in the 1991 and 1993 Ryder Cup and won three tournaments. These, though, were hardly an accurate yardstick with which to judge him. He ought to have won more. Between his second and third victories he had a torrid run of seven second place finishes.

Then came Valderrama 1993 and the Volvo Masters, the tournament where Montgomerie came of age. He likes the immaculately-prepared course at Sotogrande because it is a driver's course and he is a good driver. To cope with greens that have a Stimpmeter reading of at least ten requires a velvet touch, which he has. It is also a course he plays well. In 1992 he lost on it to Sandy Lyle only in a play-off.

Valderrama in 1993 was not as it had been in 1992 as Jimmy Patino, the owner, continued to make improvements to the course he desperately wants to stage the 1997 Ryder Cup. The lake in front of the 17th had been completed, the hole shortened to 500 yards and a

sweeping bank round the back of the green and down the side of the fairway had been built to provide viewing space for 12,000 spectators. One other alteration: the fluffy bentgrass around the greens had been overseeded with rye making the ball sit up more and thus it was easier to impart spin to chip shots.

Many of the players came on from Madrid where the previous week's tournament had only ended on the Monday. They arrived to find that Seve Ballesteros had withdrawn because of lumbago and Nick Faldo had announced that he would not compete in the following week's World Cup by Heineken because of tendonitis in his arm and wrists.

Rain, which had wiped out the pro-am, was expected to dominate the week and preferred lies were in order. Instead, the Costa del Sol lived up to its name – at least for the first day. David Gilford, despite arriving from Madrid too late for a practice round, took the lead with a 68, one of only six sub-par rounds on the first day. Gilford may have been boosted by the news that he was replacing Faldo in the World Cup. He led by one stroke from Darren Clarke and Montgomerie.

These three men, an Englishman, Irishman and a Scot were to be locked together for most of the remaining 54 holes, dominating the first day and the last. Clarke and Montgomerie are two heavyweights who weigh in at 16 and 15 stone respectively. Gilford is slighter and lighter and quietly spoken. Not one of them is over 30.

'I like the challenge of a course where you have to keep the ball in play,' Montgomerie said. 'I like it here and I am not surprised by my round today. My last four rounds have been 70, 72, 69 and now 69 again. I am confident of going out and doing well.' Boosting his own confidence was a deliberate ploy by Montgomerie who had tended to lack confidence in his own ability.

Certainly he, Gilford and Clarke were too good for the rest of the 54-man field. José Maria Olazabal flickered into life with a 70 in the opening round but faded thereafter with three over-par rounds. He finished 23rd, equal with Bernhard Langer. Faldo was clearly affected by aching arms and hands and came 25th, seven over par. 'My arms are screaming at me 'take me home'. They've had enough.'

Right, Colin Montgomerie clinches victory on the final green.

David Feherty is trapped on the 17th.

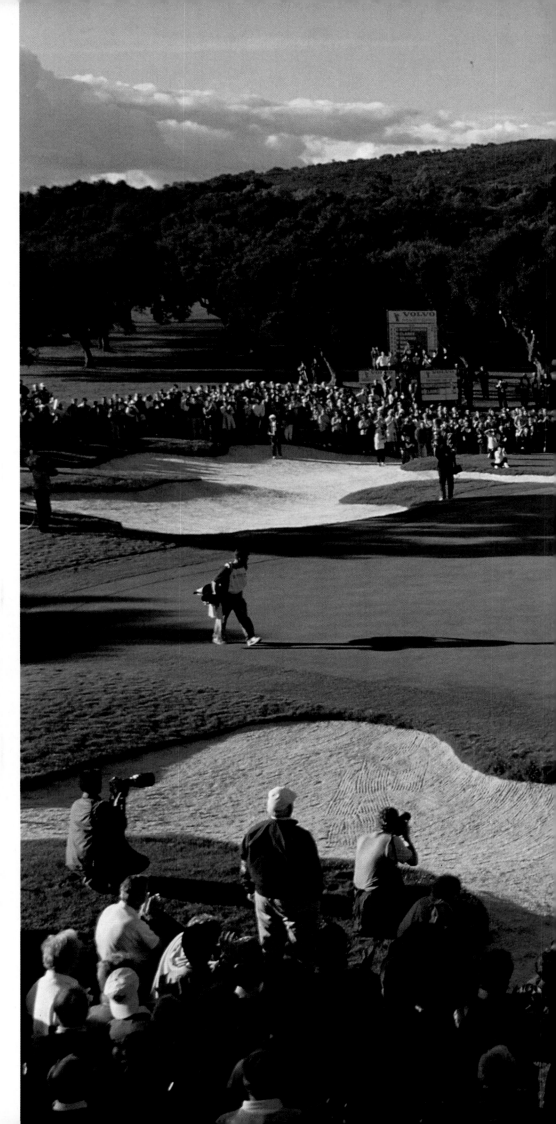

Above, David Gilford was steady as a rock

Left, Darren Clarke snatched second place.

Woosnam, making a late bid for the Volvo Order of Merit, had a superb 67 in the second round to lead by one stroke at that stage. Like Faldo, he was like one of the walking wounded. His problem was a recurrence of the spondylitis he had been suffering from since he was 16. Although he said it felt like a knife sticking in his back he said that it was forcing him to play within himself.

Again and again during the tournament the conversation turned to the 1997 Ryder Cup and the likelihood of its being staged at Valderrama. 'I'm not going to be sucked into that one,' Woosnam said. Faldo sighed when he was asked about it for the umpteenth time. 'There are 700 days to the next Ryder Cup,' he said wearily, 'Let's leave it at that.'

Montgomerie and Gilford, who both had 67s (Montgomerie coming back in 31), and Clarke who had a record-equalling 65, dominated the third day. Only a 66 by Peter Baker and 67s by Vijay Singh and Mark McNulty rivalled them. Montgomerie seven under par, led by one stroke from Clarke and Gilford.

Now Montgomerie faced his biggest test. All he had to do to win the £125,000 first prize and as much again from the Volvo bonus pool was to prove he had the temperament and skill to cope with the pressure of leading his peers for the final 18 holes of a tournament, something he had never done before. If he did this, then he would probably win the Volvo Order of Merit as well.

Knowing all that, he went out and

played the round of his life. He led by two strokes at the ninth and though Gilford and Clarke both birdied the 18th to close in on him, Montgomerie's 68 was good enough for victory by one stroke. He was ten under par and nobody had bettered par by so many at Valderrama.

Clarke, who was watched every step of the way by his mother and a happy band of supporters from Dungannon, his golf club, grabbed second place from Gilford by holing a putt of 18 feet on the 72nd hole.

'I have never been under such pressure,' Montgomerie said. 'I had only six bogeys in four rounds and that is a tribute to my driving. To win here means a lot to me. Nobody gives you a win here. You have got to earn it. I am sorry that Faldo was not completely 100 per cent. But knowing that I am number one, Faldo is second, Woosnam third and Langer fourth means a lot to me. I am very proud to be number one on this pile. I happened to play very, very well this week.'

Below, Paul Way putts on the re-designed 17th.

Vijay Singh drives from the 15th. Right, Ian Woosnam led after two rounds.

Above, Sam Torrance and Peter Baker take a different view.

Above, view across Valderrama. Top, Mark McNulty, Des Smyth and Nick Faldo take time out.

Right, marshal calls for quiet. Far right, like father, like son: Carl Mason and offspring practise at the Volvo Masters.

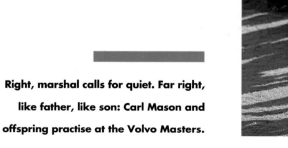

Home James as another season draws to a close.

								PRIZE
COURSE: VALDERRAMA, SOTOGRANDE				**YARDAGE: 6833**			**PAR: 71**	
POS	NAME	CTY	1	2	3	4	TOTAL	MONEY
1	Colin MONTGOMERIE	Scot	69	70	67	68	274	£125000
2	Darren CLARKE	N.Ire	69	73	65	68	275	83400
3	David GILFORD	Eng	68	72	67	69	276	46950
4	Vijay SINGH	Fij	72	72	67	70	281	37500
5	Ian WOOSNAM	Wal	71	67	71	73	282	32100
6	Mark McNULTY	Zim	73	73	67	71	284	26800
7	Carl MASON	Eng	76	70	72	67	285	23000
8	Costantino ROCCA	It	75	71	72	68	286	18250
	Jesper PARNEVIK	Swe	70	75	69	72	286	18250
10	Retief GOOSEN	SA	72	75	71	69	287	13560
	Miguel Angel JIMENEZ	Sp	73	70	75	69	287	13560
	Ernie ELS	SA	73	72	71	71	287	13560
	Rodger DAVIS	Aus	74	74	70	69	287	13560
	José COCERES	Arg	74	73	70	70	287	13560
15	Anders FORSBRAND	Swe	72	75	72	69	288	10610
	David FEHERTY	N.Ire	72	74	74	68	288	10610
	Barry LANE	Eng	73	74	73	68	288	10610
	Paul WAY	Eng	71	69	73	75	288	10610
	Gordon BRAND Jnr	Scot	71	76	70	71	288	10610
20	Sandy LYLE	Scot	78	70	70	71	289	9400
	Howard CLARK	Eng	72	74	75	68	289	9400
	Sam TORRANCE	Scot	74	70	71	74	289	9400
23	José Maria OLAZABAL	Sp	70	74	73	73	290	8775
	Bernhard LANGER	Ger	72	71	74	73	290	8775
25	Gary ORR	Scot	76	73	72	70	291	8025
	Eduardo ROMERO	Arg	70	75	73	73	291	8025
	Mark JAMES	Eng	79	72	70	70	291	8025
	Nick FALDO	Eng	74	70	75	72	291	8025
29	Mark ROE	Eng	72	76	70	74	292	7200
	Jean VAN DE VELDE	Fr	73	74	70	75	292	7200
	José RIVERO	Sp	76	80	70	66	292	7200
32	Peter FOWLER	Aus	73	74	77	69	293	6650
	Frank NOBILO	NZ	72	75	74	72	293	6650
	Paul BROADHURST	Eng	71	79	71	72	293	6650
35	Per-Ulrik JOHANSSON	Swe	77	71	72	74	294	6125
	Peter MITCHELL	Eng	76	77	70	71	294	6125
	Peter BAKER	Eng	75	74	66	79	294	6125
	Joakim HAEGGMAN	Swe	73	72	73	76	294	6125
39	Andrew OLDCORN	Eng	72	75	75	73	295	5600
	Ian PALMER	SA	76	74	75	70	295	5600
	Greg TURNER	NZ	73	77	73	72	295	5600
42	Jim PAYNE	Eng	75	78	72	72	297	5075
	Roger CHAPMAN	Eng	71	72	77	77	297	5075
	Ronan RAFFERTY	N.Ire	77	77	72	71	297	5075
	Paul McGINLEY	Ire	76	73	77	71	297	5075
46	De Wet BASSON	SA	77	76	73	73	299	4400
	Robert KARLSSON	Swe	75	75	71	78	299	4400
	Wayne WESTNER	SA	77	73	75	74	299	4400
	Steven RICHARDSON	Eng	77	77	74	71	299	4400
	Des SMYTH	Ire	77	70	80	72	299	4400
51	Stephen AMES	T&T	80	79	75	W/D	234	3725
	Jamie SPENCE	Eng	75	72	78	W/D	225	3725
	Brian MARCHBANK	Scot	82	W/D			82	3725
	Tony JOHNSTONE	Zim	72	77	79	W/D	228	3725

INTRODUCING
THE MOST EXCITING WAY
TO IMPROVE YOUR DRIVE.

THE VOLVO 850 ESTATE HAS BEEN SPECIALLY

DESIGNED TO GIVE YOU THE SPACIOUS INTERIOR

AND THE TOTAL FLEXIBILITY YOU NEED IN

YOUR LIFE. THE COMFORT AND PERFORMANCE

YOU EXPECT FROM A SEDAN IS COMBINED

WITH AMPLE INTERIOR SPACE AND VERSABILITY,

ENSURING THE VOLVO 850 ESTATE MEETS

YOUR MOST DEMANDING REQUIREMENTS.

VOLVO 850 ESTATE, 5 CYL., 20 VALVE, 2L5 ENGINE.   **VOLVO**

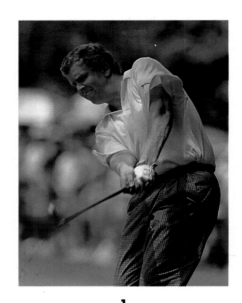

2
Nick
FALDO
England
£558,738.33

1
Colin
MONTGOMERIE
Scotland
£613,682.70

3
Ian
WOOSNAM
Wales
£501,353.41

4
Bernhard
LANGER
Germany
£469,569.64

5
Sam
TORRANCE
Scotland
£421,328.19

6
Costantino
ROCCA
Italy
£403,866.48

7
Peter
BAKER
England
£387,988.84

8
Darren
CLARKE
Northern Ireland
£369,675.08

9
Gordon
BRAND Jnr
Scotland
£367589.10

10
Barry
LANE
England
£339,218.47

POS	NAME	CTY	PRIZE MONEY	POS	NAME	CTY	PRIZE MONEY	POS	NAME	CTY	PRIZE MONEY
11	Mark JAMES	Eng	£335589.34	64	Andrew SHERBORNE	Eng	£81210.12	117	Mike HARWOOD	Aus	£40494.15
12	Ronan RAFFERTY	N.Ire	£311125.03	65	Glen DAY	USA	£79944.60	118	David RAY	Eng	£40273.12
13	Steven RICHARDSON	Eng	£304015.12	66	Gary EVANS	Eng	£79809.17	119	Christy O'CONNOR Jnr	Ire	£39906.87
14	Frank NOBILO	NZ	£294598.76	67	Sandy LYLE	Scot	£79224.67	120	Miguel Angel MARTIN	Sp	£39638.21
15	Joakim HAEGGMAN	Swe	£287370.84	68	Sven STRUVER	Ger	£79133.91	121	Robert LEE	Eng	£39193.33
16	David GILFORD	Eng	£273301.31	69	Jorge BERENDT	Arg	£78492.06	122	Juan QUIROS	Sp	£37614.27
17	Jesper PARNEVIK	Swe	£272511.73	70	Robert ALLENBY	Aus	£77150.00	123	Mikael KRANTZ	Swe	£37110.41
18	José Maria OLAZABAL	Sp	£249493.14	71	Anders GILLNER	Swe	£71780.90	124	Giuseppe CALI	It	£36053.71
19	Paul BROADHURST	Eng	£243588.17	72	Domingo HOSPITAL	Sp	£67577.83	125	Glenn RALPH	Eng	£36048.30
20	Wayne WESTNER	SA	£226297.89	73	Mark DAVIS	Eng	£66986.00	126	David WILLIAMS	Eng	£36008.96
21	Greg TURNER	NZ	£222296.56	74	Anders SORENSEN	Den	£66081.78	127	Ricky WILLISON	Eng	£35952.22
22	David FEHERTY	N.Ire	£216479.84	75	Silvio GRAPPASONNI	It	£64280.55	128	Michel BESANCENEY	Fr	£35819.56
23	Anders FORSBRAND	Swe	£213509.72	76	Magnus SUNESSON	Swe	£61956.39	129	Martin POXON	Eng	£35442.00
24	Mark ROE	Eng	£199994.47	77	Peter O'MALLEY	Aus	£61039.33	130	Antoine LEBOUC	Fr	£35129.00
25	Jean VAN DE VELDE	Fr	£199437.49	78	José Maria CANIZARES	Sp	£60283.83	131	Heinz P THUL	Ger	£34704.73
26	Rodger DAVIS	Aus	£198180.33	79	Russell CLAYDON	Eng	£60271.96	132	Chris MOODY	Eng	£32276.13
27	Carl MASON	Eng	£183757.65	80	Paul CURRY	Eng	£59900.62	133	Jon ROBSON	Eng	£31429.25
28	Eduardo ROMERO	Arg	£175430.55	81	John McHENRY	Ire	£58799.43	134	Patrick HALL	Eng	£29598.25
29	José COCERES	Arg	£174679.04	82	Wayne RILEY	Aus	£57786.71	135	Tom PERNICE	USA	£29314.10
30	Gary ORR	Scot	£173979.45	83	Mike McLEAN	Eng	£57748.91	136	Paul AFFLECK	Wal	£28749.50
31	Peter FOWLER	Aus	£173073.92	84	Andrew MURRAY	Eng	£56345.84	137	Ross McFARLANE	Eng	£28407.12
32	Des SMYTH	Ire	£169729.42	85	Paul EALES	Eng	£55425.81	138	Bill MALLEY	USA	£27457.75
33	De Wet BASSON	SA	£163858.37	86	Pierre FULKE	Swe	£54895.68	139	Ian GARBUTT	Eng	£26715.08
34	Ernie ELS	SA	£162827.10	87	Derrick COOPER	Eng	£54320.27	140	Stephen FIELD	Eng	£26588.10
35	Miguel Angel JIMÉNEZ	Sp	£162572.69	88	Eamonn DARCY	Ire	£53865.83	141	Gabriel HJERTSTEDT	Swe	£26345.83
36	Jim PAYNE	Eng	£160570.83	89	Martin GATES	Eng	£52578.99	142	Stuart LITTLE	Eng	£25729.40
37	José RIVERO	Sp	£159897.37	90	Richard BOXALL	Eng	£52365.22	143	Jonathan SEWELL	Eng	£25343.75
38	Paul McGINLEY	Ire	£159786.04	91	Vicente FERNANDEZ	Arg	£51228.88	144	Gavin LEVENSON	SA	£24505.50
39	Vijay SINGH	Fij	£159110.17	92	Philip WALTON	Ire	£49902.82	145	Ruben ALVAREZ	Arg	£23755.24
40	Mark McNULTY	Zim	£152097.86	93	Mark MOULAND	Wal	£48340.71	146	Andrew HARE	Eng	£22711.17
41	Tony JOHNSTONE	Zim	£151223.33	94	Jeremy ROBINSON	Eng	£48223.21	147	Danny MIJOVIC	Can	£22710.90
42	Seve BALLESTEROS	Sp	£148854.97	95	André BOSSERT	Swi	£47994.16	148	Torsten GIEDEON	Ger	£21777.45
43	Robert KARLSSON	Swe	£147386.54	96	Marc FARRY	Fr	£47555.85	149	Ove SELLBERG	Swe	£21365.86
44	Retief GOOSEN	SA	£147256.20	97	Adam HUNTER	Scot	£46901.49	150	Haydn SELBY-GREEN	Eng	£21138.21
45	Ian PALMER	SA	£139420.83	98	Ross DRUMMOND	Scot	£46361.60	151	Brian BARNES	Scot	£20768.46
46	Per-Ulrik JOHANSSON	Swe	£136592.09	99	David CURRY	Eng	£46211.74	152	David J RUSSELL	Eng	£19679.85
47	Peter MITCHELL	Eng	£133127.88	100	David A RUSSELL	Eng	£45627.29	153	Alexander CEJKA	Ger	£19476.90
48	Roger CHAPMAN	Eng	£131769.03	101	Paul MAYO	Wal	£45596.42	154	Chris WILLIAMS	Eng	£18572.50
49	Stephen AMES	T&T	£131743.10	102	Stephen McALLISTER	Scot	£45465.58	155	Stephen BENNETT	Eng	£18444.94
50	Jamie SPENCE	Eng	£125887.49	103	Fredrik LINDGREN	Swe	£44993.11	156	Keith WATERS	Eng	£18059.33
51	Howard CLARK	Eng	£120086.21	104	Justin HOBDAY	SA	£44807.77	157	Robin MANN	Eng	£14508.33
52	Andrew OLDCORN	Eng	£115705.00	105	José Manuel CARRILES	Sp	£44263.00	158	José ROZADILLA	Sp	£14053.13
53	Brian MARCHBANK	Scot	£113888.73	106	Mike CLAYTON	Aus	£43617.72	159	Jamie TAYLOR	Aus	£13470.00
54	Paul WAY	Eng	£113148.04	107	Craig CASSELLS	Eng	£43105.67	160	Roger WINCHESTER	Eng	£13362.00
55	Mats LANNER	Swe	£106765.54	108	Eoghan O'CONNELL	Ire	£43080.73	161	Roy MACKENZIE	Chil	£13277.00
56	Olle KARLSSON	Swe	£103919.33	109	Alberto BINAGHI	It	£43016.57	162	Ole ESKILDSEN	Den	£12095.59
57	Paul LAWRIE	Scot	£95067.07	110	Thomas LEVET	Fr	£42827.00	163	Eric GIRAUD	Fr	£12023.87
58	Jay TOWNSEND	USA	£90012.27	111	Jeff HAWKES	SA	£42796.10	164	Philip TALBOT	Eng	£11902.50
59	Johan RYSTROM	Swe	£88949.47	112	Steve BOWMAN	USA	£41967.27	165	Charles RAULERSON	USA	£11271.64
60	Phillip PRICE	Wal	£86901.12	113	Manuel PINERO	Sp	£41931.89	166	Yago BEAMONTE	Sp	£10800.00
61	Santiago LUNA	Sp	£86333.16	114	Mike MILLER	Scot	£41623.23	167	Peter TERAVAINEN	USA	£10597.50
62	Gordon J BRAND	Eng	£83842.85	115	Malcolm MACKENZIE	Eng	£41080.06	168	Rick HARTMANN	USA	£10553.21
63	Steen TINNING	Den	£83409.00	116	David R JONES	Eng	£40771.00	169	Antonio GARRIDO	Sp	£10225.00

THE PGA EUROPEAN TOUR
(A Company Limited by Guarantee)

Board of Directors
N C Coles, MBE – Group Chairman
A Gallardo (Tour, Enterprise, Properties)
B Gallacher (Tour, Enterprises, Properties)
T A Horton (Properties)
D Jones (Tour)
M G King (Enterprises, Properties)
B Langer (Enterprises)
J E O'Leary (Tour, Enterprises, Properties)
C Moody (Tour)
G W Ralph (Tour)
P M P Townsend (Enterprises, Properties)
K R Waters (Tour)

Executive Director
K D Schofield

Deputy Executive Director
G C O'Grady

General Counsel
M D Friend

Group Company Secretary
M Bray

**PGA European Tour
Tournament Committee**
J E O'Leary – Chairman
A Gallardo – Vice Chairman
A Binaghi
E Dussart
I Gervas
M James

D Jones (co-opted)
B Langer
M Lanner
C Mason
C Moody
G W Ralph
O Sellberg
K Waters

PGA European Seniors Tour
A Stubbs – Managing Director

**Director of Tour Operations and
Chief Referee**
J N Paramor

Senior Tournament Directors
A N McFee (Director of Tour Qualifying
School Programme)
M R Stewart

Tournament Directors
D Garland
D Probyn

Challenge Tour Director
Alan de Soultrait

Tournament Administrators
M Eriksson
M Haarer
K Williams
G Hunt (Referee)
M Vidaor

J M Zamora

PGA European Tour Enterprises Ltd
G C O'Grady - Managing Director
S Kelly - Marketing Director
I Barker - Account Director
G Oosterhuis – Corporate Sponsorship
Manager
C Perring – Event Staging Manager

PGA European Tour Properties Ltd
R G Hills – Managing Director

PGA European Tour (South)
A Gallardo – President

Communications Division
M Platts – Director of Communications
and Public Relations
M Wilson – Consultant to Executive
Director

Group Finance Controller
C Allamand

Group Financial Planner
J Orr

Group Accounts Executive
C Dyce

**Corporate Relations
Consultant**
H Wickham

THE CONTRIBUTORS

Mike Britten
Turespana Iberia – Open de Canarias
Turespana Masters – Open de Andalucia
Turespana Iberia – Open de Baleares
Honda Open
Matthew Chancellor (Golf Weekly)
Open V33 du Grand Lyon
Jersey European Airways Open
Jeremy Chapman (The Sporting Life)
Toyota World Match-Play Championship
Peter Corrigan (Independent on Sunday)
Volvo Order of Merit Winner
Norman Dabell (The Observer)
Heineken Open Catalonia
Hohe Brücke Austrian Open
Bill Elliott (The Daily Star)
GA European Open
Andrew Farrell (Golf Weekly)
Turespana Open Mediterrania – The Land of Valencia
Canon European Masters, Madrid Open
Mercedes German Masters

Melanie Garrett (Golf World)
Roma Masters
Mark Garrod (Press Association)
Air France Cannes Open
Dermot Gilleece (Irish Times)
Carrolls Irish Open
David Hamilton (Golf Weekly)
Portuguese Open
Benson and Hedges International Open
Peter Higgs (Mail on Sunday)
Madeira Island Open
John Hopkins (The Times)
Peugeot Open de Espana
Trophée Lancôme, Volvo Masters
Renton Laidlaw (The Evening Standard)
Lancia Martini Italian Open
Alfred Dunhill Open, Canon Shoot-Out
Derek Lawrenson (Birmingham Post and Mail)
Dunhill British Masters
Michael McDonnell (The Daily Mail)
Murphy's English Open
The Year in Retrospect

Chris Plumridge (The Sunday Telegraph)
Kronenbourg Open
Volvo PGA Championship
122nd Open Championship
The Ryder Cup by Johnnie Walker
Bob Rodney (The Daily Telegraph)
Shell Scottish Seniors, Seniors British Open
Gordon Simpson (Press Association)
Heineken Dutch Open
Graham Spiers (Scotland on Sunday)
Alfred Dunhill Cup
Lauren St John (The Sunday Times)
Moroccan Open
Scandinavian Masters
Mel Webb (The Times)
Dubai Desert Classic
Johnnie Walker Classic
Peugeot Open de France
BMW International Open
Michael Williams (The Daily Telegraph)
Volvo German Open
Ian Wood (The Scotsman)
Bell's Scottish Open

THE PHOTOGRAPHERS

Contents - Phil Inglis, Chicot Agency, Charles Briscoe-Knight
The Year in Retrospect - Margot Briscoe-Knight, Phil Sheldon, Allsport/Stephen Munday/David Cannon/Dave Rogers/Anton Want/John Gichigi, Mego Foto/Manuel Pinella, Phil Inglis.
Volvo Order of Merit Winner - Allsport/Stephen Munday, Charles Briscoe-Knight, Margot Briscoe-Knight, Chicot Agency, Phil Sheldon
Canon Shoot-Out - Phil Inglis, Charles Briscoe-Knight, Allsport/David Cannon
The Apollo Week - Phil Inglis
Madeira Island Open - Chicot Agency
Dubai Desert Classic - C. Briscoe-Knight
Johnnie Walker Classic - C. Briscoe-Knight
Turespana Iberia-Open de Canarias - Allsport
Moroccan Open - Allsport
Turespana Masters-Open de Andalucia - Allsport, Mega Foto
Turespana Open Mediterrania-The Land of Valencia - Allsport, Mega Foto/Manuel Pinella
Turespana Iberia-Open de Baleares - Allsport
Portuguese Open - Allsport
Kronenbourg Open - Allsport

Open V33 du Grand Lyon - Allsport, Chicot Agency
Roma Masters - Allsport
Heineken Open Catalonia - Allsport, Mega Foto/Manuel Pinella
Cannes Open - Allsport
Benson and Hedges International Open - Phil Sheldon, Allsport
Peugeot Open de Espana - Allsport, Mega Foto/Manuel Pinella
Lancia Martini Italian Open - Allsport/John Gichigi
Volvo PGA Championship - Charles Briscoe-Knight
Dunhill British Masters - Charles Briscoe-Knight, Margot Briscoe-Knight
Honda Open - Allsport
Jersey European Airways Open - Allsport/Howard Boylan, Stuart McAlister
Peugeot Open de France - Chicot Agency
Carrolls Irish Open - C Briscoe-Knight
Shell Scottish Seniors - Phil Sheldon
Bell's Scottish Open - Phil Inglis
122nd Open Championship - Charles Briscoe-Knight, Margot Briscoe-Knight
Seniors British Open - Phil Sheldon
Heineken Dutch Open - Allsport/David Cannon/Stephen Munday
Scandinavian Masters - Allsport

BMW International Open - Phil Inglis
Hohe Brücke Austrian Open - Allsport
Murphy's English Open - Charles Briscoe-Knight
Volvo German Open - Allsport/Anton Want, Charles Briscoe-Knight
Canon European Masters - Phil Inglis, Chicot Agency
GA European Open - C Briscoe-Knight
Trophée Lancôme - Chicot Agency
The Ryder Cup by Johnnie Walker - Charles Briscoe-Knight, Margot Briscoe-Knight, Allsport/David Cannon
Mercedes German Masters - Allsport/Stephen Munday
Alfred Dunhill Open - Phil Sheldon, Mathew Harris
Alfred Dunhill Cup - Phil Sheldon
Toyota World Match-Play Championship - Charles Briscoe-Knight
Madrid Open - Allsport/Stephen Munday
Volvo Masters - Charles Briscoe-Knight, Margot Briscoe-Knight, Phil Inglis
Volvo Order of Merit - C Briscoe-Knight, M Briscoe-Knight, Chicot Agency, Phil Sheldon, Allsport/Stephen Munday
Page 246 - Charles Briscoe-Knight
End Page - Allsport